DATE DUE

DEMCO 38-296

The Baby Boom

AMERICANS AGED 35 TO 54

The Baby Boom

AMERICANS AGED 35 TO 54

2nd edition

by Cheryl Russell

New Strategist Publications, Inc.

Ithaca, New York

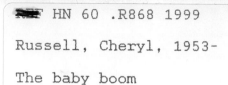
607 / 273-0913

www.newstrategist.com

ISBN 1-885070-22-5

Printed in the United States of America

Table of Contents

Chapter 7. Population

Chapter 8. Spending

Chapter 9. Wealth

Tables

Chapter 3. Health

Chapter 4. Income

Chapter 5. Labor Force

Chapter 6. Living Arrangements

Chapter 7. Population

Chapter 8. Spending

Chapter 9. Wealth

Illustrations

Introduction

Chapter 1. Attitudes & Behavior

Chapter 2. Education

Chapter 3. Health

Chapter 4. Income

Chapter 5. Labor Force

Chapter 6. Living Arrangements

Introduction

The mood of the nation—our problems and concerns, hopes and fears—is influenced by the age structure of the population. Today, the middle-aged share of the population is at an all-time high. Never before have so many Americans—both numerically and proportionately—been in the 35-to-54 age group. For the next few decades, the wants and needs of the middle-aged will shape consumer markets.

Those who want to understand the changing dynamics of the all-important middle-aged population hold in their hands the key to the market. *The Baby Boom: Americans Aged 35 to 54* is your strategic guide, revealing the unique characteristics of today's middle-aged and how those characteristics are remaking our society.

The middle aged of today are baby boomers. The baby-boom generation, born between 1946 and 1964, spans the ages from 35 to 53—almost entirely filling the 35-

Population aged 35 to 54

(percent of people aged 35 to 54 in the population, 1920 to 2020)

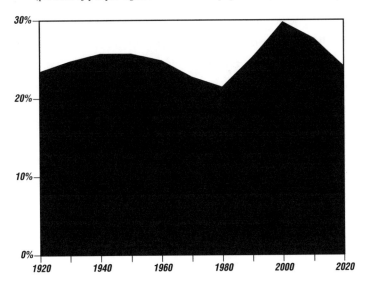

to-54 age group. For years, the nation's 78 million boomers have determined what's hot and what's not simply because of their numbers. Now there is an even more compelling reason to pay attention to boomers—they are in their peak earning, spending, and saving years. The generation that brought us sport utility vehicles is behind the stock market boom. The generation that put Orlando on the map with its quasi-religious zeal for anything Disney has yet to reach the peak years of travel spending. In industry after industry—automotive, home furnishings, entertainment, apparel—the baby-boom generation has only just begun to make its mark.

Twenty years ago, young adults dominated the demographic landscape. Now it is the middle-aged. This shift is not only unprecedented, but a youth-dominant culture is all most of us have ever known. Few Americans can even remember a time when young adults did not wield the greatest influence on consumer markets. Most business strategies, marketing campaigns, products, and services have been designed to serve the wants and needs of youth.

In 1980, the youth market was in its heyday. The share of the population in the 35-to-54 age group was at a low of 21 percent. At that time, the large baby-boom generation was aged 16 to 34. Now the tide has turned: the 35-to-54 share of the population reached 25 percent in 1990 and is nearing 30 percent today.

This shift has not gone unnoticed, but its importance has been ignored. Many businesses still pursue the young-adult market as though it was the only one that mattered, obsessively targeting youth even as sales fall. In the apparel industry, revenues have faltered as manufacturers and retailers offer styles for teens and young adults rather than the middle-aged. The network television audience is shrinking because producers create shows for the young rather than the burgeoning middle-aged—all because misinformed advertisers demand a youthful audience. Many businesses are asleep at the wheel while the consumer landscape changes around them. Since 1990, the number of people aged 35 to 54 has grown 28 percent, expanding by 19 million. Marketers who are on top of this trend have a once-in-a-lifetime opportunity to capture the baby-boom market from their competitors.

One of the most important truths about boomers is that they are still the youth market. In their teens and twenties, more than three decades ago, boomers created the youth market. As they enter their forties and fifties, millions of self-indulgent, demanding, and fun-loving boomers are proving the youth market to be a state of mind rather than a stage of life. Most boomers still live in that state, refusing to adopt the attitudes and lifestyles of their parents. As the baby-boom generation brings youthful attitudes and values to middle age, their fierce independence and self-indulgence is reshaping products and services. Businesses savvy enough to determine what boomers want will catch a wave of consumer demand that will be the ride of a lifetime. *The Baby Boom* points the way, providing the statistics you need to target boomers as well as the trends behind them.

How to Use This Book

The Baby Boom: Americans Aged 35 to 54 is designed for easy use. It is divided into nine chapters, organized alphabetically: Attitudes and Behavior, Education, Health, Income, Labor Force, Living Arrangements, Population, Spending, and Wealth.

Most of the tables in the book are based on data collected and published by the federal government, in particular the Bureau of the Census, the Bureau of Labor Statistics, the National Center for Education Statistics, and the National Center for Health Statistics. The federal government continues to be the best source of up-to-date, reliable information on the changing characteristics of Americans. To explore the opinions of 35-to-54-year-olds, most of the tables in the Attitudes and Behavior chapter are based on data from the nationally representative General Social Survey of the University of Chicago's National Opinion Research Center (NORC). Attitudinal data for all age groups are shown for comparative purposes. NORC is the oldest nonprofit, university-affiliated national survey research facility in the nation. It conducted the General Social Survey annually from 1972 through 1994, except for the years 1979, 1981, and 1992. It now conducts the survey every two years, with 1996 being the latest year for which data are available.

While most of the data in this book are produced by the federal government, the tables in *The Baby Boom* are not simply reprints of government spreadsheets—as is the case in many other reference books. Instead, each table is individually compiled and created by New Strategist's editors, with calculations designed to reveal the trends. Each chapter of *The Baby Boom* includes the demographic and lifestyle data most important to researchers. Each table tells a story about people aged 35 to 54, a story explained by the accompanying text, which analyzes the data and highlights future trends. If you need more statistical detail than the tables provide, you can plumb the original source listed at the bottom of each table.

The book contains a lengthy table list to help researchers locate the information they need. For a more detailed search, an index is at the back of the book. Also there is the glossary, which defines the terms commonly used in the tables and text. A list of telephone and web site contacts also appears at the end of the book, allowing researchers to access government specialists and web sites.

The baby-boom market continues to be the most powerful consumer force this nation has ever known. Not only is the 35-to-54 age group large, but its influence extends into the younger and older generations as it guides its children and aids its parents. With *The Baby Boom: Americans Aged 35 to 54* at hand, you hold the baby-boom market in your hands.

1

Attitudes & Behavior

◆ In middle-age, most baby boomers are "pretty" or "very" happy. They are more likely than both younger and older Americans to feel rushed, but the majority think life is exciting.

◆ Boomers are cynical about the motives of other people. The majority of 35-to-44-year-olds think other people are looking out only for themselves, as do 45 percent of 45-to-54-year-olds.

◆ In mid-life, most people must cope with the death of one or both parents. Among people aged 45 to 54, 65 percent have living mothers, but only 34 percent have fathers who are still alive.

◆ The stresses of juggling work and childrearing responsibilities take their toll on relationships in middle-age: the percentage of couples who say their marriage is "very" happy bottoms out in the 35-to-54 age group.

◆ Many boomers are preparing for retirement: 27 percent of those born from 1946 through 1953 already have at least $100,000 in retirement savings.

◆ The majority of baby boomers believe in God without any doubts, but one in eight believes instead in a "higher power of some kind."

◆ People who identify themselves as political independents outnumber both Democrats and Republicans among younger boomers, while among older boomers independents are a close second to Democrats.

Boomer Outlook Positive

While many boomers feel rushed, most say life is exciting.

Americans aged 55 or older are happier than younger generations. While 39 percent of people aged 65 to 74 are "very happy," the figure is less than 30 percent among people aged 35 to 54. The stresses of juggling work and family are behind the slightly lower levels of happiness among boomers. Once their children are grown and work has become a distant memory, the happiness of boomers is likely to grow.

Another factor contributing to the lower level of happiness among 35-to-54-year-olds is the pressure to do more in less time. While 30 percent of all Americans aged 18 or older always feel rushed, the figure peaks in the 35-to-54 age group at 37 to 39 percent. Only 9 percent of 35-to-54-year-olds and 11 percent of 45-to-54-year-olds say they "almost never feel rushed."

Despite, or perhaps because of, the frantic pace of their lives, half the people aged 35 to 54 say life is exciting. The proportion of the middle-aged who find life exciting has grown over the past few decades along with the speed of social and technological change.

◆ Many boomers occasionally feel overwhelmed by their responsibilities and the speed at which they must manage them. Businesses hoping to attract baby-boom customers should make their products and services simple and convenient.

Feeling rushed peaks in the 45-to-54 age group

(percent of people aged 18 or older who always feel rushed, by age, 1996)

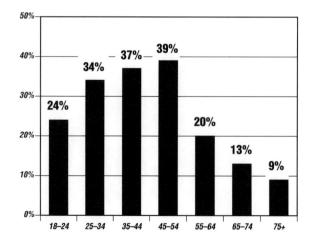

Personal Happiness, 1996

"Taken all together, how would you say things are these days—would you say that you are very happy, pretty happy, or not too happy?"

(percent of people aged 18 or older responding by age, 1996)

	very happy	pretty happy	not too happy
Total people	**30%**	**57%**	**12%**
Aged 18 to 24	24	62	13
Aged 25 to 34	30	59	10
Aged 35 to 44	27	59	13
Aged 45 to 54	29	58	13
Aged 55 to 64	37	50	11
Aged 65 to 74	39	51	10
Aged 75 or older	32	53	16

Note: Numbers may not add to 100 because "don't know" and no answer are not shown.
Source: 1996 General Social Survey, National Opinion Research Center, University of Chicago; calculations by New Strategist

Feeling Rushed, 1996

"In general, how do you feel about your time—would you say you feel rushed even to do things you have to do, only sometimes feel rushed, or almost never feel rushed?"

(percent of people aged 18 or older responding by age, 1996)

	always	sometimes	almost never
Total people	**30%**	**52%**	**18%**
Aged 18 to 24	24	63	13
Aged 25 to 34	34	56	9
Aged 35 to 44	37	53	9
Aged 45 to 54	39	48	11
Aged 55 to 64	20	49	30
Aged 65 to 74	13	48	39
Aged 75 or older	9	34	57

Note: Numbers may not add to 100 because "don't know" and no answer are not shown.
Source: 1996 General Social Survey, National Opinion Research Center, University of Chicago; calculations by New Strategist

Is Life Exciting? 1996

"In general, do you find life exciting, pretty routine, or dull?"

(percent of people aged 18 or older responding by age, 1996)

	exciting	pretty routine	dull
Total people	**49%**	**45%**	**4%**
Aged 18 to 24	47	46	6
Aged 25 to 34	52	45	2
Aged 35 to 44	50	45	4
Aged 45 to 54	50	45	4
Aged 55 to 64	53	42	5
Aged 65 to 74	43	54	1
Aged 75 or older	43	43	14

Note: Numbers may not add to 100 because "no opinion" and no answer are not shown.
Source: 1996 General Social Survey, National Opinion Research Center, University of Chicago; calculations by New Strategist

Many People Aged 35 to 54 Are Wary of Others

Younger boomers are more cynical than older members of the generation.

Americans under age 35 are least likely to think well of others, while those aged 65 or older are most likely to believe other people are helpful and fair. Boomers are in the middle of this continuum. That may explain why the generation is split on questions about the fairness, helpfulness, and trustworthiness of others.

The 53 percent majority of boomers aged 35 to 44 think other people are looking out only for themselves. In contrast, a 45 percent minority of 45-to-54-year-olds think so poorly of others, while the 47 percent plurality believe people try to be helpful.

Regarding the fairness of others, the 54 percent majority of older boomers believe others try to be fair, while a 48 percent minority of younger boomers agree. Forty-seven percent of older boomers believe most people can be trusted. In contrast, the 59 percent majority of younger boomers say you can't be too careful in dealing with other people.

◆ The wariness of boomers makes them a difficult target for marketers. Before boomers can hear an advertising message, businesses must break through their cynicism.

Opinion of Others, 1996

"Would you say most people can be trusted or you can't be too careful in dealing with people? Would you say most of the time people try to be helpful, or they are mostly just looking out for themselves? Would you say most people would try to take advantage of you if they got a chance, or would they try to be fair?"

(percent of people aged 18 or older responding by age, 1996)

	trust		helpfulness		fairness	
	most people can be trusted	you can't be too careful	try to be helpful	just look out for themselves	would try to be fair	would take advantage
Total people	**34%**	**61%**	**43%**	**49%**	**50%**	**42%**
Aged 18 to 24	18	77	28	67	29	66
Aged 25 to 34	25	70	35	56	45	46
Aged 35 to 44	35	59	39	53	48	41
Aged 45 to 54	47	48	47	45	54	37
Aged 55 to 64	46	50	60	33	62	32
Aged 65 to 74	29	62	54	40	57	35
Aged 75 or older	33	59	56	32	59	31

Note: Numbers may not add to 100 because "depends," "don't know," and no answer are not shown.
"Depends" was not included because it was a volunteered response.
Source: 1996 General Social Survey, National Opinion Research Center, University of Chicago; calculations by New Strategist

Lifestyles Have Changed

Boomers have been transformed by the social change they helped create over the past 40 years.

Among all generations, boomers are most likely to have been raised by both parents. Seventy-four percent of people aged 35 to 44 and 76 percent of those aged 45 to 54 were living with both parents at age 16. Unfortunately, boomers have not been able to provide the same stability to their children. Among young adults, only 60 percent were living with both parents at age 16.

As boomers grew up, women were entering the workforce. The proportion of Americans whose mother worked for pay for at least one year while they were children is less than half among people aged 65 or older. It reaches the two-thirds level among 35-to-54-year-olds.

When boomers established their own households, they revolutionized relationships between men and women—making cohabitation before marriage common. While 20 percent of married people aged 45 to 54 lived with their spouse before marriage, the proportion jumps to 39 percent among 35-to-44-year-olds.

◆ Today's middle-aged have both benefited and suffered from the social change of the last few decades. While some wax nostalgic for the way things used to be, few would choose to return to the lifestyles of the 1950s.

Most boomers were raised by two parents

(percent of people aged 18 or older who were living with both parents at age 16, by age, 1996)

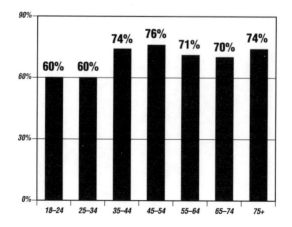

Living with Both Parents during Childhood? 1996

"Were you living with both your own mother and father around the time you were 16?"

(percent of people aged 18 or older responding by age, 1996)

	both parents	mother only or mother/ stepfather	father only or father/ stepmother	other
Total people	**69%**	**19%**	**5%**	**7%**
Aged 18 to 24	60	26	7	7
Aged 25 to 34	60	29	6	5
Aged 35 to 44	74	15	5	6
Aged 45 to 54	76	16	4	5
Aged 55 to 64	71	14	5	11
Aged 65 to 74	70	14	4	13
Aged 75 or older	74	10	6	10

Note: Numbers may not add to 100 because "don't know" and no answer are not shown.
Source: 1996 General Social Survey, National Opinion Research Center, University of Chicago; calculations by New Strategist

Did Your Mother Work? 1996

"Did your mother ever work for pay for as long as a year while you were growing up?"

(percent of people aged 18 or older responding by age, 1996)

	yes	*no*
Total people	**63%**	**35%**
Aged 18 to 24	82	18
Aged 25 to 34	78	21
Aged 35 to 44	67	32
Aged 45 to 54	62	37
Aged 55 to 64	50	48
Aged 65 to 74	44	54
Aged 75 or older	27	71

Note: Numbers may not add to 100 because "don't know" and no answer are not shown.
Source: 1996 General Social Survey, National Opinion Research Center, University of Chicago; calculations by New Strategist

Cohabitation before Marriage, 1994

"Did you live with your husband/wife before you got married?"

(percent of people aged 18 or older responding by age, 1994)

	yes	*no*
Total people	**29%**	**70%**
Aged 18 to 24	47	53
Aged 25 to 34	48	52
Aged 35 to 44	39	58
Aged 45 to 54	20	78
Aged 55 to 64	9	89
Aged 65 to 74	11	89
Aged 75 or older	2	93

Note: Asked only of those married at the time. Numbers may not add to 100 because no answer is not shown.
Source: 1994 General Social Survey, National Opinion Research Center, University of Chicago; calculations by New Strategist

Middle-Aged Most Likely to Live in Suburbs

Big cities hold little appeal to those raising children.

Only 13 percent of Americans aged 45 to 54 live in a big city. Forty-one percent live in a small city or town, while 28 percent—the highest share among all age groups—live in the suburbs or outskirts of a big city. In this age group, many people have teenaged children and the income to afford bigger homes. They move from crowded urban areas to more spacious surroundings in the suburbs or small towns outside of metropolitan areas. Fifteen percent even move to the country—again, a higher share than in any other age group. More than two out of three 45-to-54-year-olds live in a single-family detached home.

People aged 35 to 44 are almost as likely as older boomers to live in the suburbs, with 27 percent located there. But they are less likely that 45-to-54-year-olds to live in small towns (36 percent) and more likely to live in big cities (20 percent). As they age into their forties and fifties, younger boomers will likely make the move to more spacious surroundings as well.

♦ With computers and online services allowing people to more easily work from home and cut down on daily commutes, the proportion of Americans living in small towns and cities may rise in the years ahead.

Community Type, 1994

"Would you describe the place where you live as . . . "

(percent of people aged 18 or older responding by age, 1994)

	a big city	suburbs or outskirts of a big city	small city or town	country village	farm or home in the country
Total people	**19%**	**24%**	**40%**	**4%**	**10%**
Aged 18 to 24	26	23	39	5	6
Aged 25 to 34	21	23	43	3	8
Aged 35 to 44	20	27	36	6	9
Aged 45 to 54	13	28	41	2	15
Aged 55 to 64	23	23	34	6	11
Aged 65 to 74	18	17	44	7	11
Aged 75 or older	17	19	42	4	13

Note: Numbers may not add to 100 because "don't know" and no answer are not shown.
Source: 1994 General Social Survey, National Opinion Research Center, University of Chicago; calculations by New Strategist

Type of Dwelling Unit, 1996

"In what type of dwelling do you live?"

(percent of people aged 18 or older by type of dwelling unit in which they live, by age, 1996)

	detached single-family home	apartment house (5+ units)	two-to-four-family house	mobile home	rowhouse	other
Total people	**59%**	**18%**	**8%**	**8%**	**5%**	**2%**
Aged 18 to 24	40	26	10	11	8	2
Aged 25 to 34	43	25	13	9	6	1
Aged 35 to 44	63	15	8	7	5	1
Aged 45 to 54	68	13	6	5	4	2
Aged 55 to 64	72	9	5	7	5	1
Aged 65 to 74	72	13	4	7	3	0
Aged 75 or older	56	27	4	5	5	3

Note: Numbers may not add to 100 because "don't know" and no answer are not shown.
Source: 1996 General Social Survey, National Opinion Research Center, University of Chicago; calculations by New Strategist

Many Boomers Must Cope with Trauma

The majority have experienced a traumatic event in the past five years.

Six out of 10 people aged 35 to 54 have experienced a traumatic event in the past five years. Trauma is defined as the death of a close relative, divorce, unemployment, hospitalization, or disability.

No age group is immune from trauma. The proportion of those who experienced a traumatic event rises from 53 percent among those aged 18 to 24 to a peak of 79 percent among those aged 65 to 74. One traumatic event experienced by many is the death of a relative. One-third of all Americans have experienced the death of a relative in the past five years, including 29 percent of 35-to-44-year-olds and 38 percent of 45-to-54-year-olds.

One of the most traumatic events now facing boomers is the death of a parent. While most boomers have living mothers, a minority of those aged 45 to 54 have living fathers. The proportion of boomers whose mother has died climbs from 19 percent among 35-to-44-year-olds to 33 percent among 45-to-54-year-olds. Sixty-two percent of the older group have experienced the death of their father compared to just 39 percent of the younger group.

♦ As boomers age, they will have to face the death of their parents, and many will encounter illness. Look for a growing number of businesses to offer them a helping hand in coping with these events.

Oldest boomers likely to have experienced death of father

(percent of people aged 35 to 54 whose father is no longer alive, 1996)

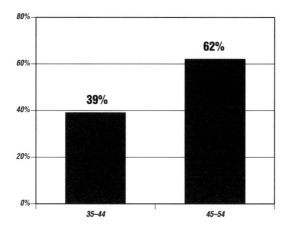

Traumatic Events during Past Five Years, 1994

**"Have you experienced a death, divorce, unemployment,
or other traumatic event during the past five years?"**

(percent of people aged 18 or older responding by age, 1994)

	none	one or more
Total people	32%	63%
Aged 18 to 24	45	53
Aged 25 to 34	40	58
Aged 35 to 44	34	59
Aged 45 to 54	28	62
Aged 55 to 64	23	73
Aged 65 to 74	15	79
Aged 75 or older	33	63

Note: Traumatic events are death, divorce, unemployment, and hospitalization/disability.
Numbers may not add to 100 because no answer is not shown.
Source: 1994 General Social Survey, National Opinion Research Center, University of Chicago; calculations by New Strategist

Deaths of Relatives in Past Five Years, 1994

"Have you experienced the death of a relative in the past five years?"

(percent of people aged 18 or older responding by age, 1994)

	none	one or more
Total people	**67%**	**32%**
Aged 18 to 24	97	3
Aged 25 to 34	81	18
Aged 35 to 44	70	29
Aged 45 to 54	59	38
Aged 55 to 64	48	52
Aged 65 to 74	46	52
Aged 75 or older	53	42

Note: Numbers may not add to 100 because no answer is not shown.
Source: 1994 General Social Survey, National Opinion Research Center, University of Chicago; calculations by New Strategist

Parents Living, 1994

"Is your mother/father alive?"

(percent of people aged 18 or older responding by age, 1994)

	mother		father	
	yes	*no*	*yes*	*no*
Total people	**63%**	**37%**	**46%**	**51%**
Aged 18 to 24	97	3	93	3
Aged 25 to 34	91	9	80	18
Aged 35 to 44	81	19	59	39
Aged 45 to 54	65	33	34	62
Aged 55 to 64	35	64	10	87
Aged 65 to 74	5	93	2	96
Aged 75 or older	2	97	0	98

Note: Numbers may not add to 100 because "don't know" and no answer are not shown.
Source: 1994 General Social Survey, National Opinion Research Center, University of Chicago; calculations by New Strategist

Most Boomers Are Happily Married

But marital happiness reaches a low in middle-age.

Among the nation's married couples, 61 percent say their marriage is "very happy." The proportion of couples who are very happy bottoms out in the 35-to-54 age group, at 53 to 58 percent. Behind this dip in happiness are the dual demands of career and children. After children have grown up, couples who have managed to stay together usually find renewed satisfaction in their relationship.

Boomers involved in a romantic relationship rather than marriage are less happy than the married, with only 38 to 40 percent saying they are "very happy." There is a reason for this: In most cases, the happiest couples end up tying the knot, leaving the less happy behind.

When the oldest boomers married, wives were expected to care for the home while husbands were expected to earn the living. Then the rules changed. On the whole, boomers are happy about the revolution in sex roles. Most prefer the new arrangement, and 68 to 74 percent say they would rather husbands and wives share responsibilities than have separate spheres. More than 80 percent of boomers do not think that a wife's career should take a backseat to her husband's.

♦ One reason for the high divorce rate among boomers—particularly those aged 45 to 54—are changing expectations regarding the roles of husbands and wives. This group entered marriage fully expecting a traditional lifestyle but discovered the rules had changed. Nevertheless, many are now enthusiastic proponents of the more egalitarian lifestyle.

Marital and Relationship Happiness, 1996

"Taking all things together, how would you describe your marriage/romantic relationship? Would you say it is very happy, pretty happy, or not too happy?"

(percent of people aged 18 or older responding by age, 1996)

	marriage			romantic relationship		
	very happy	*pretty happy*	*not too happy*	*very happy*	*pretty happy*	*not too happy*
Total people	**61%**	**36%**	**2%**	**42%**	**44%**	**5%**
Aged 18 to 24	60	35	3	49	46	3
Aged 25 to 34	69	28	2	46	43	3
Aged 35 to 44	53	44	3	38	52	6
Aged 45 to 54	58	39	2	40	38	5
Aged 55 to 64	67	32	1	33	33	13
Aged 65 to 74	72	26	2	33	22	11
Aged 75 or older	62	34	2	11	44	11

Note: Asked of people who were married or involved in a romantic relationship at the time of the survey.
Numbers may not add to 100 because "don't know" is not shown.
Source: 1996 General Social Survey, National Opinion Research, University of Chicago; calculations by New Strategist

Traditional or Modern Relationship? 1996

"Which type of relationship with a spouse or partner would you prefer? One in which the man has the main responsibility for providing the household income and the woman has the main responsibility for taking care of home and family or one in which the man and woman equally share responsibilities?"

(percent of people aged 18 or older responding by age, 1996)

	man provides income, woman cares for home and family	responsibilities are shared
Total people	**30%**	**70%**
Aged 18 to 24	17	83
Aged 25 to 34	23	76
Aged 35 to 44	31	68
Aged 45 to 54	26	74
Aged 55 to 64	40	60
Aged 65 to 74	37	61
Aged 75 or older	47	52

Note: Numbers may not add to 100 because "don't know" and no answer are not shown.
Source: 1996 General Social Survey, National Opinion Research, University of Chicago; calculations by New Strategist

Husband's Career More Important? 1996

"It is more important for a wife to help her husband's career than to have one herself—do you agree or disagree?"

(percent of people aged 18 or older responding by age, 1996)

	strongly agree	agree	disagree	strongly disagree	agree, total	disagree, total
Total people	3%	17%	53%	24%	20%	77%
Aged 18 to 24	2	12	54	30	14	84
Aged 25 to 34	2	10	56	30	12	86
Aged 35 to 44	3	11	54	29	14	83
Aged 45 to 54	2	12	58	24	14	82
Aged 55 to 64	3	24	51	18	27	69
Aged 65 to 74	6	38	44	7	44	51
Aged 75 or older	7	45	34	5	52	39

Note: Numbers may not add to 100 because "don't know" and no answer are not shown.
Source: 1996 General Social Survey, National Opinion Research Center, University of Chicago; calculations by New Strategist

Do Young Children Suffer If Mother Works? 1996

"A preschool child is likely to suffer if his or her mother works—do you agree or disagree?"

(percent of people aged 18 or older responding by age, 1996)

	strongly agree	agree	disagree	strongly disagree	agree, total	disagree, total
Total people	**8%**	**36%**	**41%**	**11%**	**45%**	**52%**
Aged 18 to 24	2	31	52	12	33	64
Aged 25 to 34	7	27	52	12	34	64
Aged 35 to 44	10	34	39	14	44	53
Aged 45 to 54	7	38	40	11	45	51
Aged 55 to 64	10	43	37	6	53	43
Aged 65 to 74	12	50	27	5	62	32
Aged 75 or older	13	50	26	3	63	29

Note: Numbers may not add to 100 because "don't know" and no answer are not shown.
Source: 1996 General Social Survey, National Opinion Research Center, University of Chicago; calculations by New Strategist

Many Boomer Couples Share Control of Finances

While wives frequently control the purse strings, husbands rarely do.

Businesses often wonder who makes the financial decisions—husband or wife—when they target married couples. Statistics from the General Social Survey provide the answer: both husband and wife, or the wife alone. Rarely do husbands control family finances. This is just as true among boomers as it is among both older and younger Americans.

The most common method of controlling finances among 35-to-54-year-olds is that husband and wife pool their money, with each spouse taking out what he or she needs. The second most common arrangement among boomers (practiced by 25 to 31 percent) is for the wife to manage the money, while the husband has some personal spending money. The husband is the money manager in only 16 percent of boomer couples.

Many boomers are not all that happy with the amount of money they are managing. Three out of 10 people aged 35 to 54 say they are not at all satisfied with their financial situation. Only 22 to 28 percent say they are pretty well satisfied. Those most satisfied with their finances are the oldest Americans.

◆ With so many boomers unhappy with their finances, many would welcome products and services that could help them improve the situation, such as job training, debt consolidation, savings plans, and discounts on goods and services.

Who Controls Family Finances? 1996

"Which of the following comes closest to describing the system that you and your husband/wife use to organize your finances?"

(percent of people aged 18 or older responding by age, 1996)

	all money pooled, each takes out what he/she needs	wife manages money, except husband's personal spending money	some money pooled, each partner has some separate	husband manages money, except wife's personal spending money	wife has housekeeping allowance, husband manages rest of money	keep finances completely separate
Total people	**37%**	**28%**	**13%**	**9%**	**8%**	**5%**
Aged 18 to 24	53	22	11	11	0	3
Aged 25 to 34	36	29	12	11	9	4
Aged 35 to 44	40	31	11	7	9	4
Aged 45 to 54	34	25	18	8	8	5
Aged 55 to 64	32	30	14	11	10	2
Aged 65 to 74	37	24	11	4	11	11
Aged 75 or older	30	41	7	7	4	11

Note: Asked of people who were married at the time of the survey. Numbers may not add to 100 because no answer is not shown.
Source: 1996 General Social Survey, National Opinion Research, University of Chicago; calculations by New Strategist

Satisfaction with Financial Situation, 1996

"So far as you and your family are concerned, would you say that you are pretty well satisfied with your present financial situation, more or less satisfied, or not satisfied at all?"

(percent of people aged 18 or older responding by age, 1996)

	pretty well satisfied	more or less satisfied	not at all satisfied
Total people	**28%**	**44%**	**28%**
Aged 18 to 24	23	42	35
Aged 25 to 34	20	50	29
Aged 35 to 44	22	47	31
Aged 45 to 54	28	42	30
Aged 55 to 64	34	42	23
Aged 65 to 74	45	33	21
Aged 75 or older	45	41	13

Note: Numbers may not add to 100 because "don't know" and no answer are not shown.
Source: 1996 General Social Survey, National Opinion Research Center, University of Chicago; calculations by New Strategist

Many Are Confident in Their Financial Preparation for Retirement

Few boomers have not started saving for retirement.

Among older boomers, those who have saved $100,000 or more for retirement far outnumber those who have saved nothing (27 versus 12 percent). Among younger boomers, 15 percent have saved nothing while 10 percent have saved $100,000 or more. Most younger boomers have at least $10,000 in their retirement account.

Twenty-seven percent of the oldest boomers say they are very confident in having enough money for a comfortable retirement. (This may be the same 27 percent who have saved $100,000 or more.) Another 49 percent are somewhat confident. Younger boomers are slightly less confident in having enough money for retirement, but the great majority are at least somewhat confident.

The largest share of older boomers (43 percent) and the majority of younger boomers (55 percent) believe personal savings will be their most important source of income in retirement. Most, from 69 to 78 percent, expect to work part-time in retirement.

◆ While boomers believe their peers are not preparing adequately for retirement, they feel far more confident in their own preparations. But enough people lack confidence to create an enormous market for retirement planning.

Many older boomers have substantial retirement savings

(percent distribution of people born between 1946 and 1953 by amount saved for retirement, 1997)

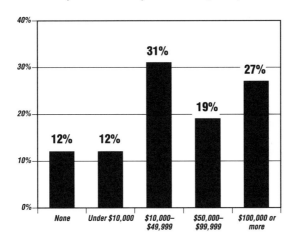

Attitudes of Boomers toward Retirement, 1997

(percent of working people responding by birth cohort, 1997)

	older boomers (born 1946–53)	younger boomers (born 1954–64)
Amount saved for retirement		
None	12%	15%
Under $10,000	12	20
$10,000–$49,999	31	43
$50,000–$99,999	19	13
$100,000 or more	27	10
Confidence in having enough money for a comfortable retirement		
Very confident	27	19
Somewhat confident	49	47
Not too confident	14	18
Not at all confident	12	13
Expected most important source of retirement income		
Personal savings	43	55
Employer-provided money	32	21
Social Security	14	10
Expect to retire at age 55 or younger	**10**	**17**
Want to retire at age 55 or younger	**28**	**37**
Expect to work part-time in retirement	**69**	**78**

Source: 1997 Retirement Confidence Survey, *Employee Benefit Research Institute, Mathew Greenwald & Associates, Inc., and American Savings Education Council*

The Middle-Aged Have the Least Time for TV

But most watch television at least two hours a day.

Among all age groups, boomers watch the least TV. Between 28 and 30 percent watch for no more than one hour a day, on average. In contrast, among people aged 65 or older, only 11 percent watch TV for no more than one hour a day. With work and family responsibilities, boomers have little time to sit in front of the tube. In contrast, older Americans have the most free time and spend the most time watching TV. While boomers are least likely to watch a lot of TV, the majority put in two to four hours a day.

With so little free time, many boomers are forgoing reading the daily newspaper in favor of other activities. Only 39 percent of people aged 35 to 44 read the newspaper every day. A larger 51 percent of those aged 45 to 54 are daily newspaper readers. Daily newspaper readership climbs with age to a peak of 71 percent in the 65-to-74 age group.

♦ People aged 35 to 54 are busier than ever, making them hard to reach through traditional media—television and newspapers. Marketers targeting this age group must either broadcast their message so widely that it can't be missed or narrowly target certain segments of boomers where they live, work, and play.

Television Viewing, 1996

"On the average day, about how many hours do you personally watch television?"

(percent of people aged 18 or older responding by age, 1996)

	one hour or less	two to four hours	five or more hours
Total people	**24%**	**60%**	**16%**
Aged 18 to 24	23	60	17
Aged 25 to 34	26	62	13
Aged 35 to 44	28	58	13
Aged 45 to 54	30	57	13
Aged 55 to 64	22	64	15
Aged 65 to 74	11	64	25
Aged 75 or older	11	57	33

Note: Numbers may not add to 100 due to rounding.
Source: 1996 General Social Survey, National Opinion Research Center, University of Chicago; calculations by New Strategist

Newspaper Readership, 1996

"How often do you read the newspaper?"

(percent of people aged 18 or older responding by age, 1996)

	every day	a few times a week	once a week	less than once a week	never
Total people	**42%**	**24%**	**16%**	**11%**	**6%**
Aged 18 to 24	17	33	21	21	7
Aged 25 to 34	22	33	23	17	6
Aged 35 to 44	39	30	15	11	6
Aged 45 to 54	51	19	15	10	4
Aged 55 to 64	58	17	9	9	6
Aged 65 to 74	71	9	11	3	5
Aged 75 or older	66	10	8	3	12

Note: Numbers may not add to 100 because no answer is not shown.
Source: 1996 General Social Survey, National Opinion Research Center, University of Chicago; calculations by New Strategist

Most Boomers Believe in God without a Doubt

A substantial number believe in a higher power rather than God, however.

People aged 35 to 54 are just as likely as the average person to believe in God without any doubts. Between 62 and 64 percent agree with the statement, "I know God really exists and I have no doubts about it." Only 2 to 3 percent of boomers say they don't believe in God at all. Between these two extremes are the 12 percent of 35-to-54-year-olds who believe in a higher power rather than God, a larger share than in any other age group.

Slightly more than one-half of people aged 35 to 54 identify themselves as Protestants, a share substantially smaller than the Protestant share among older Americans, which peaks at 71 percent among those aged 55 to 64. The proportion of boomers who are Catholic is about average. The age group is slightly more likely than older Americans to be of "other religion," while more than 10 percent of boomers say they have no religious affiliation.

The middle-aged attend religious services less frequently than older Americans, but more frequently than young adults. Between 29 and 30 percent of people aged 35 to 54 attend services weekly or more often, compared with 36 to 45 percent of people aged 55 or older and only 18 to 21 percent of people under age 35. The majority of boomers attend religious services only a few times a year or never.

♦ Many baby boomers turned away from traditional religious practices in their youth, hoping to create for themselves a more personal belief system. Those who are marching to the beat of a different drummer have created an enormous market for products and services that promote spirituality.

Belief in God, 1994

**"Which statement comes closest to expressing what you believe about God?
1) I don't believe in God; 2) I don't know whether there is a God and I don't
believe there is any way to find out; 3) I don't believe in a personal
God, but I do believe in a higher power of some kind; 4) I find myself
believing in God some of the time, but not at others;
5) While I have doubts, I feel that I do believe in God;
6) I know God really exists and I have no doubts about it."**

(percent of people aged 18 or older responding by age, 1994)

	no doubts	believe, but have doubts	believe sometimes	higher power	don't know, no way to find out	don't believe
Total people	**62%**	**15%**	**4%**	**9%**	**3%**	**2%**
Aged 18 to 24	47	25	4	8	5	5
Aged 25 to 34	58	21	4	7	4	2
Aged 35 to 44	62	14	3	12	3	2
Aged 45 to 54	64	13	4	11	3	3
Aged 55 to 64	72	12	2	10	1	1
Aged 65 to 74	66	9	6	6	1	4
Aged 75 or older	64	13	3	8	0	2

Note: Numbers may not add to 100 because "don't know" and no answer are not shown.
Source: 1994 General Social Survey, National Opinion Research Center, University of Chicago; calculations by New Strategist

Religious Preference, 1996

"What is your religious preference? Is it Protestant, Catholic, Jewish, some other religion, or no religion?"

(percent of people aged 18 or older responding by age, 1996)

	Protestant	Catholic	Jewish	other	none
Total people	**57%**	**24%**	**2%**	**5%**	**12%**
Aged 18 to 24	41	29	1	7	22
Aged 25 to 34	53	23	1	7	15
Aged 35 to 44	54	25	3	6	12
Aged 45 to 54	57	24	3	5	11
Aged 55 to 64	71	20	1	2	6
Aged 65 to 74	69	24	2	1	4
Aged 75 or older	70	17	6	2	5

Note: Numbers may not add to 100 because "don't know" and no answer is not shown.
Source: 1996 General Social Survey, National Opinion Research Center, University of Chicago; calculations by New Strategist

Attendance at Religious Services, 1996

"How often do you attend religious services?"

(percent of people aged 18 or older responding by age, 1996)

	weekly or more	one to three times a month	up to several times a year	never
Total people	**29%**	**16%**	**37%**	**15%**
Aged 18 to 24	18	17	43	18
Aged 25 to 34	21	18	42	16
Aged 35 to 44	30	15	38	14
Aged 45 to 54	29	17	37	15
Aged 55 to 64	36	15	34	12
Aged 65 to 74	45	14	27	11
Aged 75 or older	41	11	26	19

Note: Numbers may not add to 100 because no answer is not shown.
Source: 1996 General Social Survey, National Opinion Research Center, University of Chicago; calculations by New Strategist

Privacy Is Threatened by Computers

The majority of 35-to-54-year-olds think computers threaten individual privacy.

While most 35-to-54-year-olds think the information stored in the federal government's computers poses some threat to individual privacy, they are less likely to see this as a serious threat than older Americans. Between 33 and 41 percent of boomers regard it as a "very serious threat" compared to 45 to 46 percent of people aged 55 or older. Nevertheless, fully 65 percent of 35-to-44-year-olds and 74 percent of those aged 45 to 54 regard computerized information held by the federal government as at least a fairly serious threat to individual privacy.

Interestingly, the proportion of Americans who regard computer information as a threat to individual privacy is much lower among younger Americans, many of whom grew up with computers. The demarcation occurs within the baby-boom generation. Among people under age 45, between 27 and 28 percent say computer information is not a serious threat to individual privacy. This proportion drops to between 16 and 18 percent among people aged 45 or older.

♦ As younger boomers and Generation Xers grow older, the public's resistance to the collection and sharing of computer information may decline.

Younger generations are less threatened

(percent of people aged 18 or older who think information about people in the federal government's computers is not a serious threat to individual privacy, by age, 1996)

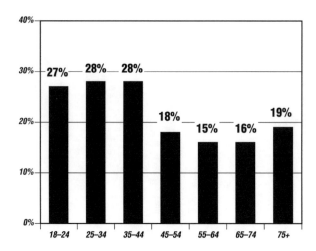

Privacy and Personal Information, 1996

"The federal government has a lot of different pieces of information about people, which computers can bring together very quickly. Is this a very serious threat to individual privacy, a fairly serious threat, not a serious threat, or not a threat at all to individual privacy?"

(percent of people aged 18 or older responding by age, 1996)

	very serious threat	fairly serious threat	not a serious threat	not a threat at all	can't choose
Total people	**36%**	**32%**	**19%**	**4%**	**7%**
Aged 18 to 24	24	35	26	1	11
Aged 25 to 34	30	34	25	3	7
Aged 35 to 44	33	32	23	5	6
Aged 45 to 54	41	33	14	4	6
Aged 55 to 64	45	31	11	4	7
Aged 65 to 74	45	25	9	7	11
Aged 75 or older	46	25	10	9	6

Note: Numbers may not add to 100 because no answer is not shown.
Source: 1996 General Social Survey, National Opinion Research Center, University of Chicago; calculations by New Strategist

American Electorate Highly Cynical of Politics

Boomers are about as cynical as the average person.

Only about one-third of people aged 35 to 54 believe the average citizen has considerable influence on politics. A larger share—more than 40 percent—think the average citizen has little or no influence. Americans of all ages are similarly divided, with the largest share feeling powerless. Despite this cynicism, most (60 to 66 percent) 35-to-54-year-olds went to the polls in November 1996. The voting rate peaked at 73 percent in the 65-to-74 age group.

Despite their reputation as rebels, the political leanings of boomers mirror those of the public as a whole. Between 34 and 36 percent of 35-to-54-year-olds regard themselves as moderates, while 34 percent identify themselves as conservatives—shares similar to those among all adults. Boomers are slightly more liberal than the population as a whole (26 to 28 percent identify themselves as liberal versus 24 percent of all adults). While conservatives outnumber liberals among the baby-boom generation, boomers are more liberal and less conservative than older Americans. This fact may account for their reputation as upstarts.

Political cynicism has turned many Americans—particularly younger generations—away from political parties. The proportion of people who identify themselves as independents rather than Republicans or Democrats rises with age, from just 24 percent of the oldest Americans to the 51 percent majority of the youngest adults. Boomers stand in the middle of this continuum; 36 to 38 percent identify themselves as independents.

♦ To win elections in the future, political parties must capture the votes of independents. This puts independents in control of the policies of both parties, which may pull Democrats and Republicans towards the political middle.

Political Influence of Average Citizen, 1996

"The average citizen has considerable influence on politics—do you agree or disagree?"

(percent of people aged 18 or older responding by age, 1996)

	strongly agree	agree	neither	disagree	strongly disagree	agree, total	disagree, total
Total people	**4%**	**27%**	**19%**	**36%**	**10%**	**31%**	**46%**
Aged 18 to 24	3	23	21	36	9	26	45
Aged 25 to 34	3	22	18	39	13	25	52
Aged 35 to 44	5	26	22	35	10	31	45
Aged 45 to 54	5	30	20	31	10	35	41
Aged 55 to 64	4	27	15	41	7	31	48
Aged 65 to 74	2	35	14	32	9	37	41
Aged 75 or older	6	30	10	33	6	36	39

Note: Numbers may not add to 100 because "don't know" and no answer are not shown.
Source: 1996 General Social Survey, National Opinion Research Center, University of Chicago; calculations by New Strategist

Political Leanings, 1996

"We hear a lot of talk these days about liberals and conservatives. On a seven-point scale from extremely liberal to extremely conservative, where would you place yourself?"

(percent of people aged 18 or older responding by age, 1996)

	slightly to extremely liberal	moderate, middle of the road	slightly to extremely conservative
Total people	**24%**	**36%**	**35%**
Aged 18 to 24	25	36	31
Aged 25 to 34	26	35	34
Aged 35 to 44	28	34	34
Aged 45 to 54	26	36	34
Aged 55 to 64	19	38	39
Aged 65 to 74	16	38	40
Aged 75 or older	18	41	31

Note: Numbers may not add to 100 because "don't know" and no answer are not shown.
Source: 1996 General Social Survey, National Opinion Research Center, University of Chicago; calculations by New Strategist

Political Party Identification, 1996

"Generally speaking, do you usually think of yourself as a Republican, Democrat, Independent, or what?"

(percent of people aged 18 or older responding by age, 1996)

	Democrat	independent	Republican
Total people	**34%**	**37%**	**28%**
Aged 18 to 24	27	51	20
Aged 25 to 34	28	41	29
Aged 35 to 44	31	38	30
Aged 45 to 54	37	36	25
Aged 55 to 64	36	32	31
Aged 65 to 74	42	25	31
Aged 75 or older	48	24	26

Note: Numbers may not add to 100 because "other" and no answer are not shown.
Source: 1996 General Social Survey, National Opinion Research Center, University of Chicago; calculations by New Strategist

Voting Rate by Age, 1996

(total number of U.S. citizens aged 18 or older, and percent who reported being registered and having voted in the election of November, by age, 1996; numbers in thousands)

	total	percent registered	percent voted
Total citizens	**179,936**	**70.9%**	**58.4%**
Aged 18 to 19	6,788	46.7	32.4
Aged 20 to 24	15,686	56.4	36.9
Aged 25 to 29	17,050	61.3	44.9
Aged 30 to 34	18,801	65.5	51.1
Aged 35 to 44	39,935	72.2	59.6
Aged 45 to 54	30,828	76.4	66.0
Aged 55 to 64	19,959	79.8	71.4
Aged 65 to 74	17,559	81.0	72.6
Aged 75 to 84	10,533	79.5	67.9
Aged 85 or older	2,797	70.1	52.2

Source: Bureau of the Census, Voting and Registration in the Election of November 1996, *Current Population Reports P20-504, 1998*

Volunteering Peaks among Boomers

People aged 35 to 54 are most likely to volunteer for a variety of causes.

In middle-age, people must juggle myriad responsibilities—work, family, and community service. People aged 35 to 54 are more likely to volunteer in a variety of fields than older and younger Americans.

Religious organizations benefit the most from volunteers. Overall, 24 percent of Americans gave some of their time to a religious organization in 1996. Among boomers, 28 to 30 percent volunteered in this area.

Educational organizations also find a lot of boomer volunteers. From 22 to 24 percent of 35-to-54-year-olds volunteered for an educational organization in 1996, a much higher share than that in any other age group. Behind this high level of volunteering is the fact that many 35-to-54-year-olds have school-aged children, and they volunteer in classrooms to benefit their children. This same personal motivation also accounts for the high level of youth development volunteering among boomers.

People aged 45 to 54 are more likely than other age groups to volunteer in the area of arts, culture, and humanities. Twelve percent did so in 1996. A nearly equal share volunteered in the health area. Only in the environmental area are boomers outdone by another age group: people aged 18 to 24 are most likely to volunteer for environmental organizations.

◆ As women went to work and the lives of the middle-aged became much busier, many community organizations have found it difficult to round up volunteers. To remedy this situation, organizations dependent on volunteers need to rethink their practices to make it easier for busy people to lend a hand.

Volunteer Work, 1996

"In which, if any, of these areas have you done some volunteer work in the past 12 months?"

(percent of people aged 18 or older responding by age, 1996)

	religious organizations	education	youth development	health	environment	arts, culture, humanities	political organizations or campaigns
Total people	**24%**	**17%**	**15%**	**10%**	**7%**	**7%**	**5%**
18 to 24	16	16	18	8	11	7	4
25 to 34	21	17	16	13	6	5	3
35 to 44	28	24	20	12	7	6	6
45 to 54	30	22	17	13	9	12	6
55 to 64	29	10	11	5	6	9	5
65 to 74	24	6	3	6	4	4	5
75 or older	9	6	3	7	4	2	3

Note: Numbers may not add to 100 because no answer is not shown.
Source: 1996 General Social Survey, National Opinion Research Center, University of Chicago; calculations by New Strategist

The Arts Are Important to Boomers

Boomers are more likely to attend arts events and participate in art activities than is the average American.

People aged 35 to 54 are more likely to attend almost every type of art event than is the average person. This age group is also more likely than average to read literature, and to participate in a variety of art activities such as weaving, photography, and pottery. One reason for the avid interest of boomers in the arts is their high level of education. The more educated the person, the more likely he or she is to attend art events and participate in art activities, according to a 1997 survey by the National Endowment for the Arts.

Arts participation is on a par with other leisure activities, the survey finds. Among 45-to-54-year-olds, for example, the proportion visiting an art museum in the past 12 months is about the same as the proportion who attended a sporting event. Among those aged 35 to 44, the proportion visiting an arts and crafts fair or an historic park in the past year exceeds the proportion who played a sport, did volunteer work, went to a sporting event, or used a computer for entertainment.

♦ As the well-educated baby-boom generation ages and gains more leisure time, expect to see a surge in arts attendance and participation among older people.

Attendance at Arts Events, 1997

(percent of people aged 18 or older and people aged 35 to 54 attending art event or reading literature at least once in the past 12 months, 1997)

	total	aged 35 to 44	aged 45 to 54
Read literature*	63.1%	64.3%	65.5%
Visited art/craft fair	47.5	54.2	55.9
Visited historic park	46.9	52.3	53.8
Visited art museum	34.9	37.3	40.2
Musical play	24.5	25.8	29.2
Non-musical play	15.8	14.7	19.8
Classical music	15.6	14.3	20.4
Dance, except ballet	12.4	13.6	14.0
Jazz performance	11.9	14.3	13.0
Ballet	5.8	6.6	7.2
Opera	4.7	4.4	6.0

* Literature is defined as plays, poetry, novels, or short stories.
Source: National Endowment for the Arts, 1997 Survey of Public Participation in the Arts, Summary Report, Internet web site <http://arts.endow.gov/pub/Survey/SurveyPDF.html>

Participation in the Arts, 1997

(percent of people aged 18 or older and people aged 35 to 54 participating in art activity at least once in the past 12 months, 1997)

	total	aged 35 to 44	aged 45 to 54
Buying art	35.1%	39.9%	36.6%
Weaving	27.6	29.4	28.6
Photography	16.9	17.9	18.0
Drawing	15.9	15.3	12.8
Pottery	15.1	17.5	17.6
Dance, except ballet	12.6	12.7	11.1
Writing	12.1	11.7	9.5
Classical music	11.0	11.3	15.2
Singing in groups	10.4	8.7	12.7
Musical play	7.7	8.2	6.8
Non-musical play	2.7	2.3	2.5
Jazz	2.2	2.9	2.4
Opera	1.8	1.7	2.5
Ballet	0.5	0.3	0.4

Source: National Endowment for the Arts, 1997 Survey of Public Participation in the Arts, Summary Report, Internet web site <http://arts.endow.gov/pub/Survey/SurveyPDF.html>

Participation in Leisure Activities, 1997

(percent of people aged 18 or older and people aged 35 to 54 participating in leisure activities at least once in the past 12 months, 1997)

	total	aged 35 to 44	aged 45 to 54
Exercise program	75.7%	78.5%	76.9%
Home improvement/repair	65.9	75.6	74.6
Went out to the movies	65.5	73.3	65.0
Gardening	65.4	71.4	70.7
Went to an amusement park	57.0	68.3	53.3
Played a sport	44.9	51.6	40.0
Outdoor activities	44.3	54.5	44.7
Volunteer or charity work	43.2	49.6	46.3
Went to a sporting event	41.2	46.4	42.3
Used a computer for entertainment	40.4	47.1	39.9

Source: National Endowment for the Arts, 1997 Survey of Public Participation in the Arts, Summary Report, Internet web site <http://arts.endow.gov/pub/Survey/SurveyPDF.html>

2

Education

♦ Men aged 50 to 54 are the most highly educated cohort in American history, with 32 percent having a bachelor's degree.

♦ One in four women aged 35 to 54 is a college graduate, and over half have at least some college experience.

♦ Among men aged 35 to 54, 30 percent of whites, 16 percent of blacks, and 13 percent of Hispanics are college graduates.

♦ Only 59 percent of Hispanic women aged 35 to 54 are high school graduates, versus 84 percent of black women and 89 percent of white women.

♦ Four percent of 35-to-54-year-olds are currently enrolled in school, accounting for 35 percent of the nation's part-time college students.

♦ Nearly half the people aged 35 to 54 have taken adult education courses in the past 12 months, and most have done so for job advancement.

Boomer Men Are Most Educated

More than 30 percent of men aged 45 to 54 have bachelor's degrees.

Men aged 45 to 54 are the most highly educated Americans. Nearly one-third have a college diploma, and more than 1 in 10 has an advanced degree. Behind this high level of education is the Vietnam War. To avoid being drafted during the 1960s and early 1970s, many young men opted for college deferments. Those men are now in their forties and early fifties.

When the war ended, so did the incentive to stay in school. Consequently, men aged 35 to 44 are less educated than those aged 45 to 54. Twenty-eight percent of men aged 40 to 44 and 26 percent of those aged 35 to 44 have a bachelor's degree. But more than half have at least some college experience.

♦ The lofty educational level of baby-boom men has transformed the middle-aged market. Educated middle-aged consumers are driving the demand for a variety of products and services, including computers, sport utility vehicles, and mutual funds.

Men aged 50 to 54 are the best educated

(percent of men aged 35 to 54 who have a college degree, by age, 1998)

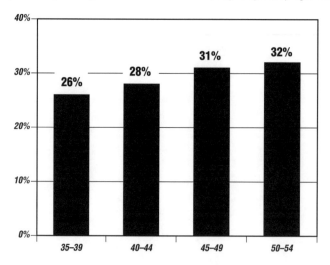

Educational Attainment of Men Aged 35 to 54, 1998

(number and percent distribution of total men aged 25 or older and men aged 35 to 54 by highest level of education, 1998; numbers in thousands)

	total	35 to 54	35 to 39	40 to 44	45 to 49	50 to 54
Total men	**82,376**	**38,654**	**11,299**	**10,756**	**9,116**	**7,483**
Not a high school graduate	14,175	5,103	1,572	1,301	1,067	1,163
High school graduate	26,575	12,239	4,003	3,535	2,600	2,101
Some college, no degree	14,122	6,890	1,855	2,040	1,728	1,267
Associate's degree	5,670	3,208	893	927	859	529
Bachelor's degree	14,090	7,062	2,014	1,957	1,719	1,372
Master's degree	4,640	2,515	596	578	695	646
Professional degree	1,749	925	227	247	257	194
Doctoral degree	1,353	712	139	172	190	211
High school graduate or more	68,199	33,551	9,727	9,456	8,048	6,320
Some college or more	41,624	21,312	5,724	5,921	5,448	4,219
Bachelor's degree or more	21,832	11,214	2,976	2,954	2,861	2,423
Total men	**100.0%**	**100.0%**	**100.0%**	**100.0%**	**100.0%**	**100.0%**
Not a high school graduate	17.2	13.2	13.9	12.1	11.7	15.5
High school graduate	32.3	31.7	35.4	32.9	28.5	28.1
Some college, no degree	17.1	17.8	16.4	18.0	18.0	16.9
Associate's degree	6.9	8.3	7.9	8.6	9.4	7.1
Bachelor's degree	17.1	18.3	17.8	18.2	18.9	18.3
Master's degree	5.6	6.5	5.3	5.4	7.6	8.6
Professional degree	2.1	2.4	2.0	2.3	2.8	2.6
Doctoral degree	1.6	1.8	1.2	1.6	2.1	2.8
High school graduate or more	82.8	86.8	86.1	87.9	88.3	84.5
Some college or more	50.5	55.1	50.7	55.1	59.8	56.4
Bachelor's degree or more	26.5	29.0	26.3	27.5	31.4	32.4

Source: Bureau of the Census, Educational Attainment in the United States: March 1998, *detailed tables from Current Population Report P20-513, 1998; calculations by New Strategist*

Most Boomer Women Have College Experience

About one in four is a college graduate.

Unlike their male counterparts, women aged 35 to 54 did not have the threat of being drafted and sent to Vietnam to keep them in college. Older baby-boom women are significantly less educated than their male counterparts. Among women aged 50 to 54, for example, only 25 percent are college graduates, versus 32 percent of men in the age group.

But baby-boom women are much more educated than older generations of women. Unlike men, whose educational attainment peaks in the 45-to-54 age group, younger boomer women are no less educated than those in their late forties and early fifties. Among women aged 40 to 44, 27 percent are college graduates—almost equal to the 28 percent of men in the age group who have graduated from college.

♦ Because men and women tend to marry people like themselves, many college-educated men and women are married to each other. With earnings closely linked to education, college-educated dual-income couples in the 35-to-54 age group are the nation's most affluent households.

Educational Attainment of Women Aged 35 to 54, 1998

(number and percent distribution of total women aged 25 or older and women aged 35 to 54 by highest level of education, 1998; numbers in thousands)

	total	35 to 54	35 to 39	40 to 44	45 to 49	50 to 54
Total women	**89,835**	**39,866**	**11,392**	**11,015**	**9,518**	**7,941**
Not a high school graduate	15,381	4,561	1,299	1,154	1,049	1,059
High school graduate	31,599	13,841	3,906	3,693	3,299	2,943
Some college, no degree	15,516	7,322	2,171	2,081	1,691	1,379
Associate's degree	7,198	3,846	1,165	1,161	928	592
Bachelor's degree	14,215	7,043	2,084	2,101	1,618	1,240
Master's degree	4,592	2,504	581	623	737	563
Professional degree	820	411	88	138	110	75
Doctoral degree	515	335	97	63	86	89
High school graduate or more	74,455	35,302	10,092	9,860	8,469	6,881
Some college or more	42,856	21,461	6,186	6,167	5,170	3,938
Bachelor's degree or more	20,142	10,293	2,850	2,925	2,551	1,967
Total women	**100.0%**	**100.0%**	**100.0%**	**100.0%**	**100.0%**	**100.0%**
Not a high school graduate	17.1	11.4	11.4	10.5	11.0	13.3
High school graduate	35.2	34.7	34.3	33.5	34.7	37.1
Some college, no degree	17.3	18.4	19.1	18.9	17.8	17.4
Associate's degree	8.0	9.6	10.2	10.5	9.7	7.5
Bachelor's degree	15.8	17.7	18.3	19.1	16.0	15.6
Master's degree	5.1	6.3	5.1	5.7	7.7	7.1
Professional degree	0.9	1.0	0.8	1.3	1.2	0.9
Doctoral degree	0.6	0.8	0.9	0.6	0.9	1.1
High school graduate or more	82.9	88.6	88.6	89.5	88.0	86.7
Some college or more	47.7	53.8	54.3	55.0	54.3	49.6
Bachelor's degree or more	22.4	25.8	25.0	26.6	26.8	24.8

Source: Bureau of the Census, Educational Attainment in the United States: March 1998, *detailed tables from* Current Population Report P20-513, 1998; *calculations by New Strategist*

White Men Are Twice As Likely to Be College Graduates

Only 16 percent of black men aged 35 to 54 have a college degree.

Among men aged 35 to 54, whites are much better educated than blacks or Hispanics. The 30 percent share of white men in the age group who have a college degree is nearly twice as great as the 16 percent share among blacks and more than twice the 13 percent share among Hispanics.

Black and white men aged 35 to 54 are almost equally likely to have graduated from high school (88 percent of white men and 80 percent of black men are high school graduates). The divergence in educational attainment between blacks and whites occurs after high school, when family income strongly determines who remains in school and who does not.

Only 58 percent of Hispanic men graduated from high school, a rate far below the rates for whites and blacks. One reason for the low educational level of Hispanics is that many are poorly educated immigrants.

♦ Because white men are much better educated than blacks or Hispanics, their incomes are higher. Until the gap in education closes, the earnings of black and Hispanic men, on average, will remain below the earnings of white men.

Blacks are almost as likely as whites to have a high school diploma

(percent of men aged 35 to 54 who have a high school diploma, by race and Hispanic origin, 1998)

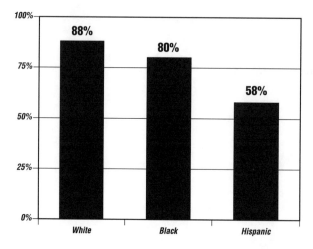

Educational Attainment of Men Aged 35 to 54 by Race and Hispanic Origin, 1998

(number and percent distribution of men aged 35 to 54 by educational attainment, race, and Hispanic origin, 1998; numbers in thousands)

	white	black	Hispanic
Total men aged 35 to 54	**32,748**	**4,153**	**3,686**
Not a high school graduate	4,046	845	1,548
High school graduate	10,223	1,607	976
Some college, no degree	5,842	809	496
Associate's degree	2,818	240	195
Bachelor's degree	6,161	499	286
Master's degree	2,194	101	108
Professional degree	828	37	55
Doctoral degree	633	14	24
High school graduate or more	28,699	3,307	2,140
Some college or more	18,476	1,700	1,164
Bachelor's degree or more	9,816	651	473
Total men aged 35 to 54	**100.0%**	**100.0%**	**100.0%**
Not a high school graduate	12.4	20.3	41.0
High school graduate	31.2	38.7	26.5
Some college, no degree	17.8	19.5	13.5
Associate's degree	8.6	5.8	5.3
Bachelor's degree	18.8	12.0	7.8
Master's degree	6.7	2.4	2.9
Professional degree	2.5	0.9	1.5
Doctoral degree	1.9	0.3	0.7
High school graduate or more	87.6	79.6	58.1
Some college or more	56.4	40.9	31.6
Bachelor's degree or more	29.0	15.7	12.8

Source: Bureau of the Census, Educational Attainment in the United States: March 1998, *detailed tables from Current Population Report P20-513, 1998; calculations by New Strategist*

Hispanic Women Lag in Educational Attainment

Only 59 percent of Hispanic women aged 35 to 54 are high school graduates.

Among women aged 35 to 54, whites and blacks are almost equally likely to have graduated from high school (89 percent of whites and 84 percent of blacks). But while 27 percent of white women in the age group are college graduates, only 18 percent of blacks have a college degree. Black women are more likely than black men to be college graduates, however, while white women are less likely to have graduated from college than their male counterparts.

Only 58 percent of Hispanic women aged 35 to 54 graduated from high school, and just 12 percent have a bachelor's degree. Behind the low educational level of Hispanics is the fact that many are poorly educated immigrants.

♦ Until women's educational level equals that of men, the average woman won't earn as much as the average man.

Black and white women are almost equally likely to be high school graduates

(percent of women aged 35 to 54 who have a high school diploma, by race and Hispanic origin, 1998)

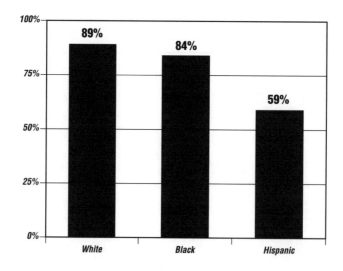

Educational Attainment of Women Aged 35 to 54 by Race and Hispanic Origin, 1998

(number and percent distribution of women aged 35 to 54 by educational attainment, race, and Hispanic origin, 1998; numbers in thousands)

	white	black	Hispanic
Total women aged 35 to 54	**32,859**	**5,009**	**3,618**
Not a high school graduate	3,483	787	1,499
High school graduate	11,394	1,865	977
Some college, no degree	5,988	1,050	488
Associate's degree	3,295	418	210
Bachelor's degree	5,929	594	345
Master's degree	2,134	252	62
Professional degree	354	29	20
Doctoral degree	284	14	14
High school graduate or more	29,378	4,222	2,116
Some college or more	17,984	2,357	1,139
Bachelor's degree or more	8,701	889	441
Total women aged 35 to 54	**100.0%**	**100.0%**	**100.0%**
Not a high school graduate	10.6	15.7	41.4
High school graduate	34.7	37.2	27.0
Some college, no degree	18.2	20.0	13.5
Associate's degree	10.0	8.3	5.8
Bachelor's degree	18.0	11.9	9.5
Master's degree	6.5	5.0	1.7
Professional degree	1.1	0.6	0.6
Doctoral degree	0.9	0.3	0.4
High school graduate or more	89.4	84.3	58.5
Some college or more	54.7	47.1	31.5
Bachelor's degree or more	26.5	17.7	12.2

Source: Bureau of the Census, Educational Attainment in the United States: March 1998, *detailed tables from Current Population Report P20-513, 1998; calculations by New Strategist*

Nearly 3 Million Boomers Still in School

Of the nation's 70 million students, 2.7 million are aged 35 to 54.

Four percent of people aged 35 to 54 are currently enrolled in school. While this figure is a small percentage of the population in the age group, the number of middle-aged Americans attending school has expanded enormously over the past few decades.

Among students, boomer women outnumber boomer men, 1.7 million to 1 million. While 2.8 percent of men aged 35 to 54 are in school, the proportion is 4.4 percent among women—peaking at 5.7 percent of women aged 35 to 39.

◆ As well-educated boomers age into their fifties and sixties, expect to see school enrollment rise among older Americans.

Women outnumber men in school

(number of people aged 35 to 54 enrolled in school, by sex, 1996)

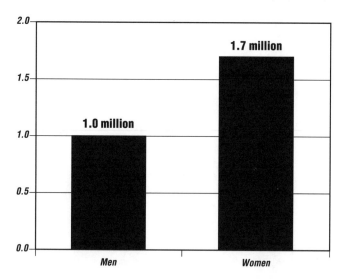

School Enrollment of People Aged 35 to 54, 1996

(number of people aged 3 or older and people aged 35 to 54, and number and percent enrolled in school by sex, fall 1996; numbers in thousands)

	total	enrolled	
		number	*percent*
Total people	**253,175**	**70,297**	**27.8%**
Total aged 35 to 54	75,835	2,725	3.6
Aged 35 to 39	22,373	1,138	5.1
Aged 40 to 44	20,908	797	3.8
Aged 45 to 49	18,466	531	2.9
Aged 50 to 54	14,088	259	1.8
Total males	**123,103**	**35,092**	**28.5**
Total aged 35 to 54	37,172	1,029	2.8
Aged 35 to 39	11,020	494	4.5
Aged 40 to 44	10,300	300	2.9
Aged 45 to 49	9,026	161	1.8
Aged 50 to 54	6,826	74	1.1
Total females	**130,073**	**35,205**	**27.1**
Total aged 35 to 54	38,664	1,696	4.4
Aged 35 to 39	11,353	644	5.7
Aged 40 to 44	10,608	497	4.7
Aged 45 to 49	9,441	370	3.9
Aged 50 to 54	7,262	185	2.6

Source: Bureau of the Census, School Enrollment—Social and Economic Characteristics of Students: October 1996, *detailed tables from Current Population Report P20-500, 1998; calculations by New Strategist*

Most College Students Aged 35 to 54 Attend School Part-Time

With families to support, boomers cannot afford to go to school full-time.

As the number of older college students has grown, so has the number of students attending college part-time. Most boomers have families to support and cannot afford the luxury of full-time study, but have to juggle daytime jobs and nighttime classes. In 1996, 74 percent of college students aged 35 to 54 attended school part-time.

Overall, 2.6 million people aged 35 to 54 are in college, accounting for a significant 17 percent of total college enrollment. People aged 35 to 54 are a 7 percent share of full-time students, but a 35 percent share of part-timers.

♦ Because the most highly educated people are the ones most likely to seek even more education, boomers will continue to be found on college campuses even as they age into their fifties and sixties.

Among boomers in college, most attend part-time

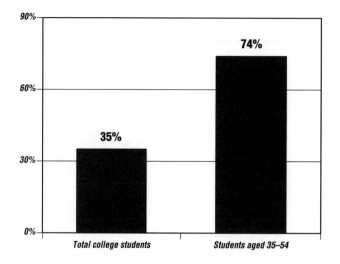

*(percent of total college students and students aged
35 to 54 who attend school part-time, 1996)*

College Students Aged 35 to 54 by Attendance Status, 1996

(number and percent distribution of people aged 15 or older and people aged 35 to 54 enrolled in institutions of higher education, by full- or part-time attendance status, 1996; numbers in thousands)

	total	full-time	part-time
Total people enrolled	**15,226**	**9,839**	**5,388**
Total aged 35 to 54	2,554	667	1,886
Aged 35 to 39	1,068	333	735
Aged 40 to 44	742	161	579
Aged 45 to 49	501	119	383
Aged 50 to 54	243	54	189
Percent distribution by attendance status			
Total people enrolled	**100.0%**	**64.6%**	**35.4%**
Total aged 35 to 54	100.0	26.1	73.8
Aged 35 to 39	100.0	31.2	68.8
Aged 40 to 44	100.0	21.7	78.0
Aged 45 to 49	100.0	23.8	76.4
Aged 50 to 54	100.0	22.2	77.8
Percent distribution by age			
Total people enrolled	**100.0%**	**100.0%**	**100.0%**
Total aged 35 to 54	16.8	6.8	35.0
Aged 35 to 39	7.0	3.4	13.6
Aged 40 to 44	4.9	1.6	10.7
Aged 45 to 49	3.3	1.2	7.1
Aged 50 to 54	1.6	0.5	3.5

Source: Bureau of the Census, School Enrollment—Social and Economic Characteristics of Students: October 1996, detailed tables from Current Population Report P20-500, 1998; calculations by New Strategist

Adult Education Is Popular among Boomers

Professional advancement is the primary reason they go to school.

Fully 40 percent of people aged 17 or older took some type of adult education course in 1995, including nearly one-half of those aged 35 to 54. The courses they took range from bachelor's degree programs to money management seminars. Overall, 34 million people aged 35 to 54 took part in adult education during the past year, accounting for 46 percent of total participants.

Two out of three boomers who took adult education courses cite professional advancement as their motivation for participating. Four out of 10 cite personal or social reasons. Few boomers take adult education courses to train for a new job or to complete a degree or diploma.

◆ Boomers value education for it's own sake as well as for its professional benefits. Enrollment in adult education among older Americans will rise as boomers age.

Adult Education by Age, 1995

(number and percent of people aged 17 or older not attending elementary or secondary school full-time who have been enrolled in any educational activity in the past 12 months, and percent distribution by reason for taking course, by age, 1995; numbers in thousands)

		participants in adult education					
				reason for taking course (percent)			
	total	*total*		*personal/ social*	*advance on the job*	*train for a new job*	*complete degree or diploma*
		number	*percent*				
Total people	**189,543**	**76,261**	**40%**	**44%**	**54%**	**11%**	**10%**
Aged 17 to 24	22,407	10,539	47	39	33	21	19
Aged 25 to 34	40,326	19,508	48	41	56	14	8
Aged 35 to 44	42,304	20,814	49	40	64	10	9
Aged 45 to 54	31,807	14,592	46	39	65	7	10
Aged 55 to 64	21,824	6,117	28	52	54	4	6
Aged 65 or older	30,876	4,691	15	86	14	1	3

Note: Percent distribution by reason will not add to 100 because some participants took more than one course or had more than one reason for participating.
Source: Bureau of the Census, Statistical Abstract of the United States: 1998

3

Health

♦ Because boomers are more involved in exercise and fitness activities than older generations were at their age, they may be healthier in old age than is the current generation of elderly.

♦ The 12 million people aged 35 to 54 who are without health insurance account for 29 percent of the nation's uninsured.

♦ Women aged 35 or older accounted for only 7 percent of first births in 1997, 12 percent of second births, 18 percent of third births, and 29 percent of fourth or subsequent births.

♦ The eating habits of people in middle age are driven more by taste and convenience than by health benefits.

♦ Boomer men are twice as likely to exercise daily as boomer women.

♦ More than half of people aged 30 to 44 have smoked marijuana. Nearly one in four 30-to-39-year-olds has used cocaine.

♦ The most prevalent chronic condition among 45-to-64-year-olds is arthritis (experienced by 23 percent), followed by high blood pressure (22 percent).

♦ At age 40, men have 36 years of life left, on average, while women have another 40 years.

The Middle-Aged Feel Better Than Ever

There has been a big increase in the percentage of fiftysomethings who feel "excellent."

The percentage of Americans aged 50 to 59 who say their health is excellent rose from 23 percent in 1976 to 30 percent in 1996. There was also a gain for people in their forties, with the proportion of those who report excellent health growing from 27 percent in 1976 to 32 percent in 1996. Today, the proportion of people in their forties and fifties who believe they are in excellent health matches the national average, while two decades earlier it was below average. Among all Americans aged 18 or older, 31 percent report being in excellent health.

The proportion of people who say their health is excellent peaks in the 18-to-29 age group at 36 percent. It is lowest among people in their seventies at 17 percent. Nevertheless, even in the oldest age group the proportion of those who report being in good or excellent health grew from 54 to 63 percent between 1976 and 1996. Only 8 percent of people aged 70 or older reported being in poor health in 1996, down from 15 percent in 1976.

♦ Because the baby-boom generation is more involved in exercise and fitness than were previous generations in middle age, boomers may be healthier in old age than is the current generation of elderly.

Health Status, 1976 and 1996

"Would you say your own health, in general, is excellent, good, fair, or poor?"

(percent of people aged 18 or older responding by age, 1976–96)

	excellent		good		fair		poor	
	1996	*1976*	*1996*	*1976*	*1996*	*1976*	*1996*	*1976*
Total people	**31%**	**31%**	**49%**	**42%**	**16%**	**20%**	**4%**	**7%**
Aged 18 to 29	36	44	49	44	14	10	1	2
Aged 30 to 39	35	41	52	44	10	11	2	3
Aged 40 to 49	32	27	50	47	15	19	3	7
Aged 50 to 59	30	23	44	44	19	23	7	9
Aged 60 to 69	23	18	49	32	18	37	9	12
Aged 70 or older	17	17	46	37	29	31	8	15

Note: Numbers may not add to 100 because no answer is not included.
Source: General Social Surveys, National Opinion Research Center, University of Chicago

Women Are More Likely to Eat Yogurt Than Men

The food consumption of boomer men and women differs, but not by much.

While many boomers claim to follow a healthy diet, a look at what they really eat reveals otherwise. Twenty-five percent of men aged 30 to 39 eat crackers, popcorn, pretzels, or corn chips on an average day, while only 12 percent eat dark green vegetables. Among women in their forties, 40 percent eat cakes, cookies, pastries, or pies on an average day, while only 26 percent consume citrus fruits or juices.

Women aged 30 to 49 are more likely than men to eat fruit, while men are more likely to eat French fries. Women in their thirties are almost twice as likely as their male counterparts to eat yogurt, 6.4 versus 3.7 percent. Men are more likely than women to eat beef or hot dogs on an average day, while women are more likely to drink skim milk. Despite all the dieting advice directed at women, they are more likely than men to eat sweets.

The biggest difference between boomer men and women is in their beverage consumption. Men are much more likely than women to drink beer, while women are more likely to drink wine or tea. Men are more likely than women to drink regular carbonated soft drinks, while women are more likely to drink diet sodas.

◆ Most boomers know what it means to eat a healthy diet. But more often than not, they eat what they want rather than what they should. With age, however, health concerns may prompt many to control their impulses.

Food Consumption of People Aged 30 to 49 by Sex, 1994–95

(percent of total people and people aged 30 to 49 consuming selected types of foods on an average day, by sex, 1994–95)

	total people	aged 30 to 39		aged 40 to 49	
		men	women	men	women
Grain products	**97.1%**	**98.1%**	**96.4%**	**96.2%**	**96.1%**
Yeast breads and rolls	66.5	68.1	65.0	67.9	64.2
Cereals and pastas	47.0	37.4	39.2	37.6	38.7
Ready-to-eat cereals	28.8	18.8	19.1	18.4	18.8
Rice	11.3	13.8	12.9	12.6	11.5
Pasta	7.0	6.8	7.5	9.1	7.9
Quick breads, pancakes, French toast	22.6	22.6	20.5	24.6	25.3
Cakes, cookies, pastries, pies	40.8	38.0	37.8	36.6	40.1
Crackers, popcorn, pretzels, corn chips	28.0	25.4	29.2	25.0	28.1
Mixtures, mainly grain	35.9	41.4	37.9	31.1	30.1
Vegetables	**82.9**	**88.0**	**81.0**	**86.7**	**84.4**
White potatoes	43.7	50.2	39.3	42.7	39.5
Fried	26.3	32.5	21.8	25.3	21.2
Dark-green vegetables	9.7	12.1	9.1	10.5	11.8
Deep-yellow vegetables	12.9	11.6	14.8	12.0	15.4
Tomatoes	38.3	42.0	41.1	44.0	40.0
Lettuce, lettuce-based salads	24.6	27.2	27.8	30.1	30.1
Green beans	8.1	5.8	8.8	6.4	8.1
Corn, green peas, lima beans	11.7	8.9	12.0	13.0	11.1
Other vegetables	42.8	49.4	41.2	50.5	48.9
Fruits	**54.2**	**41.8**	**46.7**	**47.2**	**52.3**
Citrus fruits and juices	26.7	21.7	21.5	23.2	25.5
Juices	20.5	15.5	15.3	16.9	18.6
Other fruits, mixtures, and juices	39.5	29.0	33.9	33.0	39.7
Apples	12.2	10.1	10.4	8.3	12.8
Bananas	13.1	12.8	11.7	13.7	13.1
Melons and berries	7.9	4.6	6.4	7.7	12.2
Other fruits and mixtures, mainly fruit	13.9	11.4	10.4	12.1	14.1
Noncitrus juices and nectars	8.7	3.8	5.6	4.6	4.4

(continued)

(continued from previous page)

	total people	aged 30 to 39		aged 40 to 49	
		men	women	men	women
Milk and milk products	**79.1%**	**74.8%**	**75.2%**	**75.6%**	**76.8%**
Milk, milk drinks, yogurt	60.8	51.9	53.2	52.1	52.2
Fluid milk	56.0	48.3	48.8	48.6	48.4
Whole	19.3	15.9	13.4	17.4	13.6
Low fat	26.7	25.5	24.1	20.5	20.7
Skim	10.7	6.3	11.8	12.2	14.4
Yogurt	3.9	3.7	6.4	3.1	4.6
Milk desserts	18.1	18.2	13.9	19.7	18.0
Cheese	32.5	34.2	34.7	33.5	32.6
Meat, poultry, and fish	**86.5**	**89.9**	**84.5**	**89.6**	**85.5**
Beef	21.6	28.9	22.9	25.9	20.2
Pork	15.9	14.3	15.0	19.8	15.9
Frankfurters, sausages, luncheon meats	28.6	31.3	25.7	32.7	23.8
Poultry	23.1	25.5	17.7	23.9	23.3
Chicken	19.4	22.8	15.2	19.5	18.5
Fish and shellfish	7.7	11.6	7.2	6.7	6.8
Mixtures, mainly meat, poultry, fish	35.8	38.1	34.9	37.2	34.0
Eggs	19.2	19.5	17.8	21.0	18.4
Legumes	13.2	15.9	15.6	16.0	14.7
Nuts and seeds	9.9	7.7	6.6	9.2	8.7
Fats and oils	54.7	57.0	58.8	57.2	63.9
Table fats	30.8	31.0	28.8	32.2	33.2
Salad dressings	29.1	30.3	32.4	34.7	34.1
Sugars and sweets	53.6	49.9	56.5	52.9	61.4
Sugars	28.2	32.1	36.1	33.8	37.9
Candy	15.4	12.3	11.3	12.6	15.7
Beverages	**87.2**	**94.4**	**90.9**	**95.9**	**93.3**
Alcoholic	12.6	24.3	12.2	23.4	10.8
Wine	3.6	4.1	5.3	5.1	5.6
Beer and ale	7.8	20.1	4.8	17.9	3.7
Nonalcoholic	86.1	93.1	90.2	94.6	92.6
Coffee	39.7	53.4	46.8	62.9	61.2
Tea	23.3	27.4	30.6	25.5	32.0
Fruit drinks and ades	19.3	13.1	13.2	13.3	11.5
Carbonated soft drinks	50.4	63.1	57.2	53.7	53.0
Regular	39.0	50.6	39.8	40.5	28.7
Low calorie	13.0	14.8	18.5	15.7	26.0

Source: USDA, ARS Food Surveys Research Group, 1994 and 1995 Continuing Survey of Food Intakes by Individuals, 1997; Internet web site <http://www.barc.usda.gov/bhnrc>

Most 30-to-49-Year-Olds Eat Out Daily

Boomers eat away from home more than the average American.

Fifty-seven percent of Americans eat out on an average day, but the proportion is an even higher 66 percent among men aged 30 to 49. Women aged 30 to 49 are more likely to eat out than the average woman, 55 to 56 percent versus 51 percent.

Eating out does not necessarily mean going to a restaurant. Many people eat away from home at stores or other people's homes, for example. On an average day, about one-third of 30-to-49-year-olds eat at fast-food restaurants. An almost equal share eat at sit-down restaurants, while slightly fewer eat at stores. From 14 to 24 percent eat at someone else's home. A small percentage of boomers even eat at school cafeterias—some are attending school themselves while others are working at schools.

◆ Many boomers eat away from home because their busy schedules often do not permit home cooking. Responding to this need, supermarkets are offering more prepared foods as well as in-store dining—eroding the restaurant share of the food dollar.

Two-thirds of boomer men eat out on an average day

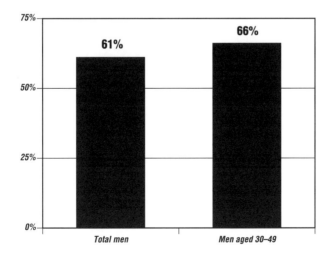

(percent of total men aged 20 or older and men aged 30 to 49 who eat away from home on an average day, 1994–95)

People Aged 30 to 49 Consuming Food
Away from Home by Location, 1994–95

(percent of total people and people aged 30 to 49 eating away from home on an average day, and percent distribution of those eating away from home by location, by sex, 1994–95)

	total people	men			women		
		total	30 to 39	40 to 49	total	30 to 39	40 to 49
Percent eating away from home	57.1%	61.2%	66.5%	66.4%	51.3%	56.0%	55.2%
Total eating away from home	100.0	100.0	100.0	100.0	100.0	100.0	100.0
Fast-food restaurant	32.4	37.2	37.1	34.8	29.5	33.3	31.1
Sit-down restaurant	26.8	31.7	27.5	30.5	33.7	28.0	34.4
Store	24.1	28.1	30.4	29.2	22.0	22.1	25.9
Someone else/gift	22.6	16.9	18.4	14.2	22.9	19.4	23.8
School cafeteria	11.4	1.6	1.6	2.7	2.0	2.0	3.2
Cafeteria	7.0	8.5	10.2	9.2	10.2	13.2	7.6
Day care	2.3	0.2	0.0	0.0	1.0	1.6	0.1
Other	23.3	29.5	32.4	28.0	25.3	28.1	27.3

Note: Numbers will not add to 100 because food may be eaten at more than one location during the day.
Source: USDA, ARS Food Surveys Research Group, 1994 and 1995 Diet and Health Knowledge Survey, 1997; Internet web site <http://www.barc.usda.gov/bhnrc>

Taste and Convenience More Important Than Health Benefits

Boomers are often too busy to eat well.

While most people in their thirties and forties claim to eat healthy foods, in fact few are giving up their favorite foods for health benefits. And a minority of them say they will trade taste or convenience for health. In part, the busy lifestyles of people aged 30 to 49 prevent them from closely watching their diets. In addition, many health foods lack the taste boomers crave and the convenience they need.

There are important differences in the eating habits of thirty- and fortysomethings. People in their forties are more concerned with healthy eating than those in their thirties. Forty-nine percent of the older group say they maintain a low-fat, low-cholesterol diet compared with just 38 percent of people in their thirties. The older group is also more likely to avoid some favorite foods to eat healthier, 40 to 32 percent.

♦ Although many baby boomers want to follow a healthy diet, they aren't willing to sacrifice to gain health benefits. As the health concerns of boomers grow with age, the most successful food marketers will be the ones who can offer health benefits in tasty and convenient packages.

Eating Habits of People Aged 30 to 49, 1996

(percent of people aged 18 or older and aged 30 to 49 who always or usually follow selected practices, by age, 1996)

	total persons 18+	30 to 39	40 to 49
Eat healthy foods	79%	72%	81%
Read food package labels	66	64	66
Choose low-fat dairy foods	53	43	53
Maintain a low-cholesterol diet	51	38	49
Maintain a low-fat diet	50	38	49
Choose products made with whole grains	49	44	53
Balance healthy foods with less healthy foods I enjoy more	43	45	44
Avoid some favorite foods to eat healthier	39	32	40
Try new food products	34	37	37
Avoid some favorite foods to lose weight	32	32	34
Give up convenience for health benefits	28	21	27
Maintain a low-calorie diet	26	16	28
Avoid foods that contain red meat	22	19	23
Give up good taste for health benefits	15	8	11
Choose foods/beverages to improve mental performance	14	11	14
Maintain a vegetarian diet	9	7	8
Choose foods/beverages to improve athletic performance	9	9	9

Source: 1997 HealthFocus Trend Report, HealthFocus, Des Moines, Iowa, 1997

Few Boomers Are Still Having Children

Now that the youngest boomers are in their mid-thirties, the generation accounts for a tiny share of births.

Among the nearly 4 million babies born to American women in 1997, only 12.5 percent had mothers aged 35 or older. Even though many baby boomers delayed having children until their thirties, most babies are born to women in their twenties.

Women aged 35 or older accounted for only 6.7 percent of first births in 1997. The proportion rises to 12 percent for second births and 18 percent for third births. Even among fourth and subsequent births, however, only 29 percent of mothers are aged 35 or older.

Among boomers giving birth in 1997, 68 percent were non-Hispanic whites. This compares with a non-Hispanic white share of just 59 percent for younger women who had babies in 1997. Minorities are a larger share of young adults than of the baby-boom generation, which accounts for this difference.

Boomer women are much less likely than younger women to be unmarried when they give birth. In 1996, one in three new mothers under age 35 was not married, versus only 16 percent of new mothers aged 35 or older.

Older mothers are more likely to deliver their babies by Caesarean section than younger women. Overall, 28 percent of births to women aged 35 or older in 1996 were by Caesarean. The figure was nearly one-third for births to women aged 40 or older.

♦ As the large and vocal baby-boom generation ages beyond the childbearing years, menopause will replace infertility as the hot topic in the reproductive arena.

Births to Women Aged 35 or Older
by Race and Hispanic Origin, 1997

(number and percent distribution of births to women by age, race, and Hispanic origin, 1997)

		race				Hispanic origin	
	total	white	black	Asian	Native American	Hispanic	non-Hispanic white
Total births	**3,894,970**	**3,085,477**	**600,898**	**170,110**	**38,486**	**711,753**	**2,343,636**
Under age 35	3,408,872	2,685,300	547,685	140,653	35,235	650,201	2,011,747
Aged 35 or older	486,098	400,177	53,213	29,457	3,251	61,552	331,889
Aged 35 to 39	408,111	336,982	44,316	24,131	2,682	51,025	280,414
Aged 40 to 44	74,778	60,646	8,572	5,019	541	10,116	49,397
Aged 45 to 49	3,209	2,549	325	307	28	411	2,078
Percent distribution by race and Hispanic origin							
Total births	**100.0%**	**79.2%**	**15.4%**	**4.4%**	**1.0%**	**18.3%**	**60.2%**
Under age 35	100.0	78.8	16.1	4.1	1.0	19.1	59.0
Aged 35 or older	100.0	82.3	10.9	6.1	0.7	12.7	68.3
Aged 35 to 39	100.0	82.6	10.9	5.9	0.7	12.5	68.7
Aged 40 to 44	100.0	81.1	11.5	6.7	0.7	13.5	66.1
Aged 45 to 49	100.0	79.4	10.1	9.6	0.9	12.8	64.8
Percent distribution by age							
Total births	**100.0%**	**100.0%**	**100.0%**	**100.0%**	**100.0%**	**100.0%**	**100.0%**
Under age 35	87.5	87.0	91.1	82.7	91.6	91.4	85.8
Aged 35 or older	12.5	13.0	8.9	17.3	8.4	8.6	14.2
Aged 35 to 39	10.5	10.9	7.4	14.2	7.0	7.2	12.0
Aged 40 to 44	1.9	2.0	1.4	3.0	1.4	1.4	2.1
Aged 45 to 49	0.1	0.1	0.1	0.2	0.1	0.1	0.1

Note: Numbers will not add to total because Hispanics may be of any race.
Source: National Center for Health Statistics, Births and Deaths: Preliminary Data for 1997, *National Vital Statistics Reports, Vol. 47, No. 4, 1998; calculations by New Strategist*

Births to Women aged 35 or Older by Birth Order, 1997

(number and percent distribution of births to women by age and birth order, 1997)

	total births	first child	second child	third child	fourth or more
Total births	**3,894,970**	**1,581,178**	**1,259,107**	**630,672**	**404,756**
Under age 35	3,408,872	1,474,886	1,107,042	519,499	307,445
Aged 35 or older	486,098	106,292	152,065	111,173	116,568
Aged 35 to 39	408,111	89,983	131,062	95,126	89,722
Aged 40 to 44	74,778	15,621	20,305	15,510	22,871
Aged 45 to 49	3,209	688	698	537	1,252
Percent distribution by birth order					
Total births	**100.0%**	**40.6%**	**32.3%**	**16.2%**	**10.4%**
Under age 35	100.0	43.3	32.5	15.2	9.0
Aged 35 or older	100.0	21.9	31.3	22.9	24.0
Aged 35 to 39	100.0	22.0	32.1	23.3	22.0
Aged 40 to 44	100.0	20.9	27.2	20.7	30.6
Aged 45 to 49	100.0	21.4	21.8	16.7	39.0
Percent distribution by age					
Total births	**100.0%**	**100.0%**	**100.0%**	**100.0%**	**100.0%**
Under age 35	87.5	93.3	87.9	82.4	76.0
Aged 35 or older	12.5	6.7	12.1	17.6	28.8
Aged 35 to 39	10.5	5.7	10.4	15.1	22.2
Aged 40 to 44	1.9	1.0	1.6	2.5	5.7
Aged 45 to 49	0.1	0.0	0.1	0.1	0.3

Note: Numbers will not add to total because not stated is not included.
Source: National Center for Health Statistics, Births and Deaths: Preliminary Data for 1997, *National Vital Statistics Reports, Vol. 47, No. 4, 1998; calculations by New Strategist*

Births to Women Aged 35 or Older by Marital Status, 1996

(total number of births to women, and number and percent to unmarried women, by age of mother, 1996)

	total	births to unmarried women	
		number	percent
Total births	**3,891,494**	**1,260,306**	**32.4%**
Under age 35	3,417,135	1,107,514	32.4
Aged 35 or older	474,359	76,396	16.1
Aged 35 to 39	399,510	62,656	15.7
Aged 40 or older	74,849	13,740	18.4

Source: National Center for Health Statistics, Report of Final Natality Statistics, 1996, *Monthly Vital Statistics Report, Vol. 46, No. 11(S), 1998; calculations by New Strategist*

Birth Delivery Method for Women Aged 35 or Older, 1996

(number and percent distribution of births to women by age and method of delivery, 1996)

		vaginal		Caesarean		
	total	*total*	*after previous Caesarean*	*total*	*first*	*repeat*
Total births	**3,891,494**	**3,061,092**	**116,045**	**797,119**	**503,724**	**293,395**
Under age 35	3,417,135	2,723,295	96,057	665,030	432,244	232,786
Aged 35 or older	474,359	337,797	19,988	132,089	71,480	60,609
Aged 35 to 39	399,510	287,146	17,302	108,640	57,806	50,834
Aged 40 to 49	74,849	50,651	2,686	23,449	13,674	9,775
Percent distribution by delivery method						
Total births	**100.0%**	**78.7%**	**3.0%**	**20.5%**	**12.9%**	**7.5%**
Under age 35	100.0	79.7	2.8	19.5	12.6	6.8
Aged 35 or older	100.0	71.2	4.2	27.8	15.1	12.8
Aged 35 to 39	100.0	71.9	4.3	27.2	14.5	12.7
Aged 40 to 49	100.0	67.7	3.6	31.3	18.3	13.1
Percent distribution by age						
Total births	**100.0%**	**100.0%**	**100.0%**	**100.0%**	**100.0%**	**100.0%**
Under age 35	87.8	89.0	82.8	83.4	85.8	79.3
Aged 35 or older	12.2	11.0	17.2	16.6	14.2	20.7
Aged 35 to 39	10.3	9.4	14.9	13.6	11.5	17.3
Aged 40 to 49	1.9	1.7	2.3	2.9	2.7	3.3

Note: Numbers will not add to total because not stated is not included.
Source: National Center for Health Statistics, Report of Final Natality Statistics, 1996, *Monthly Vital Statistics Report, Vol. 46, No. 11(S), 1998; calculations by New Strategist*

Boomer Men Exercise More Than Women

Nearly half of women aged 40 to 49 rarely or never exercise.

Nearly one in four men aged 30 to 49 exercises vigorously on a daily basis. Only half as many boomer women exercise that frequently. Forty-one percent of women aged 40 to 49 say they rarely or never exercise, compared with only 27 percent of men in that age group.

Behind women's lower level of participation in exercise are their continuing childrearing responsibilities. While most no longer have toddlers at home, they are too busy juggling their own and their children's busy schedules to have time to work out on a regular basis.

Forty-eight percent of women in their thirties say they exercise vigorously at least twice a week, as do 42 percent of women in their forties. The majority of men aged 30 to 49 exercise vigorously at least twice a week—63 percent of men in their thirties and 58 percent of those in their forties.

♦ As their children grow up, boomer women will have more time to exercise. Look for a surge in the number of fitness enthusiasts among fiftysomething women.

Many boomer women are couch potatoes

(percent of people aged 30 to 49 who rarely or never exercise by sex, 1994–95)

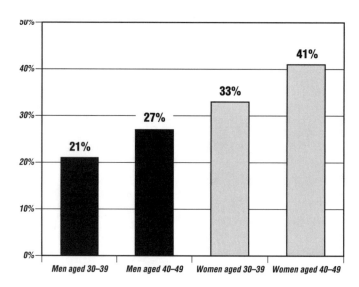

People Aged 30 to 49 by Frequency of Vigorous Exercise, 1994–95

(percent distribution of people aged 20 or older and aged 30 to 49 by frequency of vigorous exercise, 1994–95)

	total	daily	5–6 times per week	2–4 times per week	once a week	1–3 times per month	rarely or never
Total people	**100.0%**	**18.5%**	**6.8%**	**23.9%**	**8.2%**	**5.8%**	**36.5%**
Total men	**100.0**	**24.6**	**7.9**	**25.7**	**8.3**	**4.9**	**28.2**
Aged 30 to 39	100.0	23.5	9.8	29.2	10.0	6.3	21.2
Aged 40 to 49	100.0	22.6	8.3	27.1	9.1	5.4	26.8
Total women	**100.0**	**12.9**	**5.8**	**22.3**	**8.0**	**6.5**	**44.2**
Aged 30 to 39	100.0	12.4	7.1	28.1	10.4	9.1	32.9
Aged 40 to 49	100.0	12.3	6.1	23.1	9.6	7.5	40.8

Source: USDA, ARS Food Surveys Research Group, 1994 and 1995 Diet and Health Knowledge Survey, 1997; Internet web site <http://www.barc.usda.gov/bhnrc>

Walking Is the Most Popular Recreational Activity

Nearly three in four people aged 30 to 49 walk for exercise.

Seventy-five percent of people aged 30 to 39 and 72 percent of those aged 40 to 49 have walked for exercise at least once in the past year, according to the National Survey on Recreation and the Environment. Walking is by far the most popular recreational activity not only in these age groups, but among Americans of all ages.

Other recreational activities popular among 30-to-49-year-olds include sedentary pursuits such as picnicking, fishing, and birdwatching. But more strenuous activities also appear in the top ten, such as swimming, bicycling, hiking, and running.

Many recreational activities that receive a lot of media attention are not very popular among thirty- and fortysomethings. Only 18 percent of people in their thirties and 15 percent of those in their forties have played golf in the past 12 months, for example. The percentages of those who participate in tennis stand at just 12 percent among thirtysomethings and 10 percent among fortysomethings. Only 1 percent of 30-to-49-year-olds have been kayaking in the past year, and fewer than 1 percent have been snowboarding.

♦ As boomers age into their fifties, recreational activities that appeal to older Americans will boom. These are likely to include fitness walking, birdwatching, and golf.

Participation in Outdoor Recreational Activities by People Aged 30 to 49, 1994–95

(percent of people aged 30 to 49 participating in selected recreational activities at least once in the past 12 months, 1994–95; ranked by percent participating)

aged 30 to 39		aged 40 to 49	
Walking	74.7%	Walking	72.0%
Picnicking	59.8	Picnicking	55.4
Swimming (pool)	53.0	Swimming (pool)	44.8
Swimming (nonpool)	48.2	Swimming (nonpool)	42.4
Bicycling	37.4	Birdwatching	33.8
Hiking	29.5	Bicycling	30.6
Fishing (freshwater)	28.9	Hiking	27.0
Birdwatching	28.4	Fishing (freshwater)	26.7
Running, jogging	28.4	Motor boating	24.2
Motor boating	27.7	Running, jogging	23.3
Camping (developed area)	26.0	Camping (developed area)	22.6
Volleyball	17.8	Golf	15.4
Golf	17.7	Camping (primitive area)	13.8
Softball	17.7	Softball	12.1
Camping (primitive area)	16.6	Volleyball	11.3
Sledding	15.7	Sledding	10.5
Basketball	14.1	Saltwater fishing	10.4
Tennis	11.7	Tennis	9.7
Water skiing	10.7	Basketball	8.7
Saltwater fishing	10.1	Snorkeling	8.1
Skiing (downhill)	9.9	Skiing (downhill)	8.0
Snorkeling	9.5	Canoeing	7.4
Horseback riding	8.8	Horseback riding	7.2
Hunting (big game)	8.7	Water skiing	7.1
Floating, rafting	8.4	Backpacking	7.0
Backpacking	8.3	Hunting (big game)	6.9
Canoeing	8.2	Floating, rafting	6.3
Baseball	8.0	Baseball	6.1
Hunting (small game)	7.4	Hunting (small game)	6.0
Ice skating	6.7	Ice skating	5.6
Football	6.2	Sailing	5.3
Personal watercraft riding	5.5	Rowing	4.5
Caving	5.3	Skiing (cross-country)	4.4

(continued)

(continued from previous page)

aged 30 to 39		aged 40 to 49	
Mountain climbing	5.3%	Caving	4.3%
Sailing	5.1	Mountain climbing	3.7
Soccer	5.0	Personal watercraft riding	3.3
Snowmobiling	4.7	Soccer	3.0
Rowing	4.3	Snowmobiling	3.0
Rock climbing	3.9	Rock climbing	2.9
Skiing (cross-country)	3.7	Orienteering	2.4
Orienteering	2.7	Football	2.3
Hunting (migratory bird)	2.6	Hunting (migratory bird)	2.2
Windsurfing	1.4	Kayaking	1.4
Kayaking	1.3	Windsurfing	0.9
Surfing	1.2	Snowboarding	0.9
Snowboarding	0.9	Surfing	0.5

Source: USDA Forest Service, 1994–95 National Survey on Recreation and the Environment

Boomers More Likely to Drink Than Smoke

The middle aged are far less likely to smoke today than they were several decades ago.

A majority of men aged 35 to 44 smoked cigarettes in 1965, as did 44 percent of women in the age group. Today, only 32 percent of men and 27 percent of women aged 35 to 44 are smokers.

A far higher proportion of boomers drink than smoke. In 1994, about two-thirds of people aged 40 to 59 said they at least occasionally drink alchoholic beverages. Drinking is most common among young adults and uncommon among older Americans. Fully 81 percent of people aged 18 to 29 say they drink, while fewer than half of Americans aged 70 or older do so.

Few people aged 35 to 49 are current drug users. But most of those aged 30 to 44 have used drugs at some time during their lives. More than half have smoked marijuana, and one in five has used cocaine. Despite, or perhaps because of their experience with marijuana, most boomers do not favor its legalization.

♦ As boomers age, the proportion who smoke or drink should decline. But look for the share of older Americans who have ever used drugs to climb sharply as boomers enter their fifties.

Cigarette Smoking by Sex and Age, 1965 to 1995

(percent of people aged 18 or older who currently smoke cigarettes by sex and age, 1965 and 1995; percentage point change, 1965–95)

	1995	1965	percentage point change 1965–95
Total people	**24.7%**	**42.4%**	**−17.7**
Total men	**27.0**	**51.9**	**−24.9**
Aged 18 to 24	27.8	54.1	−26.3
Aged 25 to 34	29.5	60.7	−31.2
Aged 35 to 44	31.5	58.2	−26.7
Aged 45 to 64	27.1	51.9	−24.8
Aged 65 or older	14.9	28.5	−13.6
Total women	**22.6**	**33.9**	**−11.3**
Aged 18 to 24	21.8	38.1	−16.3
Aged 25 to 34	26.4	43.7	−17.3
Aged 35 to 44	27.1	43.7	−16.6
Aged 45 to 64	24.0	32.0	−8.0
Aged 65 or older	11.5	9.6	1.9

Source: National Center for Health Statistics, Health, United States, 1998; *calculations by New Strategist*

Alcohol Consumption by Age, 1994

"Do you ever have occasion to use any alcoholic beverages such as liquor, wine, or beer, or are you a total abstainer?"

(percent of people aged 18 or older who currently drink alcohol or abstain, by age, 1994)

	currently use	abstain
Total people	69.1%	30.9%
Aged 18 to 29	80.6	19.4
Aged 30 to 39	79.6	20.4
Aged 40 to 49	67.4	32.6
Aged 50 to 59	63.5	36.5
Aged 60 to 69	67.3	32.7
Aged 70 to 79	43.1	56.9
Aged 80 or older	40.0	60.0

Source: 1994 General Social Survey, National Opinion Research Center, University of Chicago; calculations by New Strategist

Drug Use by Age and Type of Drug, 1997

(percent of people aged 12 or older who ever used or currently use any illicit drug, marijuana, or cocaine, by age, 1997)

	any illicit drug		marijuana		cocaine	
	current user	*ever used*	*current user*	*ever used*	*current user*	*ever used*
Total people	**6.4%**	**35.6%**	**5.1%**	**32.9%**	**0.7%**	**10.5%**
Aged 12 and 13	3.8	9.1	2.5	4.4	0.3	0.6
Aged 14 and 15	11.2	24.1	9.2	18.6	0.5	1.6
Aged 16 and 17	19.2	37.8	16.3	33.3	2.2	6.9
Aged 18 to 20	17.3	43.3	15.4	40.0	1.5	8.2
Aged 21 to 25	12.9	46.7	11.1	42.4	1.0	9.4
Aged 26 to 29	7.6	47.7	6.3	44.9	0.8	12.1
Aged 30 to 34	7.2	53.1	5.7	50.2	0.9	23.2
Aged 35 to 39	8.6	58.6	6.9	55.9	1.6	24.5
Aged 40 to 44	4.9	51.3	3.7	50.2	0.7	17.4
Aged 45 to 49	5.3	45.0	3.4	42.6	0.7	12.7
Aged 50 or older	1.0	13.3	0.6	11.2	0.0	2.2

Note: Current users are those who used the drug at least once during the month prior to the survey.
Source: U.S. Substance Abuse and Mental Health Services Administration, National Household Survey on Drug Abuse, *Internet web site <http://www.samhsa.gov>*

Should Marijuana Be Legal? 1996

"Do you think the use of marijuana should be made legal or not?"

(percent of people aged 18 or older responding by age, 1996)

	should	should not	don't know
Total people	**26%**	**69%**	**5%**
Aged 18 to 29	31	65	4
Aged 30 to 39	31	64	5
Aged 40 to 49	26	70	4
Aged 50 to 59	27	66	7
Aged 60 to 69	14	83	4
Aged 70 or older	15	78	7

Source: 1996 General Social Survey, National Opinion Research Center, University of Chicago; calculations by New Strategist

Many In Middle-Age Lack Health Insurance

As boomers reach the age of vulnerability, the health care debate will heat up.

Forty-three million Americans—16 percent of the population—did not have health insurance in 1997. The share of Americans without health insurance has been creeping up, despite the booming economy of the past few years.

Among people aged 35 to 44, 17 percent did not have health insurance in 1997. The figure stood at 14 percent among 45-to-54-year-olds. Overall, the 12 million people aged 35 to 54 who were without health insurance accounted for 29 percent of uninsured Americans.

Middle-aged Americans who are without health insurance are vulnerable to financial catastrophe. Chronic illness becomes much more common as people enter their fifties. With one in seven 45-to-54-year-olds lacking insurance, a financial crisis looms for many.

◆ Baby boomers have never suffered silently. As the generation enters the ages of vulnerability, expect to hear increasingly strident demands for reform in health care financing.

Health Insurance Coverage of People Aged 35 to 54, 1997

(number and percent distribution of total people and people aged 35 to 54 by health insurance coverage status, 1997; numbers in thousands)

| | | covered by private or government health insurance | | | | | | | |
| | | private health insurance | | | government health insurance | | | | |
	total	total	total	employment based	total	Medicaid	Medicare	military	not covered
Total	**269,094**	**225,646**	**188,532**	**165,091**	**66,685**	**28,956**	**35,590**	**8,527**	**43,448**
35 to 54	78,519	66,082	60,736	56,659	7,934	4,466	2,011	2,442	12,437
35 to 44	44,462	36,763	33,673	31,560	4,257	2,700	878	1,161	7,699
45 to 54	34,057	29,319	27,063	25,099	3,677	1,766	1,133	1,281	4,738

Percent distribution by type of coverage

Total	**100.0%**	**83.9%**	**70.1%**	**61.4%**	**24.8%**	**10.8%**	**13.2%**	**3.2%**	**16.1%**
35 to 54	100.0	84.2	77.4	72.2	10.1	5.7	2.6	3.1	15.8
35 to 44	100.0	82.7	75.7	71.0	9.6	6.1	2.0	2.6	17.3
45 to 54	100.0	86.1	79.5	73.7	10.8	5.2	3.3	3.8	13.9

Percent distribution by age

Total	**100.0%**	**100.0%**	**100.0%**	**100.0%**	**100.0%**	**100.0%**	**100.0%**	**100.0%**	**100.0%**
35 to 54	29.2	29.3	32.2	34.3	11.9	15.4	5.7	28.6	28.6
35 to 44	16.5	16.3	17.9	19.1	6.4	9.3	2.5	13.6	17.7
45 to 54	12.7	13.0	14.4	15.2	5.5	6.1	3.2	15.0	10.9

Note: Numbers may not add to total because some people have more than one type of health insurance coverage.
Source: Bureau of the Census, unpublished tables from the 1998 Current Population Survey; calculations by New Strategist

Boomers Less Confident in Medicine

Fewer than half now say they have a great deal of confidence.

Only 40 percent of people aged 40 to 49 say they "have a great deal of confidence" in the people running medicine. This is down from the 55 percent majority who had a great deal of confidence 20 years earlier. Among people aged 50 to 59, the proportion of those with a great deal of confidence in the people running medicine fell from 48 to 42 percent between 1976 and 1996.

The proportion of Americans who say they have "hardly any confidence" in medicine has remained fairly stable during the past two decades. In contrast, the percentage citing "only some confidence" has climbed as fewer feel a great deal of confidence in the leaders of medicine. Among people aged 30 to 69, the proportion of those who have only some confidence in the people running medicine was larger in 1996 than the proportion of those with a great deal of confidence. Twenty years earlier, the opposite was the case.

♦ The rising cost of health care, as well as the introduction of managed care, has soured many Americans on the health care system. The loss of confidence has been particularly acute among boomers, many of whom find themselves paying more for less.

Boomers' confidence in medicine has plummeted

*(percent of people aged 30 to 49 who "have a great deal of confidence"
in the people running medicine, 1976 and 1996)*

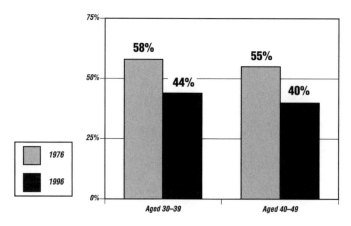

Confidence in Medicine, 1976 to 1996

"As far as the people running medicine are concerned, would you say you have a great deal of confidence, only some confidence, or hardly any confidence at all in them?"

(percent of people aged 18 or older responding by age, 1976–96)

	a great deal		only some		hardly any	
	1996	*1976*	*1996*	*1976*	*1996*	*1976*
Total people	**44%**	**54%**	**45%**	**35%**	**9%**	**9%**
Aged 18 to 29	55	60	37	32	7	7
Aged 30 to 39	44	58	50	36	6	5
Aged 40 to 49	40	55	48	34	11	11
Aged 50 to 59	42	48	45	45	12	5
Aged 60 to 69	37	47	52	36	9	16
Aged 70 or older	44	49	41	29	11	16

Note: Numbers may not add to 100 because "don't know" and no answer are not included.
Source: General Social Surveys, National Opinion Research Center, University of Chicago; calculations by New Strategist

Aches and Pains Are the Biggest Problem

More than one-third of 35-to-54-year-olds regularly experience muscle aches and pains.

It is no surprise that muscle aches and pains is the number one problem for people in midlife, whose bodies are beginning to exhibit the first signs of wear and tear. Headaches are an equally big problem for people aged 35 to 54, many of whom are juggling the dual responsibilities of job and family. Other symptoms associated with stress are also high on the list, including upset stomach and fatigue, affecting more than one in four members of this age group.

Less troubling among 35-to-54-year-olds are some health problems known to plague young adults, such as acne, premenstrual problems, and hay fever. Nevertheless, at least one in 10 experiences these problems in an average two-week period.

♦ The pharmaceutical industry has profited enormously from the everyday health problems of Americans. As the population ages, arthritis will rise in importance and headaches will fall.

Top Health Problems for People Aged 35 to 54

(percent of people aged 35 to 54 reporting health problems during the two weeks prior to the survey, by type of problem, 1992; ranked by percent reporting problem)

	percent reporting problem
Muscle aches/pains	37%
Headache	37
Overweight problems	35
Upset stomach	31
Sinus problems	31
Lip problems	30
Common cold	28
Fatigue	28
Teeth problems	25
Minor cuts/scratches	24
Eye problems	22
Back problems	22
Arthritis/rheumatism	22
Painful dry skin	20
Sleep problems	19
Acne/pimples	18
Anxiety	18
Premenstrual problems	14
Overindulgence in food	14
Bruises	13
Hay fever	13
Bunions/corns/calluses	12
Diarrhea	11
Constipation	10
Sore throat not associated with a cold	9

Source: Consumer Healthcare Products Association, Self-Medication in the '90s: Practices and Perceptions, 1992

Acute Conditions Less Likely in Middle-Age

Middle-aged Americans account for a small share of those who suffer from colds and flu each year.

People aged 45 to 64 accounted for only 13 percent of all acute conditions experienced by Americans in 1995, according to the National Center for Health Statistics. With boomers entering their fifties, they can expect to catch fewer colds and suffer fewer injuries. Because the Center uses broad, 20-year age groups in its analysis of health conditions, it is impossible to see the steady decline in the incidence of acute conditions throughout middle age. But comparing rates of acute illness for people aged 25 to 44 with those for people aged 45 to 64 shows the drop in acute conditions that accompanies aging.

Take the common cold, for example. In 1995, 19 of every 100 people aged 25 to 44 caught a cold bad enough to send them to the doctor or keep them in bed for at least half a day, but the rate was just 16 per 100 among people aged 45 to 64. The flu struck only 28 of every 100 45-to-64-year-olds in 1995, versus 45 of every 100 people in the younger age group. Only a handful of acute conditions strike 45-to-64-year-olds more frequently than 25-to-44-year-olds, including pneumonia, sprains, and strains.

♦ Fully 25 percent of acute musculoskeletal conditions are experienced by people aged 45 to 64. This relatively high share can be explained by the increasing involvement of older people in regular fitness activities. Many older Americans are overdoing it and taking their sprains and strains to the doctor.

Acute Health Conditions Experienced
by People Aged 25 to 64, 1995

(total number of acute conditions, number and rate per 100 people aged 25 to 64, and share of total acute conditions accounted for by age group, 1995; numbers in thousands)

	total	aged 25 to 44			aged 45 to 64		
		number	rate	share of total	number	rate	share of total
Total acute conditions	456,874	130,406	156.9	28.5%	61,540	119.0	13.5%
Infective and parasitic diseases	52,605	11,199	13.5	21.3	4,490	8.7	8.5
Common childhood diseases	3,105	122	0.1	3.9	–	–	–
Intestinal virus	12,447	3,247	3.9	26.1	1,015	2.0	8.2
Viral infections	16,875	3,318	4.0	19.7	1,782	3.4	10.6
Respiratory conditions	223,037	66,901	80.5	30.0	29,785	57.6	13.4
Common cold	60,564	15,434	18.6	25.5	8,349	16.1	13.8
Influenza	108,009	37,570	45.2	34.8	14,477	28.0	13.4
Acute bronchitis	13,250	3,689	4.4	27.8	1,651	3.2	12.5
Pneumonia	5,113	1,171	1.4	22.9	1,207	2.3	23.6
Digestive system conditions	15,828	4,189	5.0	26.5	2,311	4.5	14.6
Dental conditions	3,503	1,677	2.0	47.9	440	0.9	12.6
Indigestion, nausea, and vomiting	7,323	1,352	1.6	18.5	1,002	1.9	13.7
Injuries	64,619	19,434	23.4	30.1	12,024	23.3	18.6
Fractures and dislocations	8,200	2,790	3.4	34.0	1,433	2.8	17.5
Sprains and strains	12,961	4,520	5.4	34.9	2,871	5.6	22.2
Open wounds and lacerations	12,417	3,704	4.5	29.8	1,785	3.5	14.4
Contusions and superficial injuries	12,295	3,694	4.4	30.0	2,048	4.0	16.7
Selected other acute conditions							
Eye conditions	2,431	758	0.9	31.2	309	0.6	12.7
Acute ear infections	23,568	2,717	3.3	11.5	949	1.8	4.0
Acute urinary conditions	7,089	2,259	2.7	31.9	1,383	2.7	19.5
Skin conditions	5,474	1,690	2.0	30.9	609	1.2	11.1
Acute musculoskeletal conditions	7,866	3,645	4.4	46.3	1,945	3.8	24.7
Headache, excluding migraine	4,128	1,224	1.5	29.7	392	0.8	9.5
Fever, unspecified	6,282	483	0.6	7.7	75	0.1	1.2

Note: The acute conditions shown here are those that caused people to seek medical attention or to restrict their activity for at least half a day. (–) means not applicable or sample is too small to make a reliable estimate.
Source: National Center for Health Statistics, Current Estimates from the National Health Interview Survey, 1995, *Series 10, No. 199, 1998; calculations by New Strategist*

Chronic Conditions Emerge in Middle-Age

People aged 45 to 64 are much more likely than younger adults to suffer from chronic conditions.

Although the incidence of acute conditions diminishes as people enter their forties and fifties, chronic illnesses begin to emerge. Only a few chronic conditions (migraines and hay fever, for example) are more common among 18-to-44-year-olds than among those aged 45 to 64. Because the National Center for Health Statistics publishes its data on health conditions in broad age groups, it is impossible to see the steady emergence of chronic conditions as people age from their forties into their fifties and sixties. But a comparison of the prevalence of conditions in the 45-to-64 age group with the prevalence rate in the 18-to-44 age group reveals which conditions are likely to become much more common as the baby-boom generation ages.

The most prevalent chronic condition among 45-to-64-year-olds is arthritis (experienced by 233 per 1,000 people in the age group, or 23 percent), followed by high blood pressure (22 percent). The proportion of people aged 45 to 64 with these conditions is more than four times as high as the proportion among 18-to-44-year-olds. Hearing impairments and heart disease also emerge as significant problems in the 45-to-64 age group.

◆ As the large baby-boom generation ages into its fifties and sixties, expect to see an enormous increase in the number of people with arthritis, high blood pressure, heart disease, and hearing problems.

Chronic Health Conditions Experienced by People Aged 18 to 64, 1995

(total number of people with chronic conditions, number and rate per 1,000 persons aged 18 to 64, and share of total chronic conditions accounted for by age group, 1995; numbers in thousands)

		aged 18 to 44			aged 45 to 64		
	total	number	rate	share of total	number	rate	share of total
Skin and musculoskeletal conditions							
Arthritis	32,663	5,067	46.9	15.5%	12,047	232.9	36.9%
Gout, including gouty arthritis	2,478	421	3.9	17.0	1,182	22.9	47.7
Intervertebral disc disorders	5,927	2,482	23.0	41.9	2,399	46.4	40.5
Bone spur or tendinitis, unspecified	2,750	938	8.7	34.1	1,326	25.6	48.2
Disorders of bone or cartilage	1,793	324	3.0	18.1	572	11.1	31.9
Bunions	3,262	961	9.1	29.5	1,234	23.9	37.8
Bursitis, unclassified	5,372	1,814	16.8	33.8	2,013	38.9	37.5
Sebaceous skin cyst	1,288	732	6.8	56.8	372	7.2	28.9
Acne	5,339	3,137	29.0	58.8	323	6.2	6.0
Psoriasis	2,489	951	8.8	38.2	863	16.7	34.7
Dermatitis	9,333	4,101	38.0	43.9	1,852	35.8	19.8
Dry, itching skin, unclassified	6,440	2,401	22.2	37.3	1,561	30.2	24.2
Ingrown nails	5,371	2,167	20.1	40.3	1,496	28.9	27.9
Corns and calluses	4,347	1,396	12.9	32.1	1,482	28.7	34.1
Impairments							
Visual impairment	8,511	3,127	28.9	36.7	2,496	48.3	29.3
Color blindness	2,966	1,431	13.2	48.2	947	18.3	31.9
Cataracts	6,256	249	2.3	4.0	996	19.3	15.9
Glaucoma	2,478	195	1.8	7.9	636	12.3	25.7
Hearing impairment	22,465	4,994	46.2	22.2	7,484	144.7	33.3
Tinnitus	6,805	1,741	16.1	25.6	2,834	54.8	41.6
Speech impairment	2,747	756	7.0	27.5	470	9.1	17.1
Absence of extremities	1,195	479	4.4	40.1	453	8.8	37.9
Paralysis of extremities	1,509	425	3.9	28.2	374	7.2	24.8
Deformity or orthopedic impairment	31,784	14,999	138.8	47.2	9,079	175.6	28.6

(continued)

(continued from previous page)

		aged 18 to 44			aged 45 to 64		
	total	number	rate	share of total	number	rate	share of total
Digestive conditions							
Ulcer	4,297	1,918	17.8	44.6%	1,486	28.7	34.6%
Hernia of abdominal cavity	4,664	1,122	10.4	24.1	1,676	32.4	35.9
Gastritis or duodenitis	3,663	1,299	12.0	35.5	1,164	22.5	31.8
Frequent indigestion	7,196	3,475	32.2	48.3	2,129	41.2	29.6
Enteritis or colitis	2,409	943	8.7	39.1	841	16.3	34.9
Spastic colon	2,437	1,110	10.3	45.5	789	15.3	32.4
Diverticula of intestines	2,121	229	2.1	10.8	597	11.5	28.1
Frequent constipation	3,644	1,225	11.3	33.6	886	17.1	24.3
Genitourinary, nervous, endocrine, metabolic, and blood conditions							
Goiter or other thyroid disorders	4,521	1,396	12.9	30.9	1,557	30.1	34.4
Diabetes	8,693	1,231	11.4	14.2	2,399	63.8	27.6
Anemias	4,177	2,053	19.0	49.2	973	18.8	23.3
Epilepsy	1,443	623	5.8	43.2	331	6.4	22.9
Migraine headache	11,897	7,361	68.1	61.9	3,001	58.0	25.2
Neuralgia or neuritis, unspecified	373	92	0.9	24.7	83	1.6	22.3
Kidney trouble	3,022	1,371	12.7	45.4	796	15.4	26.3
Bladder disorders	4,135	1,395	12.9	33.7	1,022	19.8	24.7
Diseases of prostate	2,591	170	1.6	6.6	871	16.8	33.6
Diseases of female genital organs	5,362	3,375	31.2	62.9	1,458	28.2	27.2
Circulatory conditions							
Rheumatic fever	2,166	757	7.0	34.9	821	15.9	37.9
Heart disease	21,114	3,869	35.8	18.3	6,247	120.8	29.6
High blood pressure	29,954	5,706	52.8	19.0	11,516	222.7	38.4
Cerebrovascular disease	3,314	244	2.3	7.4	773	14.9	23.3
Hardening of the arteries	1,845	69	0.6	3.7	482	9.3	26.1
Varicose veins of lower extremities	7,396	2,449	22.7	33.1	2,390	46.2	32.3
Hemorrhoids	9,077	3,969	36.7	43.7	3,290	63.6	36.2
Respiratory conditions							
Chronic bronchitis	14,533	5,422	50.2	37.3	3,305	63.9	22.7
Asthma	14,878	5,577	51.6	37.5	2,754	53.3	18.5
Hay fever or allergic rhinitis	25,730	12,792	118.4	49.7	5,964	115.3	23.2
Chronic sinusitis	37,003	17,572	162.6	47.5	9,258	179.0	25.0
Deviated nasal septum	1,705	882	8.2	51.7	529	10.2	31.0
Chronic disease of tonsils/adenoids	2,706	1,096	10.1	40.5	246	4.8	9.1
Emphysema	1,870	127	1.2	6.8	671	13.0	35.9

Note: Chronic conditions are those that last at least three months or belong to a group of conditions that are considered to be chronic regardless of when they begin. (–) means sample is too small to make a reliable estimate.
Source: National Center for Health Statistics, Current Estimates from the National Health Interview Survey, 1995, Series 10, No. 199, 1998; calculations by New Strategist

The Middle-Aged Account for about Half of Health Care Visits

Most health care visits are to doctors' offices.

In 1996, Americans visited health care providers a total of 892 million times. Forty-eight percent of those visits were made by people aged 25 to 64. Most health care visits are to doctor's offices—83 percent of the visits made by 25-to-64-year-olds. Another 8 percent of visits are to outpatient clinics, while 10 percent are to emergency rooms.

People aged 45 to 64 are much more likely to visit a health care provider than those in the 25-to-44 age group. The older age group has a health care visit rate of 374 per 100 people (or 3.7 visits per person per year, on average), much higher than the 277-per-100 rate of the younger age group. The 25-to-44-year-olds visit emergency rooms more frequently than 45-to-64-year-olds, however.

♦ With most baby boomers still younger than age 45, the 25-to-44 age group accounts for a larger share of health care visits than the 45-to-64 age group. As boomers age, health care visits by the older age group will become a larger share of the health care market.

Health Care Visits by People Aged 25 to 64, 1996

(number, percent distribution, and annual rate of ambulatory care visits, by total people and people aged 25 to 64, by place of care, 1996; numbers in thousands)

	total	physician offices	outpatient departments	emergency departments
NUMBER OF VISITS				
Total visits	**892,025**	**734,493**	**67,186**	**90,347**
Aged 25 to 64	429,916	354,678	33,458	41,781
Aged 25 to 44	231,031	184,449	18,547	28,036
Aged 45 to 64	198,885	170,229	14,911	13,745
PERCENT DISTRIBUTION BY PLACE				
Total visits	**100.0%**	**82.3%**	**7.5%**	**10.1%**
Aged 25 to 64	100.0	82.5	7.8	9.7
Aged 25 to 44	100.0	79.8	8.0	12.1
Aged 45 to 64	100.0	85.6	7.5	6.9
PERCENT DISTRIBUTION BY AGE				
Total visits	**100.0%**	**100.0%**	**100.0%**	**100.0%**
Aged 25 to 64	48.2	48.3	49.8	46.2
Aged 25 to 44	25.9	25.1	27.6	31.0
Aged 45 to 64	22.3	23.2	22.2	15.2
VISITS PER 100 PERSONS				
Total visits	**337.3**	**277.8**	**25.4**	**34.2**
Aged 25 to 44	276.7	220.9	22.2	33.6
Aged 45 to 64	373.7	319.9	28.0	25.8

Note: Ambulatory care visits are defined as individuals seeking personal health services who are not currently admitted to any health care institution on the premises.
Source: National Center for Health Statistics, Ambulatory Care Visits to Physician Offices, Hospital Outpatient Departments, and Emergency Departments: United States, 1996, *Vital and Health Statistics, Series 13, No. 135, 1998; calculations by New Strategist*

One in Four 45-to-54-Year-Olds Is Disabled

Disability rises sharply in middle age.

The percentage of Americans who are disabled rises from 15 percent among 22-to-44-year-olds to a significant 25 percent among 45-to-54-year-olds. The rate of severe disability also rises, from 8.5 to 13 percent.

The most common problems in the 45-to-54 age group are difficulty with lifting or carrying 10 pounds, climbing stairs, or walking three city blocks. Over 7 percent of people in this age group have difficulty with or are unable to do one or more of these activities, more than double the rate in the younger age group. Among 22-to-44-year-olds, mental problems are one of the most common disabilities, with 3.8 percent experiencing them.

While the disability rate is higher in the 45-to-54 age group than in the 22-to-44 age group, few in either group experience profound problems. Only 2 percent of the younger ones and 3 percent of the older ones need personal assistance to manage their daily lives.

♦ Health-conscious boomers hope to avoid many of the limitations that accompany aging. While they may succeed at avoiding some of them, hearing loss is likely to be more widespread among boomers than among older generations thanks to the popularity of rock and roll.

People Aged 22 to 54 with Disabilities, 1994–95

(total number of people aged 15 or older and aged 22 to 54, and percent with a disability, by type of disability, 1994–1995; numbers in thousands)

	total	*22 to 44*	*45 to 54*
Total people	202,367	95,002	30,316
With any disability	**24.0%**	**14.9%**	**24.5%**
Severe	12.5	6.4	11.5
Not severe	11.5	8.5	13.0
With a mental disability	4.8	3.8	4.4
Uses wheelchair	0.9	0.3	0.4
Used cane/crutch/walker for six or more months	2.6	0.5	1.4
Difficulty with or unable to perform			
one or more functional activities	16.4	7.8	16.1
Seeing words and letters	5.8	1.6	4.2
Hearing normal conversation	6.2	2.0	4.1
Having speech understood	1.0	0.6	0.7
Lifting, carrying 10 pounds	7.9	3.2	7.4
Climbing stairs without resting	8.9	3.1	7.8
Walking three city blocks	9.1	3.3	7.7
Difficulty with or unable to perform			
one or more ADLs	4.0	1.5	3.1
Getting around inside the home	1.7	0.5	1.0
Getting in and out of bed or chair	2.7	1.0	2.2
Bathing	2.2	0.7	1.3
Dressing	1.6	0.6	1.0
Eating	0.5	0.2	0.3
Getting to/using toilet	0.9	0.3	0.5
Difficulty with or unable to perform			
one or more IADLs	6.1	2.5	4.5
Going outside alone	4.0	1.2	2.6
Keeping track of money and bills	1.9	0.9	1.3
Preparing meals	2.1	0.8	1.1
Doing light housework	3.4	1.3	2.3
Taking prescribed medicines	1.5	0.6	1.0
Using the telephone	1.3	0.4	0.6
Needs personal assistance			
with an ADL or an IADL	4.7	1.9	3.3

Note: An ADL is an activity of daily living; an IADL is an instrumental activity of daily living.
Source: Bureau of the Census, Internet web site <http://www.census.gov>

Causes of Death Shift in Middle-Age

In the 45-to-54 age group, heart disease begins to take its toll.

Heart disease, cancer, and stroke are the leading causes of death in the United States. They are not the leading killers of 35-to-44-year-olds, however. For that age group, cancer, accidents, and AIDS are the leading causes of death. Cancer is the most prevalent cause of death in the 45-to-54 age group as well, but heart disease is number two. Nearly one-third of all deaths to 45-to-54-year-olds are caused by cancer, while another 24 percent are due to heart disease.

If middle age is defined as the point when people have lived half their lives, then 35-year-olds are not quite middle-aged while 40-year-old men are. Men aged 40 can expect to live only 36 more years, on average. In contrast, women aged 40 can still expect another 41 years of life. Only when women reach age 45 is their life expectancy (36 years) less than the number of years they have already lived. With the median age of boomers at 43 this year (meaning half of boomers are older and half are younger), it's safe to say the baby-boom generation is firmly established in middle age.

♦ With death rates from AIDS falling thanks to new drug treatments, the overall number of deaths in the 35-to-44 age group has also declined. In 1995, 102,270 people aged 35 to 44 died, a figure that fell to 96,033 in 1996.

Leading Causes of Death for People Aged 35 to 44, 1996

(number and percent distribution of deaths for the 10 leading causes of death for people aged 35 to 44, 1996)

		number	percent
	All causes	**96,033**	**100.0%**
1.	Malignant neoplasms	17,049	17.8
2.	Accidents	14,267	14.9
3.	Human immunodeficiency virus infection	13,637	14.2
4.	Diseases of heart	13,217	13.8
5.	Suicide	6,741	7.0
6.	Homicide and legal intervention	3,894	4.1
7.	Chronic liver disease and cirrhosis	3,640	3.8
8.	Cerebrovascular diseases	2,722	2.8
9.	Diabetes mellitus	1,879	2.0
10.	Pneumonia and influenza	1,461	1.5
	All other causes	17,526	18.2

Source: National Center for Health Statistics, Deaths: Final Data for 1996, *National Vital Statistics Report, vol. 47, no. 9, 1998; calculations by New Strategist*

Leading Causes of Death for People Aged 45 to 54, 1996

(number and percent distribution of deaths for the 10 leading causes of death for people aged 45 to 54, 1996)

		number	percent
	All causes	**144,329**	**100.0%**
1.	Malignant neoplasms	44,627	30.9
2.	Diseases of heart	35,034	24.3
3.	Accidents	9,846	6.8
4.	Human immunodeficiency virus infection	6,259	4.3
5.	Cerebrovascular diseases	5,792	4.0
6.	Chronic liver disease and cirrhosis	5,431	3.8
7.	Suicide	4,837	3.4
8.	Diabetes mellitus	4,258	3.0
9.	Chronic obstructive pulmonary disease	2,801	1.9
10.	Pneumonia and influenza	2,093	1.5
	All other causes	23,351	16.2

Source: National Center for Health Statistics, Deaths: Final Data for 1996, *National Vital Statistics Report, vol. 47, no. 9, 1998; calculations by New Strategist*

Life Expectancy of People Aged 35 or Older by Sex and Race, 1997

(years of life remaining at birth and at ages 35 or older by sex and race, 1997)

	total	men total	men white	men black	women total	women white	women black
At birth	**76.5**	**73.6**	**74.3**	**67.3**	**79.2**	**79.8**	**74.7**
Aged 35	43.3	40.8	41.2	36.0	45.6	45.9	41.9
Aged 40	38.6	36.2	36.6	31.7	40.8	41.1	37.4
Aged 45	34.1	31.7	32.1	27.6	36.1	36.4	33.0
Aged 50	29.6	27.4	27.7	23.8	31.6	31.8	28.8
Aged 55	25.3	23.2	23.5	20.3	27.1	27.3	24.7
Aged 60	21.3	19.3	19.5	17.0	22.9	23.1	20.9
Aged 65	17.6	15.8	15.9	14.2	19.0	19.1	17.4
Aged 70	14.2	12.6	12.7	11.4	15.3	15.4	14.1
Aged 75	11.1	9.8	9.8	9.2	12.0	12.0	11.3
Aged 80	8.3	7.4	7.3	7.1	8.9	8.9	8.5
Aged 85	6.0	5.4	5.3	5.4	6.3	6.3	6.2

Source: National Center for Health Statistics, Births and Deaths: Preliminary Data for 1997, *National Vital Statistics Reports, Vol. 47, No. 4, 1998*

4

Income

♦ Nearly 10 million households have incomes of $100,000 or more, and 60 percent of them are headed by 35-to-54-year-olds. The ranks of the rich are growing because the oversized baby-boom generation is now in its peak earning years.

♦ Among the 5.8 million householders aged 35 to 54 with incomes of $100,000 or more, 85 percent are married couples.

♦ The median income of households headed by 50-to-54-year-olds was $52,045 in 1997, higher than that of any other age group.

♦ Although few black or Hispanic householders aged 35 to 54 have six-digit incomes, 27 percent have household incomes of $50,000 or more.

♦ Since 1980, the median income of men aged 35 to 44 has fallen 16 percent, after adjusting for inflation. The median income of men aged 45 to 54 fell 3 percent during those years.

♦ The median income of women aged 35 to 44 rose 48 percent from 1980 to 1997, after adjusting for inflation. The median income of women aged 45 to 54 rose an even higher 64 percent during those years.

♦ Men aged 45 to 54 are the best-educated in history. Those with college degrees, who account for 32 percent of the age group, had a median income of $53,319 in 1997.

♦ The poverty rate bottoms out among 45-to-54-year-olds. Now that the enormous baby-boom generation has filled the age group, public support for poverty programs has plummeted.

Boomer Incomes Still below Record

Householders aged 35 to 44 saw their incomes decline between 1990 and 1997.

Between 1990 and 1997, the median income of households headed by people aged 35 to 44 fell 2 percent, to $46,359, after adjusting for inflation. The median income of householders aged 45 to 54 barely changed during those years, rising 0.8 percent to reach $51,875. For both age groups, median household income is well below the record levels reached in the late 1980s. The median household income of 35-to-44-year-olds is 7 percent below its 1987 peak, while the median household income of 45-to-54-year-olds is 3 percent off its 1989 peak.

Householders aged 45 to 54 typically have the highest incomes. The erosion of the incomes of 35-to-44-year-olds makes that peak sharper today than in the past. In 1997, the median income of householders aged 45 to 54 was $5,516 greater than that of householders aged 35 to 44. In 1980, the gap had been $2,914.

◆ The 45-to-54 age group is becoming increasingly important to marketers for three reasons: the age group is expanding with boomers, its income is growing faster than that of younger age groups, and its spending on most categories of goods and services surpasses that of any other age group.

Below-average income gain for 35-to-54-year-olds

(percent change in median income of total households and households headed by people aged 35 to 54, 1980–97; in 1997 dollars)

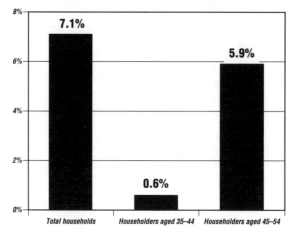

Median Income of Households Headed by People Aged 35 to 54, 1980 to 1997

(median income of total households and households headed by people aged 35 to 54, 1980 to 1997; in 1997 dollars)

	total households	householders aged 35 to 54	
		35 to 44	45 to 54
1997	$37,005	$46,359	$51,875
1996	36,306	45,439	51,630
1995	35,887	45,775	50,612
1994	34,942	45,125	51,183
1993	34,700	45,387	51,323
1992	35,047	45,591	50,834
1991	35,502	46,369	51,557
1990	36,770	47,353	51,480
1989	37,415	48,713	53,746
1988	36,937	49,594	51,844
1987	36,820	49,711	52,565
1986	36,460	48,014	52,221
1985	35,229	46,339	49,557
1984	34,626	46,009	48,684
1983	33,655	44,603	48,911
1982	33,864	44,272	46,983
1981	33,978	45,218	48,175
1980	34,538	46,077	48,991
Percent change			
1996–1997	1.9%	2.0%	0.5%
1990–1997	0.6	–2.1	0.8
1980–1997	7.1	0.6	5.9

Source: Bureau of the Census, unpublished tables from the 1998 Current Population Survey, Internet web site <http://www.census.gov>; calculations by New Strategist

Fiftysomethings Have Highest Incomes

The median household income of householders aged 50 to 54 tops $52,000.

Householders aged 35 to 54 had a median household income of $48,838 in 1997, far above the $37,005 national median. The reason for the higher incomes of 35-to-54-year-olds is that most households in this age group are headed by married couples and most of those married couples are dual-earners. In addition, middle-aged householders are at the peak of their careers, when pay levels are highest.

Householders aged 35 to 54 (most of them baby boomers) account for 60 percent of the nation's households with incomes of $100,000 or more. Within the 35-to-54 age group, household incomes are highest among 50-to-54-year-olds, at $52,045. One in six households in this age group has an income of $100,000 or more.

♦ The ranks of the rich are growing because the oversized baby-boom generation is beginning to reap the benefits of its education, work experience, and dual-income lifestyle. With demographic forces at play, the gap between rich and poor is not likely toshrink until affluent boomers begin to retire and rejoin the middle class.

♦ Consumer businesses targeting the affluent should set their sights on the oldest boomers because that's where the money is. As the entire generation moves through its peak earning years, the affluent market should grow for another decade.

Income Distribution of Households Headed by People Aged 35 to 54, 1997: Total Households

(number and percent distribution of total households and households headed by people aged 35 to 54 by income, 1997; households in thousands as of 1998)

| | | | aged 35 to 54 | | | | | |
| | | | aged 35 to 44 | | | aged 45 to 54 | | |
	total	total	total	35 to 39	40 to 44	total	45 to 49	50 to 54
Total households	**102,528**	**43,490**	**23,943**	**11,838**	**12,105**	**19,547**	**10,601**	**8,946**
Under $10,000	11,296	3,006	1,688	979	708	1,318	689	628
$10,000 to $19,999	16,163	4,290	2,459	1,226	1,233	1,831	990	841
$20,000 to $29,999	14,319	4,955	2,965	1,541	1,423	1,990	1,106	882
$30,000 to $39,999	12,784	5,202	3,020	1,546	1,475	2,182	1,168	1,014
$40,000 to $49,999	10,587	4,761	2,759	1,415	1,343	2,002	1,132	869
$50,000 to $59,999	8,728	4,394	2,522	1,264	1,258	1,872	1,048	824
$60,000 to $69,999	7,049	3,955	2,141	1,011	1,129	1,814	1,001	813
$70,000 to $79,999	5,153	3,044	1,693	789	906	1,351	725	626
$80,000 to $89,999	3,953	2,265	1,183	510	672	1,082	616	466
$90,000 to $99,999	2,834	1,798	887	395	492	911	490	420
$100,000 or more	9,661	5,822	2,629	1,162	1,466	3,193	1,635	1,559
Median income	$37,005	$48,838	$46,359	$44,281	$48,845	$51,875	$51,717	$52,045
Total households	**100.0%**	**100.0%**	**100.0%**	**100.0%**	**100.0%**	**100.0%**	**100.0%**	**100.0%**
Under $10,000	11.0	6.9	7.1	8.3	5.8	6.7	6.5	7.0
$10,000 to $19,999	15.8	9.9	10.3	10.4	10.2	9.4	9.3	9.4
$20,000 to $29,999	14.0	11.4	12.4	13.0	11.8	10.2	10.4	9.9
$30,000 to $39,999	12.5	12.0	12.6	13.1	12.2	11.2	11.0	11.3
$40,000 to $49,999	10.3	10.9	11.5	12.0	11.1	10.2	10.7	9.7
$50,000 to $59,999	8.5	10.1	10.5	10.7	10.4	9.6	9.9	9.2
$60,000 to $69,999	6.9	9.1	8.9	8.5	9.3	9.3	9.4	9.1
$70,000 to $79,999	5.0	7.0	7.1	6.7	7.5	6.9	6.8	7.0
$80,000 to $89,999	3.9	5.2	4.9	4.3	5.6	5.5	5.8	5.2
$90,000 to $99,999	2.8	4.1	3.7	3.3	4.1	4.7	4.6	4.7
$100,000 or more	9.4	13.4	11.0	9.8	12.1	16.3	15.4	17.4

Source: Bureau of the Census, unpublished tables from the 1998 Current Population Survey, Internet web site <http://www.bls.census.gov/cps/ads/1998/sdata.htm>; calculations by New Strategist

Black and Hispanic Household Incomes Well Below Average

Black, white, and Hispanic incomes peak in the 45-to-54 age group.

The median household income of blacks and Hispanics aged 45 to 54 is more than $20,000 below the $54,879 median of white householders in the age group. For blacks aged 45 to 54, median household income is $33,761, and for Hispanics it is $32,074.

The incomes of black and Hispanic households do not peak as sharply in middle age as white income does. For black households, income peaks in the 45-to-49 age group at $34,643, 38 percent greater than the median income of all black households. For Hispanic households, income peaks in the 50-to-54 age group at $33,964, 28 percent higher than the median for all Hispanic households. For whites, the $55,306 peak income of householders aged 50 to 54 is 42 percent greater than the median for all white households.

Black household incomes are substantially lower than white income because black households are less likely to be headed by a married couple. Hispanic household incomes lag those of whites because many Hispanics are recent immigrants with low earnings.

♦ The affluent market is dominated by whites. Among the 5.8 million householders aged 35 to 54 with incomes of $100,000 or more, 91 percent are white.

♦ Although few black or Hispanic households have six-digit incomes, 27 percent have incomes of $50,000 or more.

Income Distribution of Households Headed by People Aged 35 to 54, 1997: Black Households

(number and percent distribution of total black households and households headed by blacks aged 35 to 54 by income, 1997; households in thousands as of 1998)

	total	total	aged 35 to 54					
			aged 35 to 44			aged 45 to 54		
			total	35 to 39	40 to 44	total	45 to 49	50 to 54
Total black households	**12,474**	**5,467**	**3,096**	**1,608**	**1,489**	**2,371**	**1,393**	**979**
Under $10,000	2,672	828	511	339	172	317	181	136
$10,000 to $19,999	2,491	927	567	295	274	360	202	157
$20,000 to $29,999	1,996	947	583	281	302	364	214	150
$30,000 to $39,999	1,521	703	391	217	175	312	179	132
$40,000 to $49,999	1,170	573	343	172	170	230	128	104
$50,000 to $59,999	842	434	217	107	110	217	127	91
$60,000 to $69,999	598	316	142	48	94	174	103	70
$70,000 to $79,999	337	217	118	46	73	99	61	38
$80,000 to $89,999	273	174	84	30	55	90	63	27
$90,000 to $99,999	157	110	44	25	19	66	42	25
$100,000 or more	415	240	95	49	46	145	96	49
Median income	$25,050	$30,334	$27,710	$26,129	$29,859	$33,761	$34,643	$32,161
Total black households	**100.0%**	**100.0%**	**100.0%**	**100.0%**	**100.0%**	**100.0%**	**100.0%**	**100.0%**
Under $10,000	21.4	15.1	16.5	21.1	11.6	13.4	13.0	13.9
$10,000 to $19,999	20.0	17.0	18.3	18.3	18.4	15.2	14.5	16.0
$20,000 to $29,999	16.0	17.3	18.8	17.5	20.3	15.4	15.4	15.3
$30,000 to $39,999	12.2	12.9	12.6	13.5	11.8	13.2	12.8	13.5
$40,000 to $49,999	9.4	10.5	11.1	10.7	11.4	9.7	9.2	10.6
$50,000 to $59,999	6.8	7.9	7.0	6.7	7.4	9.2	9.1	9.3
$60,000 to $69,999	4.8	5.8	4.6	3.0	6.3	7.3	7.4	7.2
$70,000 to $79,999	2.7	4.0	3.8	2.9	4.9	4.2	4.4	3.9
$80,000 to $89,999	2.2	3.2	2.7	1.9	3.7	3.8	4.5	2.8
$90,000 to $99,999	1.3	2.0	1.4	1.6	1.3	2.8	3.0	2.6
$100,000 or more	3.3	4.4	3.1	3.0	3.1	6.1	6.9	5.0

Source: Bureau of the Census, unpublished tables from the 1998 Current Population Survey, Internet web site <http://www.bls.census.gov/cps/ads/1998/sdata.htm>; calculations by New Strategist

Income Distribution of Households Headed by People Aged 35 to 54, 1997: Hispanic Households

(number and percent distribution of total Hispanic households and households headed by Hispanics aged 35 to 54 by income, 1997; households in thousands as of 1998)

| | | aged 35 to 54 | | | | | | |
| | | | aged 35 to 44 | | | aged 45 to 54 | | |
	total	total	total	35 to 39	40 to 44	total	45 to 49	50 to 54
Total Hispanic households	**8,590**	**3,702**	**2,316**	**1,198**	**1,119**	**1,386**	**782**	**605**
Under $10,000	1,441	464	289	166	123	175	108	67
$10,000 to $19,999	1,756	654	421	227	193	233	132	102
$20,000 to $29,999	1,523	627	401	208	192	226	131	95
$30,000 to $39,999	1,152	523	326	168	155	197	111	86
$40,000 to $49,999	894	435	272	125	147	163	93	70
$50,000 to $59,999	536	275	178	83	92	97	56	42
$60,000 to $69,999	368	189	114	57	56	75	34	41
$70,000 to $79,999	272	157	100	51	48	57	28	28
$80,000 to $89,999	176	84	54	23	31	30	20	11
$90,000 to $99,999	123	76	49	24	26	27	15	12
$100,000 or more	351	222	117	62	54	105	51	54
Median income	$26,628	$31,495	$31,148	$29,773	$32,593	$32,074	$31,084	$33,964
Total Hispanic households	**100.0%**	**100.0%**	**100.0%**	**100.0%**	**100.0%**	**100.0%**	**100.0%**	**100.0%**
Under $10,000	16.8	12.5	12.5	13.9	11.0	12.6	13.8	11.1
$10,000 to $19,999	20.4	17.7	18.2	18.9	17.2	16.8	16.9	16.9
$20,000 to $29,999	17.7	16.9	17.3	17.4	17.2	16.3	16.8	15.7
$30,000 to $39,999	13.4	14.1	14.1	14.0	13.9	14.2	14.2	14.2
$40,000 to $49,999	10.4	11.8	11.7	10.4	13.1	11.8	11.9	11.6
$50,000 to $59,999	6.2	7.4	7.7	6.9	8.2	7.0	7.2	6.9
$60,000 to $69,999	4.3	5.1	4.9	4.8	5.0	5.4	4.3	6.8
$70,000 to $79,999	3.2	4.2	4.3	4.3	4.3	4.1	3.6	4.6
$80,000 to $89,999	2.0	2.3	2.3	1.9	2.8	2.2	2.6	1.8
$90,000 to $99,999	1.4	2.1	2.1	2.0	2.3	1.9	1.9	2.0
$100,000 or more	4.1	6.0	5.1	5.2	4.8	7.6	6.5	8.9

Source: Bureau of the Census, unpublished tables from the 1998 Current Population Survey, Internet web site <http://www.bls.census.gov/cps/ads/1998/sdata.htm>; calculations by New Strategist

Income Distribution of Households Headed by People Aged 35 to 54, 1997: White Households

(number and percent distribution of total white households and households headed by whites aged 35 to 54 by income, 1997; households in thousands as of 1998)

| | | | aged 35 to 54 | | | | | |
| | | | aged 35 to 44 | | | aged 45 to 54 | | |
	total	total	total	35 to 39	40 to 44	total	45 to 49	50 to 54
Total white households	**86,106**	**36,161**	**19,761**	**9,699**	**10,062**	**16,400**	**8,816**	**7,583**
Under $10,000	8,188	2,055	1,096	596	500	959	494	465
$10,000 to $19,999	13,152	3,161	1,782	886	896	1,379	736	641
$20,000 to $29,999	11,852	3,824	2,282	1,197	1,087	1,542	857	685
$30,000 to $39,999	10,778	4,257	2,484	1,261	1,223	1,773	929	846
$40,000 to $49,999	9,004	3,966	2,294	1,205	1,090	1,672	958	715
$50,000 to $59,999	7,590	3,812	2,222	1,123	1,099	1,590	875	714
$60,000 to $69,999	6,138	3,444	1,857	881	977	1,587	872	716
$70,000 to $79,999	4,612	2,725	1,502	711	791	1,223	646	577
$80,000 to $89,999	3,507	2,000	1,052	468	585	948	531	417
$90,000 to $99,999	2,526	1,593	795	333	462	798	428	370
$100,000 or more	8,762	5,326	2,396	1,039	1,356	2,930	1,491	1,439
Median income	$38,972	$52,046	$49,695	$47,201	$51,539	$54,879	$54,543	$55,306
Total white households	**100.0%**	**100.0%**	**100.0%**	**100.0%**	**100.0%**	**100.0%**	**100.0%**	**100.0%**
Under $10,000	9.5	5.7	5.5	6.1	5.0	5.8	5.6	6.1
$10,000 to $19,999	15.3	8.7	9.0	9.1	8.9	8.4	8.3	8.5
$20,000 to $29,999	13.8	10.6	11.5	12.3	10.8	9.4	9.7	9.0
$30,000 to $39,999	12.5	11.8	12.6	13.0	12.2	10.8	10.5	11.2
$40,000 to $49,999	10.5	11.0	11.6	12.4	10.8	10.2	10.9	9.4
$50,000 to $59,999	8.8	10.5	11.2	11.6	10.9	9.7	9.9	9.4
$60,000 to $69,999	7.1	9.5	9.4	9.1	9.7	9.7	9.9	9.4
$70,000 to $79,999	5.4	7.5	7.6	7.3	7.9	7.5	7.3	7.6
$80,000 to $89,999	4.1	5.5	5.3	4.8	5.8	5.8	6.0	5.5
$90,000 to $99,999	2.9	4.4	4.0	3.4	4.6	4.9	4.9	4.9
$100,000 or more	10.2	14.7	12.1	10.7	13.5	17.9	16.9	19.0

Source: Bureau of the Census, unpublished tables from the 1998 Current Population Survey, Internet web site <http://www.bls.census.gov/cps/ads/1998/sdata.htm>; calculations by New Strategist

Married Couples Are Most Affluent

The median income of couples in the 35-to-54 age group surpasses $63,000.

Among households headed by 35-to-54-year-olds, median income was $48,838 in 1997, well above the national median of $37,005. Married couples and male-headed families are the only household types in this age group with above-average incomes, however.

The $63,041 median household income of married couples aged 35 to 54 was more than $30,000 higher than the $26,980 median of female-headed families. The income of couples is far higher than that of female-headed families because most married couples are dual-earners while many female-headed families have only one earner. Within the 35-to-54 age group, couples aged 50 to 54 had the highest median income, $66,946 in 1997.

Men and women aged 35 to 54 who live alone have similar incomes—a median of $26,158 for women and $29,977 for men—evidence that women's incomes are catching up to men's. Among 35-to-39-year-olds who live alone, the median income of women is just $1,200 less than that of men.

◆ The affluent market is almost entirely one of married couples. Among the 5.8 million households headed by 35-to-54-year-olds with incomes of $100,000 or more, 85 percent are married couples.

◆ Two out of three married couples in this age group are dual-earners. Most also have children at home. They lead busy, high-pressured lives, which makes them difficult to reach.

Income Distribution of Households by Household Type, 1997: Total Aged 35 to 54

(number and percent distribution of households headed by people aged 35 to 54, by income and household type, 1997; households in thousands as of 1998)

	total	family households			nonfamily households			
					female householder		male householder	
		married couples	female hh, no spouse present	male hh, no spouse present	total	living alone	total	living alone
Total households	**43,490**	**25,914**	**5,897**	**1,755**	**4,284**	**3,607**	**5,640**	**4,566**
Under $10,000	3,006	486	965	112	697	662	744	704
$10,000 to $19,999	4,290	1,226	1,212	220	740	687	892	778
$20,000 to $29,999	4,955	1,843	1,099	322	769	682	918	788
$30,000 to $39,999	5,202	2,584	839	247	650	579	887	764
$40,000 to $49,999	4,761	2,961	565	201	427	345	609	458
$50,000 to $59,999	4,394	3,106	368	174	307	241	433	334
$60,000 to $69,999	3,955	2,941	344	139	210	154	320	220
$70,000 to $79,999	3,044	2,385	195	112	140	66	213	165
$80,000 to $89,999	2,265	1,905	76	60	69	35	155	99
$90,000 to $99,999	1,798	1,508	60	51	93	56	87	48
$100,000 or more	5,822	4,971	170	116	182	98	383	207
Median income	$48,838	$63,041	$26,980	$40,635	$28,817	$26,158	$32,568	$29,977
Total households	**100.0%**	**100.0%**	**100.0%**	**100.0%**	**100.0%**	**100.0%**	**100.0%**	**100.0%**
Under $10,000	6.9	1.9	16.4	6.4	16.3	18.4	13.2	15.4
$10,000 to $19,999	9.9	4.7	20.6	12.5	17.3	19.0	15.8	17.0
$20,000 to $29,999	11.4	7.1	18.6	18.3	18.0	18.9	16.3	17.3
$30,000 to $39,999	12.0	10.0	14.2	14.1	15.2	16.1	15.7	16.7
$40,000 to $49,999	10.9	11.4	9.6	11.5	10.0	9.6	10.8	10.0
$50,000 to $59,999	10.1	12.0	6.2	9.9	7.2	6.7	7.7	7.3
$60,000 to $69,999	9.1	11.3	5.8	7.9	4.9	4.3	5.7	4.8
$70,000 to $79,999	7.0	9.2	3.3	6.4	3.3	1.8	3.8	3.6
$80,000 to $89,999	5.2	7.4	1.3	3.4	1.6	1.0	2.7	2.2
$90,000 to $99,999	4.1	5.8	1.0	2.9	2.2	1.6	1.5	1.1
$100,000 or more	13.4	19.2	2.9	6.6	4.2	2.7	6.8	4.5

Source: Bureau of the Census, unpublished tables from the 1998 Current Population Survey, Internet web site <http://www.bls.census.gov/cps/ads/1998/sdata.htm>; calculations by New Strategist

Income Distribution of Households by Household Type, 1997: Aged 35 to 39

(number and percent distribution of households headed by people aged 35 to 39, by income and household type, 1997; households in thousands as of 1998)

| | | family households | | | nonfamily households | | | |
| | | | | | female householder | | male householder | |
	total	married couples	female hh, no spouse present	male hh, no spouse present	total	living alone	total	living alone
Total households	**11,838**	**6,941**	**1,818**	**493**	**971**	**772**	**1,615**	**1,251**
Under $10,000	979	147	475	33	131	119	193	185
$10,000 to $19,999	1,226	352	427	81	141	123	225	182
$20,000 to $29,999	1,541	565	339	98	212	185	328	276
$30,000 to $39,999	1,546	823	220	99	154	133	249	213
$40,000 to $49,999	1,415	928	130	51	94	72	216	160
$50,000 to $59,999	1,264	944	81	42	77	70	119	86
$60,000 to $69,999	1,011	811	58	21	44	23	78	44
$70,000 to $79,999	789	649	35	22	25	7	55	39
$80,000 to $89,999	510	420	8	18	22	12	42	26
$90,000 to $99,999	395	341	3	6	19	9	27	8
$100,000 or more	1,162	961	42	23	52	21	84	32
Median income	$44,281	$56,662	$20,178	$33,582	$30,107	$27,880	$31,990	$29,119
Total households	**100.0%**	**100.0%**	**100.0%**	**100.0%**	**100.0%**	**100.0%**	**100.0%**	**100.0%**
Under $10,000	8.3	2.1	26.1	6.7	13.5	15.4	12.0	14.8
$10,000 to $19,999	10.4	5.1	23.5	16.4	14.5	15.9	13.9	14.5
$20,000 to $29,999	13.0	8.1	18.6	19.9	21.8	24.0	20.3	22.1
$30,000 to $39,999	13.1	11.9	12.1	20.1	15.9	17.2	15.4	17.0
$40,000 to $49,999	12.0	13.4	7.2	10.3	9.7	9.3	13.4	12.8
$50,000 to $59,999	10.7	13.6	4.5	8.5	7.9	9.1	7.4	6.9
$60,000 to $69,999	8.5	11.7	3.2	4.3	4.5	3.0	4.8	3.5
$70,000 to $79,999	6.7	9.4	1.9	4.5	2.6	0.9	3.4	3.1
$80,000 to $89,999	4.3	6.1	0.4	3.7	2.3	1.6	2.6	2.1
$90,000 to $99,999	3.3	4.9	0.2	1.2	2.0	1.2	1.7	0.6
$100,000 or more	9.8	13.8	2.3	4.7	5.4	2.7	5.2	2.6

Source: Bureau of the Census, unpublished tables from the 1998 Current Population Survey, Internet web site <http://www.bls.census.gov/cps/ads/1998/sdata.htm>; calculations by New Strategist

Income Distribution of Households By Household Type, 1997: Aged 40 to 44

(number and percent distribution of households headed by people aged 40 to 44, by income and household type, 1997; households in thousands as of 1998)

| | | family households | | | nonfamily households | | | |
| | | | | | female householder | | male householder | |
	total	married couples	female hh, no spouse present	male hh, no spouse present	total	living alone	total	living alone
Total households	**12,105**	**7,239**	**1,819**	**562**	**892**	**727**	**1,593**	**1,304**
Under $10,000	708	124	248	30	135	126	170	164
$10,000 to $19,999	1,233	374	387	59	119	111	292	263
$20,000 to $29,999	1,423	529	383	114	164	144	232	214
$30,000 to $39,999	1,475	678	258	77	146	124	317	262
$40,000 to $49,999	1,343	812	186	85	108	83	154	107
$50,000 to $59,999	1,258	920	106	49	63	41	118	87
$60,000 to $69,999	1,129	818	118	57	44	36	94	66
$70,000 to $79,999	906	719	59	31	46	15	52	39
$80,000 to $89,999	672	586	27	14	12	7	34	24
$90,000 to $99,999	492	406	13	14	29	25	28	18
$100,000 or more	1,466	1,272	37	33	24	12	100	56
Median income	$48,845	$61,734	$27,181	$40,033	$31,269	$27,568	$33,043	$30,298
Total households	**100.0%**	**100.0%**	**100.0%**	**100.0%**	**100.0%**	**100.0%**	**100.0%**	**100.0%**
Under $10,000	5.8	1.7	13.6	5.3	15.1	17.3	10.7	12.6
$10,000 to $19,999	10.2	5.2	21.3	10.5	13.3	15.3	18.3	20.2
$20,000 to $29,999	11.8	7.3	21.1	20.3	18.4	19.8	14.6	16.4
$30,000 to $39,999	12.2	9.4	14.2	13.7	16.4	17.1	19.9	20.1
$40,000 to $49,999	11.1	11.2	10.2	15.1	12.1	11.4	9.7	8.2
$50,000 to $59,999	10.4	12.7	5.8	8.7	7.1	5.6	7.4	6.7
$60,000 to $69,999	9.3	11.3	6.5	10.1	4.9	5.0	5.9	5.1
$70,000 to $79,999	7.5	9.9	3.2	5.5	5.2	2.1	3.3	3.0
$80,000 to $89,999	5.6	8.1	1.5	2.5	1.3	1.0	2.1	1.8
$90,000 to $99,999	4.1	5.6	0.7	2.5	3.3	3.4	1.8	1.4
$100,000 or more	12.1	17.6	2.0	5.9	2.7	1.7	6.3	4.3

Source: Bureau of the Census, unpublished tables from the 1998 Current Population Survey, Internet web site <http://www.bls.census.gov/cps/ads/1998/sdata.htm>; calculations by New Strategist

Income Distribution of Households by Household Type, 1997: Aged 45 to 49

(number and percent distribution of households headed by people aged 45 to 49, by income and household type, 1997; households in thousands as of 1998)

| | | family households | | | nonfamily households | | | |
| | | | | | female householder | | male householder | |
	total	married couples	female hh, no spouse present	male hh, no spouse present	total	living alone	total	living alone
Total households	**10,601**	**6,239**	**1,367**	**405**	**1,197**	**1,036**	**1,393**	**1,157**
Under $10,000	689	104	150	37	211	199	189	177
$10,000 to $19,999	990	233	241	46	246	236	226	196
$20,000 to $29,999	1,106	390	251	61	194	178	212	179
$30,000 to $39,999	1,168	586	201	30	155	149	195	177
$40,000 to $49,999	1,132	686	151	49	107	89	139	108
$50,000 to $59,999	1,048	693	130	43	85	67	96	78
$60,000 to $69,999	1,001	722	91	36	71	54	80	65
$70,000 to $79,999	725	534	63	38	28	14	62	52
$80,000 to $89,999	616	493	22	18	24	10	60	39
$90,000 to $99,999	490	412	21	18	20	10	19	17
$100,000 or more	1,635	1,387	47	28	56	31	116	66
Median income	$51,717	$65,712	$31,501	$44,717	$26,629	$24,006	$33,106	$31,040
Total households	**100.0%**	**100.0%**	**100.0%**	**100.0%**	**100.0%**	**100.0%**	**100.0%**	**100.0%**
Under $10,000	6.5	1.7	11.0	9.1	17.6	19.2	13.6	15.3
$10,000 to $19,999	9.3	3.7	17.6	11.4	20.6	22.8	16.2	16.9
$20,000 to $29,999	10.4	6.3	18.4	15.1	16.2	17.2	15.2	15.5
$30,000 to $39,999	11.0	9.4	14.7	7.4	12.9	14.4	14.0	15.3
$40,000 to $49,999	10.7	11.0	11.0	12.1	8.9	8.6	10.0	9.3
$50,000 to $59,999	9.9	11.1	9.5	10.6	7.1	6.5	6.9	6.7
$60,000 to $69,999	9.4	11.6	6.7	8.9	5.9	5.2	5.7	5.6
$70,000 to $79,999	6.8	8.6	4.6	9.4	2.3	1.4	4.5	4.5
$80,000 to $89,999	5.8	7.9	1.6	4.4	2.0	1.0	4.3	3.4
$90,000 to $99,999	4.6	6.6	1.5	4.4	1.7	1.0	1.4	1.5
$100,000 or more	15.4	22.2	3.4	6.9	4.7	3.0	8.3	5.7

Source: Bureau of the Census, unpublished tables from the 1998 Current Population Survey, Internet web site <http://www.bls.census.gov/cps/ads/1998/sdata.htm>; calculations by New Strategist

Income Distribution of Households by Household Type, 1997: Aged 50 to 54

(number and percent distribution of households headed by people aged 50 to 54, by income and household type, 1997; households in thousands as of 1998)

| | | family households | | | nonfamily households | | | |
| | | | | | female householder | | male householder | |
	total	married couples	female hh, no spouse present	male hh, no spouse present	total	living alone	total	living alone
Total households	**8,946**	**5,495**	**893**	**296**	**1,224**	**1,072**	**1,038**	**855**
Under $10,000	628	111	95	15	221	219	189	175
$10,000 to $19,999	841	268	159	32	234	214	149	136
$20,000 to $29,999	882	357	126	52	199	175	148	120
$30,000 to $39,999	1,014	495	159	41	194	175	126	113
$40,000 to $49,999	869	537	97	17	119	100	100	83
$50,000 to $59,999	824	548	53	39	82	66	101	80
$60,000 to $69,999	813	589	78	24	51	42	70	44
$70,000 to $79,999	626	484	40	20	40	29	43	34
$80,000 to $89,999	466	407	19	12	12	5	18	10
$90,000 to $99,999	420	348	23	13	24	14	13	5
$100,000 or more	1,559	1,351	44	31	49	34	82	52
Median income	$52,045	$66,946	$33,677	$47,673	$28,147	$26,037	$32,197	$29,305
Total households	**100.0%**	**100.0%**	**100.0%**	**100.0%**	**100.0%**	**100.0%**	**100.0%**	**100.0%**
Under $10,000	7.0	2.0	10.6	5.1	18.1	20.4	18.2	20.5
$10,000 to $19,999	9.4	4.9	17.8	10.8	19.1	20.0	14.4	15.9
$20,000 to $29,999	9.9	6.5	14.1	17.6	16.3	16.3	14.3	14.0
$30,000 to $39,999	11.3	9.0	17.8	13.9	15.8	16.3	12.1	13.2
$40,000 to $49,999	9.7	9.8	10.9	5.7	9.7	9.3	9.6	9.7
$50,000 to $59,999	9.2	10.0	5.9	13.2	6.7	6.2	9.7	9.4
$60,000 to $69,999	9.1	10.7	8.7	8.1	4.2	3.9	6.7	5.1
$70,000 to $79,999	7.0	8.8	4.5	6.8	3.3	2.7	4.1	4.0
$80,000 to $89,999	5.2	7.4	2.1	4.1	1.0	0.5	1.7	1.2
$90,000 to $99,999	4.7	6.3	2.6	4.4	2.0	1.3	1.3	0.6
$100,000 or more	17.4	24.6	4.9	10.5	4.0	3.2	7.9	6.1

Source: Bureau of the Census, unpublished tables from the 1998 Current Population Survey, Internet web site <http://www.bls.census.gov/cps/ads/1998/sdata.htm>; calculations by New Strategist

Incomes Down for Boomer Men

Men aged 35 to 44 have been hurt more than those aged 45 to 54.

Since 1980, the median income of men aged 35 to 44 has fallen 16 percent, after adjusting for inflation—a loss of more than $6,000. The median income of all men fell 3 percent between 1980 and 1997.

Men aged 45 to 54 have fared better than those aged 35 to 44. The median income of the older men fell 3 percent between 1980 and 1997, after adjusting for inflation—a loss of $1,329. In 1980, the median income of men aged 45 to 54 was slightly below that of men aged 35 to 44. By 1997, the median income of men aged 45 to 54 was 15 percent greater than that of the younger men.

♦ Because men's incomes have been falling, the earnings of working women are increasingly important to the financial well-being of baby-boom families.

Incomes of men aged 35 to 44 still well below 1980 level

(percent change in median income of total men and men aged 35 to 54, 1980–97; in 1997 dollars)

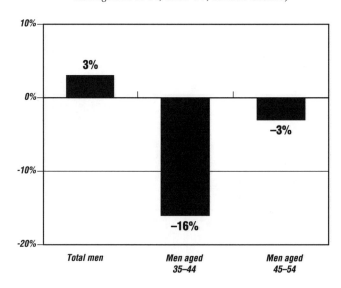

Median Income of Men Aged 35 to 54, 1980 to 1997

(median income of total men and men aged 35 to 54, 1980 to 1997; in 1997 dollars)

	total	men aged 35 to 54	
		35 to 44	45 to 54
1997	$25,212	$32,851	$37,624
1996	24,381	32,905	37,063
1995	23,761	33,090	37,477
1994	23,523	33,256	37,832
1993	23,439	33,702	36,825
1992	23,400	33,737	36,814
1991	24,121	34,529	37,449
1990	24,920	36,561	38,077
1989	25,749	38,102	40,076
1988	25,653	38,728	40,129
1987	25,129	38,206	40,248
1986	25,062	38,327	40,646
1985	24,330	37,825	38,551
1984	24,098	37,948	37,984
1983	23,577	36,161	37,249
1982	23,420	36,346	36,168
1981	24,000	37,617	37,448
1980	24,436	39,076	38,953
Percent change			
1996–1997	3.4%	−0.2%	1.5%
1990–1997	1.2	−10.1	−1.2
1980–1997	3.2	−15.9	−3.4

Source: Bureau of the Census, unpublished data from the Current Population Survey, Internet web site <http://www.census.gov>; calculations by New Strategist

Incomes of Boomer Women Have Soared

Incomes of women aged 45 to 54 have grown the most.

In contrast to the decline in the incomes of baby-boom men since 1980, women's incomes have soared. Among all women, median income grew 43 percent between 1980 and 1997, and the increase was even larger for women aged 35 to 54.

Behind the rapid rise in the median income of women is women's growing commitment to the labor force. Not only are more women working, but more are working full-time, particularly in the 35-to-54 age group. Consequently, the median income of women aged 35 to 44 rose 48 percent between 1980 and 1997. Among women aged 45 to 54, median income rose an even more impressive 64 percent, to $20,534 in 1997.

Despite these rapid income gains, the median income of women remains much lower than that of men because women are more likely to work part-time.

◆ In the 35-to-44 age group, women's income gains have almost made up for the decline in men's income over the past 17 years. The median income of men aged 35 to 44 fell $6,225 between 1980 and 1997, after adjusting for inflation, while the median income of women in the age group grew $6,098.

◆ In the 45-to-54 age group, women's income gains have far surpassed men's losses. While women's median income grew $8,047 between 1980 and 1997, after adjusting for inflation, men's income fell just $1,329.

Median Income of Women Aged 35 to 54, 1980 to 1997

(median income of total women and women aged 35 to 54, 1980 to 1997; in 1997 dollars)

	total	women aged 35 to 54	
		35 to 44	45 to 54
1997	$13,703	$18,706	$20,534
1996	13,109	18,870	19,483
1995	12,775	18,322	18,665
1994	12,418	17,533	18,466
1993	12,269	17,598	18,132
1992	12,257	17,637	18,134
1991	12,345	17,824	17,351
1990	12,366	17,811	17,474
1989	12,457	17,869	17,012
1988	12,053	17,021	16,308
1987	11,720	16,947	15,913
1986	11,144	16,202	15,201
1985	10,765	15,327	14,348
1984	10,609	14,769	13,753
1983	10,183	14,277	13,222
1982	9,884	13,181	12,595
1981	9,723	13,121	12,523
1980	9,595	12,608	12,487
Percent change			
1996–1997	4.5%	–0.9%	5.4%
1990–1997	10.8	5.0	17.5
1980–1997	42.8	48.4	64.4

Source: Bureau of the Census, unpublished data from the Current Population Survey, Internet web site <http://www.census.gov>; calculations by New Strategist

Men's Incomes Peak at Ages 50 to 54

Non-Hispanic white men aged 50 to 54 have the highest incomes.

The median income of non-Hispanic white men who work full-time peaks in the 50-to-54 age group, at $47,083 in 1997. This was nearly $12,000 more than the median income of the average man who works full-time. Among black men, peak income for full-time workers is in the 45-to-49 age group at $35,317. Peak income for Hispanic men who work full-time was just $27,034 for those aged 40 to 44.

Three out of 10 men aged 35 to 54 (including both full- and part-time workers) had an income of $50,000 or more in 1997. Six percent of men in this age group had an income of $100,000 or more. Non-Hispanic white men are much more likely to be high earners than black or Hispanic men. Thirty-four percent of non-Hispanic white men aged 35 to 54 had an income of $50,000 or more compared to 14 percent of black and 12 percent of Hispanic men in the age group.

◆ Although earnings peak in middle-age, most men aged 35 to 54 have modest incomes. Two-earner couples, rather than highly paid men, are behind the nation's record level of affluence.

Income Distribution of Men Aged 35 to 54, 1997: Total Men

(number and percent distribution of total men and men aged 35 to 54 by income, 1997; men in thousands as of 1998)

| | | aged 35 to 54 | | | | | | |
| | | | aged 35 to 44 | | | aged 45 to 54 | | |
	total	total	total	35 to 39	40 to 44	total	45 to 49	50 to 54
Total men	**101,123**	**38,652**	**22,054**	**11,299**	**10,756**	**16,598**	**9,116**	**7,483**
Without income	6,955	995	599	356	243	396	231	165
With income	94,168	37,659	21,456	10,943	10,512	16,203	8,885	7,318
Under $10,000	18,176	3,783	2,260	1,286	975	1,523	783	741
$10,000 to $19,999	19,561	5,229	3,139	1,615	1,525	2,090	1,159	930
$20,000 to $29,999	16,559	6,193	3,794	2,002	1,793	2,399	1,361	1,040
$30,000 to $39,999	12,944	6,358	3,804	2,060	1,743	2,554	1,453	1,101
$40,000 to $49,999	8,538	4,766	2,674	1,355	1,320	2,092	1,179	914
$50,000 to $74,999	10,938	6,818	3,556	1,655	1,897	3,262	1,730	1,531
$75,000 to $99,999	3,494	2,098	1,079	455	624	1,019	562	458
$100,000 or more	3,957	2,412	1,150	516	634	1,262	660	603
Median income of men with income	$25,212	$34,901	$32,851	$31,815	$35,114	$37,624	$37,142	$38,402
Median income of full-time workers	35,248	39,542	37,413	36,402	39,743	42,370	41,962	44,004
Percent working full-time	54.3%	76.5%	77.1%	76.0%	78.2%	75.8%	77.0%	74.3%
Total men	**100.0%**	**100.0%**	**100.0%**	**100.0%**	**100.0%**	**100.0%**	**100.0%**	**100.0%**
Without income	6.9	2.6	2.7	3.2	2.3	2.4	2.5	2.2
With income	93.1	97.4	97.3	96.8	97.7	97.6	97.5	97.8
Under $10,000	18.0	9.8	10.2	11.4	9.1	9.2	8.6	9.9
$10,000 to $19,999	19.3	13.5	14.2	14.3	14.2	12.6	12.7	12.4
$20,000 to $29,999	16.4	16.0	17.2	17.7	16.7	14.5	14.9	13.9
$30,000 to $39,999	12.8	16.4	17.2	18.2	16.2	15.4	15.9	14.7
$40,000 to $49,999	8.4	12.3	12.1	12.0	12.3	12.6	12.9	12.2
$50,000 to $74,999	10.8	17.6	16.1	14.6	17.6	19.7	19.0	20.5
$75,000 to $99,999	3.5	5.4	4.9	4.0	5.8	6.1	6.2	6.1
$100,000 or more	3.9	6.2	5.2	4.6	5.9	7.6	7.2	8.1

Source: Bureau of the Census, unpublished tables from the 1998 Current Population Survey, Internet web site <http://www.bls.census.gov/cps/ads/1998/sdata.htm>; calculations by New Strategist

Income Distribution of Men Aged 35 to 54, 1997: Black Men

(number and percent distribution of total black men and black men aged 35 to 54 by income, 1997; men in thousands as of 1998)

| | | | aged 35 to 54 | | | | | |
| | | | aged 35 to 44 | | | aged 45 to 54 | | |
	total	total	total	35 to 39	40 to 44	total	45 to 49	50 to 54
Total black men	**11,283**	**4,153**	**2,517**	**1,306**	**1,211**	**1,636**	**980**	**656**
Without income	1,613	297	200	121	79	97	68	29
With income	9,671	3,855	2,317	1,186	1,131	1,538	912	627
Under $10,000	2,860	744	475	253	222	269	147	122
$10,000 to $19,999	2,306	776	491	239	251	285	150	136
$20,000 to $29,999	1,840	786	509	309	201	277	164	114
$30,000 to $39,999	1,184	589	337	157	179	252	165	87
$40,000 to $49,999	633	379	235	113	123	144	95	49
$50,000 to $74,999	634	445	204	84	119	241	151	88
$75,000 to $99,999	138	82	46	19	26	36	20	17
$100,000 or more	78	51	19	10	9	32	19	13
Median income of men with income	$18,096	$25,031	$23,623	$23,147	$24,420	$27,198	$29,659	$24,122
Median income of full-time workers	26,897	31,144	28,918	27,481	30,741	34,569	35,317	31,830
Percent working full-time	45.8%	63.4%	63.1%	61.2%	65.2%	63.9%	66.8%	59.5%
Total black men	**100.0%**	**100.0%**	**100.0%**	**100.0%**	**100.0%**	**100.0%**	**100.0%**	**100.0%**
Without income	14.3	7.2	7.9	9.3	6.5	5.9	6.9	4.4
With income	85.7	92.8	92.1	90.8	93.4	94.0	93.1	95.6
Under $10,000	25.3	17.9	18.9	19.4	18.3	16.4	15.0	18.6
$10,000 to $19,999	20.4	18.7	19.5	18.3	20.7	17.4	15.3	20.7
$20,000 to $29,999	16.3	18.9	20.2	23.7	16.6	16.9	16.7	17.4
$30,000 to $39,999	10.5	14.2	13.4	12.0	14.8	15.4	16.8	13.3
$40,000 to $49,999	5.6	9.1	9.3	8.7	10.2	8.8	9.7	7.5
$50,000 to $74,999	5.6	10.7	8.1	6.4	9.8	14.7	15.4	13.4
$75,000 to $99,999	1.2	2.0	1.8	1.5	2.1	2.2	2.0	2.6
$100,000 or more	0.7	1.2	0.8	0.8	0.7	2.0	1.9	2.0

Source: Bureau of the Census, unpublished tables from the 1998 Current Population Survey, Internet web site <http://www.bls.census.gov/cps/ads/1998/sdata.htm>; calculations by New Strategist

Income Distribution of Men Aged 35 to 54, 1997: Hispanic Men

(number and percent distribution of total Hispanic men and Hispanic men aged 35 to 54 by income, 1997; men in thousands as of 1998)

| | | aged 35 to 54 | | | | | | |
| | | | aged 35 to 44 | | | aged 45 to 54 | | |
	total	total	total	35 to 39	40 to 44	total	45 to 49	50 to 54
Total Hispanic men	**10,944**	**3,687**	**2,365**	**1,339**	**1,025**	**1,322**	**726**	**596**
Without income	1,359	183	130	89	42	53	23	30
With income	9,585	3,503	2,234	1,251	984	1,269	703	566
Under $10,000	2,559	550	341	207	132	209	116	92
$10,000 to $19,999	3,116	1,061	679	391	290	382	192	190
$20,000 to $29,999	1,741	683	431	231	200	252	153	99
$30,000 to $39,999	935	494	332	181	154	162	88	75
$40,000 to $49,999	497	259	171	94	77	88	52	38
$50,000 to $74,999	486	282	176	86	93	106	62	43
$75,000 to $99,999	124	79	48	24	23	31	16	16
$100,000 or more	126	88	52	36	16	36	22	14
Median income of men with income	$16,216	$21,370	$21,533	$20,791	$22,410	$21,078	$21,383	$19,999
Median income of full-time workers	21,799	26,243	26,276	25,633	27,034	26,185	26,114	26,279
Percent working full-time	54.6%	69.9%	70.0%	68.0%	72.6%	69.8%	71.1%	68.3%
Total Hispanic men	**100.0%**	**100.0%**	**100.0%**	**100.0%**	**100.0%**	**100.0%**	**100.0%**	**100.0%**
Without income	12.4	5.0	5.5	6.6	4.1	4.0	3.2	5.0
With income	87.6	95.0	94.5	93.4	96.0	96.0	96.8	95.0
Under $10,000	23.4	14.9	14.4	15.5	12.9	15.8	16.0	15.4
$10,000 to $19,999	28.5	28.8	28.7	29.2	28.3	28.9	26.4	31.9
$20,000 to $29,999	15.9	18.5	18.2	17.3	19.5	19.1	21.1	16.6
$30,000 to $39,999	8.5	13.4	14.0	13.5	15.0	12.3	12.1	12.6
$40,000 to $49,999	4.5	7.0	7.2	7.0	7.5	6.7	7.2	6.4
$50,000 to $74,999	4.4	7.6	7.4	6.4	9.1	8.0	8.5	7.2
$75,000 to $99,999	1.1	2.1	2.0	1.8	2.2	2.3	2.2	2.7
$100,000 or more	1.2	2.4	2.2	2.7	1.6	2.7	3.0	2.3

Source: Bureau of the Census, unpublished tables from the 1998 Current Population Survey, Internet web site <http://www.bls.census.gov/cps/ads/1998/sdata.htm>; calculations by New Strategist

Income Distribution of Men Aged 35 to 54, 1997: White Men

(number and percent distribution of total white men and white men aged 35 to 54 by income, 1997; men in thousands as of 1998)

	total	aged 35 to 54 total	aged 35 to 44 total	35 to 39	40 to 44	aged 45 to 54 total	45 to 49	50 to 54
Total white men	**85,219**	**32,749**	**18,465**	**9,434**	**9,030**	**14,284**	**7,798**	**6,486**
Without income	4,819	629	354	204	149	275	157	118
With income	80,400	32,120	18,111	9,230	8,881	14,009	7,641	6,368
Under $10,000	14,431	2,843	1,661	972	688	1,182	614	567
$10,000 to $19,999	16,435	4,196	2,497	1,291	1,207	1,699	950	749
$20,000 to $29,999	13,987	5,093	3,086	1,596	1,489	2,007	1,140	866
$30,000 to $39,999	11,259	5,504	3,285	1,801	1,483	2,219	1,238	981
$40,000 to $49,999	7,540	4,173	2,323	1,176	1,147	1,850	1,021	830
$50,000 to $74,999	9,829	6,117	3,196	1,514	1,682	2,921	1,537	1,384
$75,000 to $99,999	3,195	1,920	986	404	583	934	517	417
$100,000 or more	3,726	2,271	1,075	476	599	1,196	623	572
Median income of men with income	$26,115	$37,005	$35,130	$33,186	$36,504	$39,428	$38,609	$40,176
Median income of full-time workers	36,118	41,121	38,969	37,149	40,699	43,903	42,468	45,459
Percent working full-time	55.4%	78.3%	79.2%	78.4%	80.1%	77.1%	78.1%	75.8%
Total white men	**100.0%**	**100.0%**	**100.0%**	**100.0%**	**100.0%**	**100.0%**	**100.0%**	**100.0%**
Without income	5.7	1.9	1.9	2.2	1.7	1.9	2.0	1.8
With income	94.3	98.1	98.1	97.8	98.3	98.1	98.0	98.2
Under $10,000	16.9	8.7	9.0	10.3	7.6	8.3	7.9	8.7
$10,000 to $19,999	19.3	12.8	13.5	13.7	13.4	11.9	12.2	11.5
$20,000 to $29,999	16.4	15.6	16.7	16.9	16.5	14.1	14.6	13.4
$30,000 to $39,999	13.2	16.8	17.8	19.1	16.4	15.5	15.9	15.1
$40,000 to $49,999	8.8	12.7	12.6	12.5	12.7	13.0	13.1	12.8
$50,000 to $74,999	11.5	18.7	17.3	16.0	18.6	20.4	19.7	21.3
$75,000 to $99,999	3.7	5.9	5.3	4.3	6.5	6.5	6.6	6.4
$100,000 or more	4.4	6.9	5.8	5.0	6.6	8.4	8.0	8.8

Source: Bureau of the Census, unpublished tables from the 1998 Current Population Survey, Internet web site <http://www.bls.census.gov/cps/ads/1998/sdata.htm>; calculations by New Strategist

Income Distribution of Men Aged 35 to 54, 1997: Non-Hispanic White Men

(number and percent distribution of total non-Hispanic white men and non-Hispanic white men aged 35 to 54 by income, 1997; men in thousands as of 1998)

| | | | aged 35 to 54 | | | | | |
| | | | aged 35 to 44 | | | aged 45 to 54 | | |
	total	total	total	35 to 39	40 to 44	total	45 to 49	50 to 54
Total non-Hispanic white men	**74,703**	**29,214**	**16,205**	**8,156**	**8,049**	**13,009**	**7,095**	**5,914**
Without income	3,553	470	247	139	108	223	133	90
With income	71,150	28,743	15,957	8,016	7,941	12,786	6,962	5,824
Under $10,000	11,967	2,312	1,332	767	564	980	502	478
$10,000 to $19,999	13,414	3,167	1,841	916	924	1,326	763	563
$20,000 to $29,999	12,308	4,436	2,675	1,379	1,295	1,761	990	773
$30,000 to $39,999	10,360	5,026	2,962	1,625	1,339	2,064	1,154	910
$40,000 to $49,999	7,061	3,926	2,155	1,082	1,072	1,771	976	793
$50,000 to $74,999	9,366	5,851	3,030	1,428	1,602	2,821	1,476	1,346
$75,000 to $99,999	3,074	1,842	938	379	558	904	498	405
$100,000 or more	3,600	2,183	1,023	440	583	1,160	602	558
Median income of men with income	$27,559	$38,537	$36,548	$35,396	$38,370	$41,014	$40,494	$41,702
Median income of full-time workers	37,931	42,851	40,594	38,925	41,727	45,662	44,423	47,083
Percent working full-time	55.5%	79.2%	80.4%	79.9%	80.9%	77.8%	78.8%	76.5%
Total non-Hispanic white men	**100.0%**	**100.0%**	**100.0%**	**100.0%**	**100.0%**	**100.0%**	**100.0%**	**100.0%**
Without income	4.8	1.6	1.5	1.7	1.3	1.7	1.9	1.5
With income	95.2	98.4	98.5	98.3	98.7	98.3	98.1	98.5
Under $10,000	16.0	7.9	8.2	9.4	7.0	7.5	7.1	8.1
$10,000 to $19,999	18.0	10.8	11.4	11.2	11.5	10.2	10.8	9.5
$20,000 to $29,999	16.5	15.2	16.5	16.9	16.1	13.5	14.0	13.1
$30,000 to $39,999	13.9	17.2	18.3	19.9	16.6	15.9	16.3	15.4
$40,000 to $49,999	9.5	13.4	13.3	13.3	13.3	13.6	13.8	13.4
$50,000 to $74,999	12.5	20.0	18.7	17.5	19.9	21.7	20.8	22.8
$75,000 to $99,999	4.1	6.3	5.8	4.6	6.9	6.9	7.0	6.8
$100,000 or more	4.8	7.5	6.3	5.4	7.2	8.9	8.5	9.4

Source: Bureau of the Census, unpublished tables from the 1998 Current Population Survey, Internet web site <http://www.bls.census.gov/cps/ads/1998/sdata.htm>; calculations by New Strategist

Incomes of Women Peak
in the 45-to-49 Age Group

The median income of women aged 45 to 49 who work full-time stood at $29,504 in 1997.

Women's incomes do not peak as sharply in middle-age as men's incomes do. The median income of women aged 45 to 49 who work full-time is just $3,475 greater than that of all women who work full-time. In contrast, the median income of men aged 50 to 54 who work full-time is $8,756 greater than that of all male full-time workers.

The incomes of non-Hispanic white women are higher than those of black or Hispanic women. Among non-Hispanic white women who work full-time, income peaks in the 45-to-49 age group at a median of $30,609. For black women, median income peaks in the same age group at $26,127. For Hispanic women who work full-time, median income peaks at just $22,815 in the 40-to-44 age group.

◆ The incomes of women are showing a more distinct peak in middle-age as career-oriented baby-boom women replace older generations of "just-a-job" women.

Women aged 45 to 54 make the most

(median income of total women aged 15 or older who work full-time and women aged 35 to 54 who work full-time, 1997)

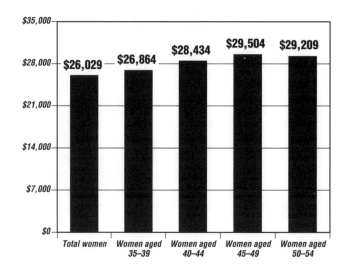

Income Distribution of Women Aged 35 to 54, 1997: Total Women

(number and percent distribution of total women and women aged 35 to 54 by income, 1997; women in thousands as of 1998)

| | | aged 35 to 54 | | | | | | |
| | | | aged 35 to 44 | | | aged 45 to 54 | | |
	total	total	total	35 to 39	40 to 44	total	45 to 49	50 to 54
Without income	**10,721**	**2,826**	**1,598**	**862**	**736**	**1,228**	**653**	**575**
With income	97,447	37,040	20,809	10,530	10,280	16,231	8,865	7,366
Under $10,000	37,533	10,179	6,021	3,222	2,798	4,158	2,196	1,962
$10,000 to $19,999	24,723	8,588	4,856	2,533	2,323	3,732	1,979	1,753
$20,000 to $29,999	15,259	6,974	3,959	2,002	1,956	3,015	1,703	1,311
$30,000 to $39,999	9,021	4,840	2,646	1,251	1,394	2,194	1,214	981
$40,000 to $49,999	4,611	2,720	1,470	694	776	1,250	716	532
$50,000 to $74,999	4,350	2,587	1,276	568	707	1,311	752	557
$75,000 to $99,999	1,026	621	309	127	182	312	169	142
$100,000 or more	922	532	274	130	144	258	132	126
Median income of women with income	$13,703	$19,507	$18,706	$17,498	$20,070	$20,534	$21,088	$19,773
Median income of full-time workers	26,029	28,330	27,524	26,864	28,434	29,364	29,504	29,209
Percent working full-time	34.9%	51.0%	49.7%	47.5%	51.9%	52.7%	54.8%	50.2%
Total women	**100.0%**	**100.0%**	**100.0%**	**100.0%**	**100.0%**	**100.0%**	**100.0%**	**100.0%**
Without income	9.9	7.1	7.1	7.6	6.7	7.0	6.9	7.2
With income	90.1	92.9	92.9	92.4	93.3	93.0	93.1	92.8
Under $10,000	34.7	25.5	26.9	28.3	25.4	23.8	23.1	24.7
$10,000 to $19,999	22.9	21.5	21.7	22.2	21.1	21.4	20.8	22.1
$20,000 to $29,999	14.1	17.5	17.7	17.6	17.8	17.3	17.9	16.5
$30,000 to $39,999	8.3	12.1	11.8	11.0	12.7	12.6	12.8	12.4
$40,000 to $49,999	4.3	6.8	6.6	6.1	7.0	7.2	7.5	6.7
$50,000 to $74,999	4.0	6.5	5.7	5.0	6.4	7.5	7.9	7.0
$75,000 to $99,999	0.9	1.6	1.4	1.1	1.7	1.8	1.8	1.8
$100,000 or more	0.9	1.3	1.2	1.1	1.3	1.5	1.4	1.6

Source: Bureau of the Census, unpublished tables from the 1998 Current Population Survey, Internet web site <http://www.bls.census.gov/cps/ads/1998/sdata.htm>; calculations by New Strategist

Income Distribution of Women Aged 35 to 54, 1997: Black Women

(number and percent distribution of total black women and black women aged 35 to 54 by income, 1997; women in thousands as of 1998)

| | | aged 35 to 54 | | | | | | |
| | | | aged 35 to 44 | | | aged 45 to 54 | | |
	total	total	total	35 to 39	40 to 44	total	45 to 49	50 to 54
Total black women	**13,715**	**5,010**	**2,982**	**1,545**	**1,437**	**2,028**	**1,180**	**847**
Without income	1,754	418	229	115	115	189	104	85
With income	11,961	4,591	2,753	1,430	1,322	1,838	1,076	763
Under $10,000	4,825	1,164	770	447	322	394	217	179
$10,000 to $19,999	3,158	1,274	753	401	353	521	306	214
$20,000 to $29,999	1,946	927	552	288	263	375	227	148
$30,000 to $39,999	1,053	625	372	171	202	253	158	96
$40,000 to $49,999	468	310	173	66	105	137	78	60
$50,000 to $74,999	414	241	112	50	61	129	77	51
$75,000 to $99,999	57	33	17	7	11	16	8	9
$100,000 or more	41	16	6	–	6	10	4	5
Median income of women with income	$13,048	$18,646	$17,681	$16,599	$19,568	$20,064	$20,426	$18,978
Median income of full-time workers	22,764	24,967	24,227	23,001	25,661	26,054	26,127	25,951
Percent working full-time	38.7%	57.0%	56.4%	55.1%	57.7%	57.9%	60.0%	55.0%
Total black women	**100.0%**	**100.0%**	**100.0%**	**100.0%**	**100.0%**	**100.0%**	**100.0%**	**100.0%**
Without income	12.8	8.3	7.7	7.4	8.0	9.3	8.8	10.0
With income	87.2	91.6	92.3	92.6	92.0	90.6	91.2	90.1
Under $10,000	35.2	23.2	25.8	28.9	22.4	19.4	18.4	21.1
$10,000 to $19,999	23.0	25.4	25.3	26.0	24.6	25.7	25.9	25.3
$20,000 to $29,999	14.2	18.5	18.5	18.6	18.3	18.5	19.2	17.5
$30,000 to $39,999	7.7	12.5	12.5	11.1	14.1	12.5	13.4	11.3
$40,000 to $49,999	3.4	6.2	5.8	4.3	7.3	6.8	6.6	7.1
$50,000 to $74,999	3.0	4.8	3.8	3.2	4.2	6.4	6.5	6.0
$75,000 to $99,999	0.4	0.7	0.6	0.5	0.8	0.8	0.7	1.1
$100,000 or more	0.3	0.3	0.2	0.0	0.4	0.5	0.3	0.6

Note: (–) means sample is too small to make a reliable estimate.
Source: Bureau of the Census, unpublished tables from the 1998 Current Population Survey, Internet web site <http://www.bls.census.gov/cps/ads/1998/sdata.htm>; calculations by New Strategist

Income Distribution of Women Aged 35 to 54, 1997: Hispanic Women

(number and percent distribution of total Hispanic women and Hispanic women aged 35 to 54 by income, 1997; women in thousands as of 1998)

		aged 35 to 54						
			aged 35 to 44			aged 45 to 54		
	total	total	total	35 to 39	40 to 44	total	45 to 49	50 to 54
Total Hispanic women	**10,485**	**3,618**	**2,241**	**1,166**	**1,075**	**1,377**	**763**	**614**
Without income	2,430	624	387	213	173	237	114	123
With income	8,055	2,994	1,854	953	902	1,140	649	491
Under $10,000	3,934	1,114	698	367	333	416	235	181
$10,000 to $19,999	2,210	916	560	297	264	356	200	156
$20,000 to $29,999	973	428	257	129	128	171	100	70
$30,000 to $39,999	502	261	157	76	82	104	63	41
$40,000 to $49,999	223	143	104	51	52	39	22	17
$50,000 to $74,999	150	100	57	24	33	43	21	20
$75,000 to $99,999	31	13	9	3	6	4	3	1
$100,000 or more	29	17	12	6	5	5	3	3
Median income of women with income	$10,260	$12,637	$12,461	$12,109	$13,555	$12,923	$13,227	$12,463
Median income of full-time workers	19,676	20,876	20,988	19,380	22,815	20,693	20,638	20,755
Percent working full-time	30.0%	42.1%	41.8%	40.6%	43.1%	42.7%	44.6%	40.4%
Total Hispanic women	**100.0%**	**100.0%**	**100.0%**	**100.0%**	**100.0%**	**100.0%**	**100.0%**	**100.0%**
Without income	23.2	17.2	17.3	18.3	16.1	17.2	14.9	20.0
With income	76.8	82.8	82.7	81.7	83.9	82.8	85.1	80.0
Under $10,000	37.5	30.8	31.1	31.5	31.0	30.2	30.8	29.5
$10,000 to $19,999	21.1	25.3	25.0	25.5	24.6	25.9	26.2	25.4
$20,000 to $29,999	9.3	11.8	11.5	11.1	11.9	12.4	13.1	11.4
$30,000 to $39,999	4.8	7.2	7.0	6.5	7.6	7.6	8.3	6.7
$40,000 to $49,999	2.1	4.0	4.6	4.4	4.8	2.8	2.9	2.8
$50,000 to $74,999	1.4	2.8	2.5	2.1	3.1	3.1	2.8	3.3
$75,000 to $99,999	0.3	0.4	0.4	0.3	0.6	0.3	0.4	0.2
$100,000 or more	0.3	0.5	0.5	0.5	0.5	0.4	0.4	0.5

Source: Bureau of the Census, unpublished tables from the 1998 Current Population Survey, Internet web site <http://www.bls.census.gov/cps/ads/1998/sdata.htm>; calculations by New Strategist

Income Distribution of Women Aged 35 to 54, 1997: White Women

(number and percent distribution of total white women and white women aged 35 to 54 by income, 1997; women in thousands as of 1998)

| | total | total | aged 35 to 54 | | | | | |
| | | | aged 35 to 44 | | | aged 45 to 54 | | |
	total	total	total	35 to 39	40 to 44	total	45 to 49	50 to 54
Total white women	**89,489**	**32,859**	**18,272**	**9,263**	**9,009**	**14,587**	**7,911**	**6,676**
Without income	8,137	2,202	1,264	680	584	938	502	435
With income	81,352	30,657	17,007	8,583	8,424	13,650	7,409	6,241
Under $10,000	31,098	8,507	4,950	2,606	2,344	3,557	1,875	1,682
$10,000 to $19,999	20,616	6,882	3,852	2,015	1,838	3,030	1,586	1,443
$20,000 to $29,999	12,728	5,769	3,242	1,649	1,594	2,527	1,423	1,103
$30,000 to $39,999	7,554	3,972	2,144	1,025	1,120	1,828	989	840
$40,000 to $49,999	3,899	2,260	1,206	577	628	1,054	612	440
$50,000 to $74,999	3,728	2,234	1,089	477	610	1,145	650	493
$75,000 to $99,999	905	559	275	117	158	284	157	127
$100,000 or more	826	477	250	116	134	227	117	110
Median income of women with income	$13,792	$19,723	$18,952	$17,959	$20,129	$20,688	$21,273	$19,965
Median income of full-time workers	26,470	28,939	28,176	27,418	29,000	29,895	29,999	29,785
Percent working full-time	34.2%	50.1%	48.6%	46.5%	50.8%	52.0%	53.9%	49.7%
Total white women	**100.0%**	**100.0%**	**100.0%**	**100.0%**	**100.0%**	**100.0%**	**100.0%**	**100.0%**
Without income	9.1	6.7	6.9	7.3	6.5	6.4	6.3	6.5
With income	90.9	93.3	93.1	92.7	93.5	93.6	93.7	93.5
Under $10,000	34.8	25.9	27.1	28.1	26.0	24.4	23.7	25.2
$10,000 to $19,999	23.0	20.9	21.1	21.8	20.4	20.8	20.0	21.6
$20,000 to $29,999	14.2	17.6	17.7	17.8	17.7	17.3	18.0	16.5
$30,000 to $39,999	8.4	12.1	11.7	11.1	12.4	12.5	12.5	12.6
$40,000 to $49,999	4.4	6.9	6.6	6.2	7.0	7.2	7.7	6.6
$50,000 to $74,999	4.2	6.8	6.0	5.1	6.8	7.8	8.2	7.4
$75,000 to $99,999	1.0	1.7	1.5	1.3	1.8	1.9	2.0	1.9
$100,000 or more	0.9	1.5	1.4	1.3	1.5	1.6	1.5	1.6

Source: Bureau of the Census, unpublished tables from the 1998 Current Population Survey, Internet web site <http://www.bls.census.gov/cps/ads/1998/sdata.htm>; calculations by New Strategist

Income Distribution of Women Aged 35 to 54, 1997: Non-Hispanic White Women

(number and percent distribution of total non-Hispanic white women and non-Hispanic white women aged 35 to 54 by income, 1997; women in thousands as of 1998)

| | | | aged 35 to 54 | | | | | |
| | | | aged 35 to 44 | | | aged 45 to 54 | | |
	total	*total*	*total*	*35 to 39*	*40 to 44*	*total*	*45 to 49*	*50 to 54*
Total non-Hispanic white women	**79,502**	**29,430**	**16,141**	**8,162**	**7,979**	**13,289**	**7,186**	**6,103**
Without income	5,793	1,606	889	475	414	717	397	320
With income	73,709	27,825	15,252	7,687	7,565	12,573	6,789	5,783
Under $10,000	27,336	7,445	4,286	2,265	2,021	3,159	1,647	1,511
$10,000 to $19,999	18,523	6,012	3,319	1,735	1,585	2,693	1,396	1,297
$20,000 to $29,999	11,809	5,357	2,997	1,524	1,474	2,360	1,327	1,034
$30,000 to $39,999	7,096	3,737	2,004	957	1,048	1,733	929	804
$40,000 to $49,999	3,687	2,122	1,105	529	578	1,017	593	423
$50,000 to $74,999	3,588	2,143	1,036	454	581	1,107	629	478
$75,000 to $99,999	875	546	266	114	152	280	154	126
$100,000 or more	800	463	239	110	129	224	116	108
Median income of women with income	$14,389	$20,644	$20,049	$18,972	$20,834	$21,366	$22,004	$20,581
Median income of full-time workers	27,149	29,668	28,997	28,284	29,756	30,484	30,609	30,343
Percent working full-time	34.8%	51.1%	49.6%	47.3%	51.9%	52.9%	54.9%	50.6%
Total non-Hispanic white women	**100.0%**	**100.0%**	**100.0%**	**100.0%**	**100.0%**	**100.0%**	**100.0%**	**100.0%**
Without income	7.3	5.5	5.5	5.8	5.2	5.4	5.5	5.2
With income	92.7	94.5	94.5	94.2	94.8	94.6	94.5	94.8
Under $10,000	34.4	25.3	26.6	27.8	25.3	23.8	22.9	24.8
$10,000 to $19,999	23.3	20.4	20.6	21.3	19.9	20.3	19.4	21.3
$20,000 to $29,999	14.9	18.2	18.6	18.7	18.5	17.8	18.5	16.9
$30,000 to $39,999	8.9	12.7	12.4	11.7	13.1	13.0	12.9	13.2
$40,000 to $49,999	4.6	7.2	6.8	6.5	7.2	7.7	8.3	6.9
$50,000 to $74,999	4.5	7.3	6.4	5.6	7.3	8.3	8.8	7.8
$75,000 to $99,999	1.1	1.9	1.6	1.4	1.9	2.1	2.1	2.1
$100,000 or more	1.0	1.6	1.5	1.3	1.6	1.7	1.6	1.8

Source: Bureau of the Census, unpublished tables from the 1998 Current Population Survey, Internet web site <http://www.bls.census.gov/cps/ads/1998/sdata.htm>; calculations by New Strategist

Earnings Soar with Education

College graduates earn much more than those with less education, making a college education well worth the cost.

For those wondering whether a college education is worth the cost, one look at the accompanying tables answers the question. Men and women with college diplomas recoup the money they spent earning their degree many times over.

Among men aged 35 to 44 who work full-time, those with at least a bachelor's degree had median earnings of $54,006 in 1997, more than $22,000 above the median earned by their counterparts who went no further than high school. Among women aged 45 to 54 who work full-time, the bonus for college graduates surpassed $18,000 ($40,476 for college graduates versus $22,340 for those with no more than a high school diploma).

◆ The nation's record level of affluence is due in large part to the high educational level of the baby-boom generation. Between 26 and 32 percent of men and women aged 35 to 54 have college degrees. They have turned those degrees into dollars.

College bonus is big

(median income of men aged 35 to 54 who work full-time by education, 1997)

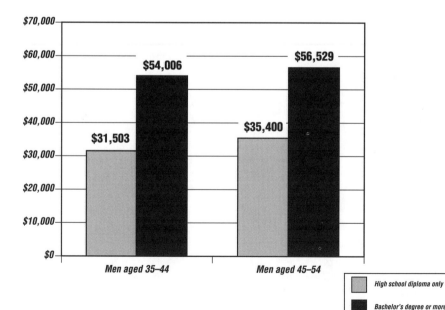

Earnings Distribution of Men by Education, 1997: Aged 35 to 44

(number and percent distribution of men aged 35 to 44 by earnings and education, 1997; men in thousands as of 1998)

	total	less than 9th grade	9th to 12th grade, no degree	high school graduate, inc. GED	some college, no degree	associate's degree	bachelor's degree or more				
							total	bachelor's degree	master's degree	professional degree	doctoral degree
Total men aged 35 to 44	22,054	926	1,946	7,537	3,895	1,820	5,929	3,971	1,174	474	311
Without earnings	1,711	188	368	684	203	106	162	109	42	9	2
With earnings	20,343	738	1,578	6,853	3,692	1,714	5,767	3,861	1,132	465	309
Under $10,000	1,687	158	264	635	280	125	228	183	29	11	6
$10,000 to $19,999	2,972	287	476	1,219	483	182	325	240	53	21	11
$20,000 to $29,999	3,723	171	401	1,588	698	298	566	481	58	13	15
$30,000 to $39,999	3,857	77	253	1,541	800	388	798	573	163	35	27
$40,000 to $49,999	2,682	18	95	955	543	308	763	538	139	51	34
$50,000 to $74,999	3,429	10	74	739	651	307	1,648	1,112	360	87	88
$75,000 to $99,999	993	8	5	93	145	73	669	372	170	74	52
$100,000 or more	1,001	10	10	81	94	36	770	361	161	171	77
Median earnings of men with earnings	$33,605	$16,033	$20,985	$29,855	$33,897	$35,798	$51,455	$47,277	$56,726	$77,194	$66,103
Median earnings of full-time workers	36,778	20,275	24,902	31,503	36,447	37,965	54,006	50,620	60,151	81,677	66,917
Percent working full-time	77.1%	50.8%	59.0%	74.1%	80.5%	81.2%	87.4%	86.5%	87.8%	90.7%	91.6%

(continued)

(continued from previous page)

| | | | 9th to | high school | some | | bachelor's degree or more | | | | |
Total men aged 35 to 44	total	less than 9th grade	12th grade, no degree	graduate, inc. GED	college, no degree	associate's degree	total	bachelor's degree	master's degree	professional degree	doctoral degree
	100.0%	100.0%	100.0%	100.0%	100.0%	100.0%	100.0%	100.0%	100.0%	100.0%	100.0%
Without earnings	7.8	20.3	18.9	9.1	5.2	5.8	2.7	2.7	3.6	1.9	0.6
With earnings	92.2	79.7	81.1	90.9	94.8	94.2	97.3	97.2	96.4	98.1	99.4
Under $10,000	7.6	17.1	13.6	8.4	7.2	6.9	3.8	4.6	2.5	2.3	1.9
$10,000 to $19,999	13.5	31.0	24.5	16.2	12.4	10.0	5.5	6.0	4.5	4.4	3.5
$20,000 to $29,999	16.9	18.5	20.6	21.1	17.9	16.4	9.5	12.1	4.9	2.7	4.8
$30,000 to $39,999	17.5	8.3	13.0	20.4	20.5	21.3	13.5	14.4	13.9	7.4	8.7
$40,000 to $49,999	12.2	1.9	4.9	12.7	13.9	16.9	12.9	13.5	11.8	10.8	10.9
$50,000 to $74,999	15.5	1.1	3.8	9.8	16.7	16.9	27.8	28.0	30.7	18.4	28.3
$75,000 to $99,999	4.5	0.9	0.3	1.2	3.7	4.0	11.3	9.4	14.5	15.6	16.7
$100,000 or more	4.5	1.1	0.5	1.1	2.4	2.0	13.0	9.1	13.7	36.1	24.8

Source: Bureau of the Census, unpublished tables from the 1998 Current Population Survey, Internet web site <http://www.bls.census.gov/cps/ads/1998/sdata.htm>; calculations by New Strategist

Earnings Distribution of Men by Education, 1997: Aged 45 to 54

(number and percent distribution of men aged 45 to 54 by earnings and education, 1997; men in thousands as of 1998)

	total	less than 9th grade	9th to 12th grade, no degree	high school graduate, inc. GED	some college, no degree	associate's degree	bachelor's degree or more				
							total	bachelor's degree	master's degree	professional degree	doctoral degree
Total men aged 45 to 54	**16,598**	**894**	**1,337**	**4,701**	**2,995**	**1,388**	**5,283**	**3,091**	**1,341**	**450**	**401**
Without earnings	1,551	207	282	538	258	99	166	121	29	3	13
With earnings	15,048	687	1,055	4,163	2,737	1,289	5,117	2,969	1,313	447	388
Under $10,000	1,110	156	150	310	193	82	217	137	59	22	–
$10,000 to $19,999	1,869	275	252	638	274	169	260	200	39	10	11
$20,000 to $29,999	2,388	133	262	848	493	228	424	307	97	11	8
$30,000 to $39,999	2,526	59	184	858	532	208	684	483	144	33	25
$40,000 to $49,999	2,138	44	96	681	457	212	648	382	179	53	34
$50,000 to $74,999	3,023	14	86	661	553	295	1,415	816	428	68	101
$75,000 to $99,999	927	5	7	103	145	50	613	290	167	69	89
$100,000 or more	1,067	2	16	59	88	46	856	357	197	182	119
Median earnings of men with earnings	$37,667	$15,715	$23,535	$32,030	$36,832	$37,255	$53,319	$49,053	$56,691	$81,989	$76,927
Median earnings of full-time workers	41,127	19,349	27,792	35,400	39,573	40,689	56,529	51,180	60,602	82,371	80,224
Percent working full-time	75.8%	52.6%	56.9%	74.6%	76.6%	77.9%	84.5%	84.5%	82.8%	90.4%	83.3%

(continued)

(continued from previous page)

| | total | less than 9th grade | 9th to 12th grade, no degree | high school graduate, inc. GED | some college, no degree | associate's degree | bachelor's degree or more | | | | |
							total	bachelor's degree	master's degree	professional degree	doctoral degree
Total men aged 45 to 54	100.0%	100.0%	100.0%	100.0%	100.0%	100.0%	100.0%	100.0%	100.0%	100.0%	100.0%
Without earnings	9.3	23.2	21.1	11.4	8.6	7.1	3.1	3.9	2.2	0.7	3.2
With earnings	90.7	76.8	78.9	88.6	91.4	92.9	96.9	96.1	97.9	99.3	96.8
Under $10,000	6.7	17.4	11.2	6.6	6.4	5.9	4.1	4.4	4.4	4.9	0.0
$10,000 to $19,999	11.3	30.8	18.8	13.6	9.1	12.2	4.9	6.5	2.9	2.2	2.7
$20,000 to $29,999	14.4	14.9	19.6	18.0	16.5	16.4	8.0	9.9	7.2	2.4	2.0
$30,000 to $39,999	15.2	6.6	13.8	18.3	17.8	15.0	12.9	15.6	10.7	7.3	6.2
$40,000 to $49,999	12.9	4.9	7.2	14.5	15.3	15.3	12.3	12.4	13.3	11.8	8.5
$50,000 to $74,999	18.2	1.6	6.4	14.1	18.5	21.3	26.8	26.4	31.9	15.1	25.2
$75,000 to $99,999	5.6	0.6	0.5	2.2	4.8	3.6	11.6	9.4	12.5	15.3	22.2
$100,000 or more	6.4	0.2	1.2	1.3	2.9	3.3	16.2	11.5	14.7	40.4	29.7

Note: (–) means sample is too small to make a reliable estimate.
Source: Bureau of the Census, unpublished tables from the 1998 Current Population Survey, Internet web site <http://www.bls.census.gov/cps/ads/1998/sdata.htm>; calculations by New Strategist

Earnings Distribution of Women by Education, 1997: Aged 35 to 44

(number and percent distribution of women aged 35 to 44 by earnings and education, 1997; women in thousands as of 1998)

	total	less than 9th grade	9th to 12th grade, no degree	high school graduate, inc. GED	some college, no degree	associate's degree	bachelor's degree or more				
							total	bachelor's degree	master's degree	professional degree	doctoral degree
Total women aged 35 to 44	**22,407**	**831**	**1,624**	**7,599**	**4,252**	**2,326**	**5,775**	**4,185**	**1,204**	**226**	**159**
Without earnings	4,588	402	602	1,601	827	343	811	638	133	29	12
With earnings	17,820	429	1,022	5,998	3,425	1,983	4,963	3,548	1,071	197	147
Under $10,000	4,004	206	434	1,601	758	313	694	571	102	13	8
$10,000 to $19,999	4,540	192	395	1,953	867	474	658	553	87	10	8
$20,000 to $29,999	3,820	23	128	1,456	843	473	896	714	140	36	8
$30,000 to $39,999	2,524	6	47	610	531	374	954	707	215	15	18
$40,000 to $49,999	1,398	2	14	252	229	203	699	430	225	24	21
$50,000 to $74,999	1,083	–	–	99	161	113	707	426	211	27	43
$75,000 to $99,999	234	–	–	17	27	14	174	84	53	17	23
$100,000 or more	218	–	2	10	8	17	181	65	41	57	18
Median earnings of women with earnings	$20,641	$10,245	$11,024	$16,580	$20,647	$23,941	$31,827	$29,083	$39,249	$50,522	$57,672
Median earnings of full-time workers	26,428	12,791	15,070	21,417	26,057	29,158	38,080	35,574	44,599	60,876	61,199
Percent working full-time	49.7%	26.2%	32.0%	49.5%	51.4%	55.0%	54.9%	51.9%	60.4%	71.7%	69.2%

(continued)

(continued from previous page)

Total women aged 35 to 44	total	less than 9th grade	9th to 12th grade, no degree	high school graduate, inc. GED	some college, no degree	associate's degree	bachelor's degree or more				
							total	bachelor's degree	master's degree	professional degree	doctoral degree
	100.0%	100.0%	100.0%	100.0%	100.0%	100.0%	100.0%	100.0%	100.0%	100.0%	100.0%
Without earnings	20.5	48.4	37.1	21.1	19.4	14.7	14.0	15.2	11.0	12.8	7.5
With earnings	79.5	51.6	62.9	78.9	80.6	85.3	85.9	84.8	89.0	87.2	92.5
Under $10,000	17.9	24.8	26.7	21.1	17.8	13.5	12.0	13.6	8.5	5.8	5.0
$10,000 to $19,999	20.3	23.1	24.3	25.7	20.4	20.4	11.4	13.2	7.2	4.4	5.0
$20,000 to $29,999	17.0	2.8	7.9	19.2	19.8	20.3	15.5	17.1	11.6	15.9	5.0
$30,000 to $39,999	11.3	0.7	2.9	8.0	12.5	16.1	16.5	16.9	17.9	6.6	11.3
$40,000 to $49,999	6.2	0.2	0.9	3.3	5.4	8.7	12.1	10.3	18.7	10.6	13.2
$50,000 to $74,999	4.8	0.0	0.0	1.3	3.8	4.9	12.2	10.2	17.5	11.9	27.0
$75,000 to $99,999	1.0	0.0	0.0	0.2	0.6	0.6	3.0	2.0	4.4	7.5	14.5
$100,000 or more	1.0	0.0	0.1	0.1	0.2	0.7	3.1	1.6	3.4	25.2	11.3

Note: (–) means sample is too small to make a reliable estimate.
Source: Bureau of the Census, unpublished tables from the 1998 Current Population Survey, Internet web site <http://www.bls.census.gov/cps/ads/1998/sdata.htm>; calculations by New Strategist

Earnings Distribution of Women by Education, 1997: Aged 45 to 54

(number and percent distribution of women aged 45 to 54 by earnings and education, 1997; women in thousands as of 1998)

	total	less than 9th grade	9th to 12th grade, no degree	high school graduate, inc. GED	some college, no degree	associate's degree	bachelor's degree or more				
							total	bachelor's degree	master's degree	professional degree	doctoral degree
Total women aged 45 to 54	**17,459**	**852**	**1,256**	**6,242**	**3,070**	**1,520**	**4,519**	**2,858**	**1,301**	**185**	**175**
Without earnings	3,790	415	497	1,513	591	213	561	405	119	25	12
With earnings	13,670	437	759	4,729	2,480	1,307	3,958	2,453	1,182	161	162
Under $10,000	2,603	175	278	1,008	466	196	480	356	97	5	22
$10,000 to $19,999	3,424	201	291	1,527	665	265	470	334	105	23	8
$20,000 to $29,999	2,947	36	136	1,250	581	316	628	472	130	8	15
$30,000 to $39,999	2,040	22	34	574	408	255	745	486	209	21	27
$40,000 to $49,999	1,185	1	15	198	196	156	618	308	261	20	29
$50,000 to $74,999	1,098	–	3	134	131	94	737	365	290	40	44
$75,000 to $99,999	208	–	–	21	18	8	160	85	47	15	12
$100,000 or more	165	–	2	16	14	15	118	46	39	29	5
Median earnings of women with earnings	$21,867	$11,194	$12,256	$18,739	$21,184	$25,787	$34,991	$30,702	$41,351	$50,798	$41,775
Median earnings of full-time workers	27,249	13,702	16,636	22,340	26,974	30,374	40,476	36,328	45,776	61,842	47,486
Percent working full-time	52.7%	29.5%	34.8%	51.3%	53.8%	59.4%	60.9%	59.3%	62.4%	66.5%	69.1%

(continued)

(continued from previous page)

Total women aged 45 to 54	total	less than 9th grade	9th to 12th grade, no degree	high school graduate, inc. GED	some college, no degree	associate's degree	bachelor's degree or more				
							total	bachelor's degree	master's degree	professional degree	doctoral degree
	100.0%	100.0%	100.0%	100.0%	100.0%	100.0%	100.0%	100.0%	100.0%	100.0%	100.0%
Without earnings	21.7	48.7	39.6	24.2	19.3	14.0	12.4	14.2	9.1	13.5	6.9
With earnings	78.3	51.3	60.4	75.8	80.8	86.0	87.6	85.8	90.9	87.0	92.6
Under $10,000	14.9	20.5	22.1	16.1	15.2	12.9	10.6	12.5	7.5	2.7	12.6
$10,000 to $19,999	19.6	23.6	23.2	24.5	21.7	17.4	10.4	11.7	8.1	12.4	4.6
$20,000 to $29,999	16.9	4.2	10.8	20.0	18.9	20.8	13.9	16.5	10.0	4.3	8.6
$30,000 to $39,999	11.7	2.6	2.7	9.2	13.3	16.8	16.5	17.0	16.1	11.4	15.4
$40,000 to $49,999	6.8	0.1	1.2	3.2	6.4	10.3	13.7	10.8	20.1	10.8	16.6
$50,000 to $74,999	6.3	0.0	0.2	2.1	4.3	6.2	16.3	12.8	22.3	21.6	25.1
$75,000 to $99,999	1.2	0.0	0.0	0.3	0.6	0.5	3.5	3.0	3.6	8.1	6.9
$100,000 or more	0.9	0.0	0.2	0.3	0.5	1.0	2.6	1.6	3.0	15.7	2.9

Note: (–) means sample is too small to make a reliable estimate.
Source: Bureau of the Census, unpublished tables from the 1998 Current Population Survey, Internet web site <http://www.bls.census.gov/cps/ads/1998/sdata.htm>; calculations by New Strategist

Self-Employment Most Common among 45-to-64-Year-Olds

Five million people aged 45 to 64 received income from nonfarm self-employment in 1997.

Among people aged 25 to 44, 87 percent had wage and salary income and 7 percent had self-employment income. In the 45-to-64 age group, the share receiving wage-and-salary income falls to 73 percent because many people in their late fifties and early sixties are retired. But in this age group, the share with self-employment income peaks at 9 percent. Self-employment is most common among older workers because they are the ones with enough experience to be in business for themselves.

More than half the Americans aged 25 to 64 receive interest income, although the amount is minimal for those aged 25 to 44—less than $1,000. People aged 45 to 64 receive more than twice as much interest income, $2,348 in 1997. Other common sources of income in these age groups are Social Security (received by 11 percent of 45-to-64-year-olds) and dividends (received by 16 to 23 percent of 25-to-64-year-olds). Five percent of people aged 25 to 44 receive child support payments.

◆ The number of people aged 45 to 64 who are self-employed should rise sharply as the baby-boom generation enters this age group during the next 10 years.

Sources of Income for People Aged 25 to 64, 1997

(number and percent of people aged 25 to 64 with income and average income for those with income, by selected sources of income and age, 1997; people in thousands as of 1998)

	aged 25 to 44			aged 45 to 64		
	number	*percent*	*average*	*number*	*percent*	*average*
Total people	**79,282**	**100.0%**	**$29,838**	**53,401**	**100.0%**	**$35,815**
Earnings	72,390	91.3	30,478	43,113	80.7	37,242
Wages and salary	68,682	86.6	30,317	39,475	73.9	37,168
Nonfarm self-employment	5,419	6.8	21,685	4,842	9.1	26,658
Social Security	1,998	2.5	7,048	5,858	11.0	7,771
Public assistance	2,186	2.8	3,509	535	1.0	3,186
Veteran benefits	358	0.5	6,446	840	1.6	8,476
Survivor benefits	213	0.3	18,487	593	1.1	11,630
Disability benefits	394	0.5	8,512	832	1.6	11,344
Pensions	517	0.7	8,303	3,864	7.2	16,452
Interest	41,504	52.3	789	33,373	62.5	2,348
Dividends	12,581	15.9	1,918	12,521	23.4	3,060
Rents, royalties, estates, or trusts	3,970	5.0	3,459	5,422	10.2	4,279
Education	3,133	4.0	3,465	495	0.9	2,403
Child support	3,708	4.7	3,592	705	1.3	5,230
Alimony	136	0.2	6,049	226	0.4	12,796

Source: Bureau of the Census, Money Income in the United States: 1997, *Current Population Reports, P60-200, 1998; calculations by New Strategist*

Poverty Unlikely among Middle-Aged

But Hispanics are more likely to be poor than whites or blacks.

While 13 percent of all Americans were poor in 1997, the poverty rate among people aged 35 to 44 was a smaller 10 percent. Only 7 percent of people aged 45 to 54 were poor.

The poverty rate for middle-aged women is slightly higher than that for middle-aged men. The greatest variation in poverty rate is by race and Hispanic origin. While only 6 percent of whites aged 45 to 54 are poor, 13 percent of blacks and 16 percent of Hispanics in that age group live in poverty.

Among 35-to-44-year-old Hispanic women, fully 25 percent are poor. This compares with just 9 percent of white women and 7 percent of white men in the age group.

♦ The poverty rate reaches a low among people aged 45 to 54. With the enormous baby-boom generation now in the age group, public support for poverty programs has plummeted.

People Aged 35 to 54 in Poverty
by Sex, Race, and Hispanic Origin, 1997

(number and percent of total people and people aged 35 to 54 in poverty, by sex, race, and Hispanic origin, 1997; persons in thousands as of 1998)

	total	white	black	Hispanic
Total people in poverty	**35,574**	**24,396**	**9,116**	**8,308**
Aged 35 to 44	4,251	2,928	1,063	992
Aged 45 to 54	2,439	1,817	489	427
Total females in poverty	**20,387**	**13,944**	**5,317**	**4,463**
Aged 35 to 44	2,566	1,724	700	559
Aged 45 to 54	1,373	1,024	273	241
Total males in poverty	**15,187**	**10,452**	**3,799**	**3,845**
Aged 35 to 44	1,686	1,204	363	433
Aged 45 to 54	1,066	793	215	185
Total people in poverty	**13.3%**	**11.0%**	**26.5%**	**27.1%**
Aged 35 to 44	9.6	8.0	19.3	21.5
Aged 45 to 54	7.2	6.3	13.3	15.8
Total females in poverty	**14.9**	**12.4**	**28.9**	**29.8**
Aged 35 to 44	11.5	9.4	23.5	24.9
Aged 45 to 54	7.9	7.0	13.5	17.5
Total males in poverty	**11.6**	**9.6**	**23.6**	**24.5**
Aged 35 to 44	7.6	6.5	14.4	18.3
Aged 45 to 54	6.4	5.5	13.2	14.0

Note: Numbers will not add to total because Hispanics may be of any race and not all races are shown.
Source: Bureau of the Census, Poverty in the United States: 1997, *Current Population Reports, P60-201, 1998*

5

Labor Force

♦ In 1950, the labor force participation rate of men aged 35 to 44 was 59 percentage points greater than that of their female counterparts. By 1998, it was only 16 points greater, as women have surged into the workforce.

♦ The 35-to-54 age group accounts for 48 percent of the nation's labor force, but for only 33 percent of the unemployed.

♦ Among the middle-aged, black men and Hispanic women have the lowest labor force participation rates. White men and black women have the highest participation rates.

♦ Seven out of 10 couples aged 35 to 54 are dual earners.

♦ Workers aged 35 to 54 account for the majority of computer system analysts, engineers, physicians, lawyers, authors, clergy, and marketing managers.

♦ Among 35-to-54-year-olds working in nonagricultural industries, 8 percent work for themselves, accounting for 57 percent of the nation's self-employed.

♦ The average job tenure of men aged 45 to 54 has fallen 3.4 years since 1983 because of widespread layoffs and more job hopping.

♦ Between 1996 and 2006, the number of workers aged 35 to 44 will decline, while the number of those aged 45 to 54 will expand.

Most Men and Women Aged 35 to 54 Work

Middle-aged men are less likely to work than in 1950, while women are more likely to have a job.

Over the past three decades, the labor force participation rates of men and women aged 35 to 54 have moved in opposite directions. Men's rate has fallen, while women's has increased sharply. Between 1950 and 1998, the labor force participation rate of women aged 35 to 54 grew 38 percentage points. In contrast, the labor force participation rate fell 5 percentage points for men aged 35 to 44 and 7 percentage points for men aged 45 to 54. As women went to work, more men could take time off to go to school or even stay home and care for their children.

Men and women aged 35 to 54 are more likely to work than the population as a whole. Among all men aged 16 or older, 75 percent were in the labor force in 1998, far below the 93 percent of men aged 35 to 44. Among all women aged 16 or older, 60 percent were in the labor force, a share well below the 77 percent rate for women aged 35 to 44. Participation rates for all men and women are lower because millions of nonworking elderly are included in the calculation of labor force participation.

◆ In 1950, the labor force participation rate of men aged 35 to 44 was 59 percentage points higher than that of their female counterparts. By 1998, it was only 16 points higher. As the labor force participation rates of men and women converge, their lifestyles are becoming more alike, changing consumer behavior.

Gap is narrowing between men's and women's labor force participation rates

(percent of people aged 35 to 44 in the labor force, by sex, 1950 and 1998)

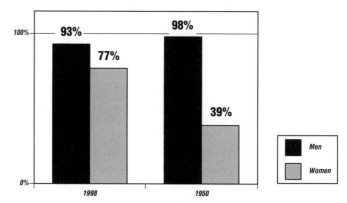

Labor Force Participation Rate of People Aged 35 to 54 by Sex, 1950 to 1998

(civilian labor force participation rate of people aged 16 or older and aged 35 to 54, by sex, 1950 to 1998; percentage point change, 1950–98)

	1998	1990	1980	1970	1960	1950	percentage point change 1950–1998
Men aged 16 or older	**74.9%**	**76.1%**	**77.4%**	**79.7%**	**83.3%**	**86.4%**	**−11.5**
Aged 35 to 44	92.6	94.4	95.5	96.9	97.7	97.6	−5.0
Aged 45 to 54	89.2	90.7	91.2	94.3	95.7	95.8	−6.6
Women aged 16 or older	**59.8**	**57.5**	**51.5**	**43.3**	**37.7**	**33.9**	**25.9**
Aged 35 to 44	77.1	76.5	65.5	51.1	43.4	39.1	38.0
Aged 45 to 54	76.2	71.2	59.9	54.4	49.9	37.9	38.3

Sources: Bureau of Labor Statistics, Employment and Earnings, *January 1999 and January 1991; and* Handbook of Labor Statistics, *Bulletin 2340, 1989; calculations by New Strategist*

Boomers Are 48 Percent of Nation's Workers

Forty-seven percent of boomer workers are women.

Among the nation's 138 million workers, 66 million are aged 35 to 54, accounting for nearly one-half of all workers. Among the 66 million workers aged 35 to 54, 31 million are women.

More than 90 percent of men aged 35 to 54 are in the labor force, as are 77 percent of women in the age group. The labor force participation rate does not vary much by age within the 35-to-54 age group, although people aged 50 to 54 are slightly less likely to work than those aged 35 to 49. Among men, 87 percent of those aged 50 to 54 work compared with a peak of 93 percent for men aged 35 to 39. Among women, 73 percent of those aged 50 to 54 work, compared with a peak of 79 percent among those aged 40 to 49.

Because unemployment is less common among the middle-aged than among young adults, people aged 35 to 54 account for a smaller share of the unemployed (33 percent) than they do of the labor force as a whole. Boomer women have a slightly higher unemployment rate than men. Half the unemployed 35-to-54-year-olds are women.

◆ During the next 10 years, affluent older boomers will begin to retire. The baby-boom share of the labor force will decline steadily as a result.

Employment Status of People Aged 35 to 54 by Sex, 1998

(number and percent of people aged 16 or older and aged 35 to 54 in the civilian labor force by sex and employment status, 1998; numbers in thousands)

| | civilian noninstitutional population | civilian labor force | | | | |
| | | total | percent of population | employed | unemployed | |
					number	percent of labor force
Total, aged 16 or older	**205,220**	**137,673**	**67.1%**	**131,463**	**6,210**	**4.5%**
Total aged 35 to 54	78,672	65,904	83.8	63,865	2,040	3.1
Aged 35 to 44	44,299	37,536	84.7	36,278	1,258	3.4
Aged 45 to 54	34,373	28,368	82.5	27,587	782	2.8
Aged 35 to 39	22,449	18,899	84.2	18,232	666	3.5
Aged 40 to 44	21,850	18,637	85.3	18,045	592	3.2
Aged 45 to 49	18,804	15,923	82.5	15,477	446	2.8
Aged 50 to 54	15,569	12,445	84.7	12,109	336	2.7
Men, aged 16 or older	**98,758**	**73,959**	**74.9**	**70,693**	**3,266**	**4.4**
Total aged 35 to 54	38,630	35,205	91.1	34,178	1,029	2.9
Aged 35 to 44	21,857	20,242	92.6	19,634	609	3.0
Aged 45 to 54	16,773	14,963	89.2	14,544	420	2.8
Aged 35 to 39	11,083	10,310	93.0	9,995	314	3.1
Aged 40 to 44	10,774	9,933	92.2	9,638	294	3.0
Aged 45 to 49	9,212	8,364	90.8	8,132	232	2.8
Aged 50 to 54	7,561	6,599	87.3	6,412	187	2.8
Women, aged 16 or older	**106,462**	**63,714**	**59.8**	**60,771**	**2,944**	**4.6**
Total aged 35 to 54	40,042	30,699	76.7	29,687	1,012	3.3
Aged 35 to 44	22,442	17,294	77.1	16,644	650	3.8
Aged 45 to 54	17,600	13,405	76.2	13,043	362	2.7
Aged 35 to 39	11,366	8,589	75.6	8,237	352	4.1
Aged 40 to 44	11,077	8,704	78.6	8,407	298	3.4
Aged 45 to 49	9,592	7,559	78.8	7,345	214	2.8
Aged 50 to 54	8,008	5,846	73.0	5,697	148	2.5

Source: Bureau of Labor Statistics, Employment and Earnings, *January 1999*

White Men Have Highest Labor Force Rate

More than 90 percent of white men aged 35 to 54 work.

Among men aged 35 to 54, whites have the highest labor force participation rate, with at least 90 percent at work or looking for work. The lowest participation rate is found among blacks—only 83 percent of black men aged 35 to 54 were in the labor force in 1998. The labor force participation rate of middle-aged Hispanic men is slightly below that of white men with nearly 90 percent of Hispanic men aged 35 to 54 in the labor force.

Despite the booming economy of the late 1990s, unemployment rates were substantially higher in 1998 for black and Hispanic men in the 35-to-54 age group than for white men. While only 2.6 percent of white men aged 35 to 39 were looking for work, the proportion was 6.5 percent among black men in the age group.

♦ Even in the best of times, black and Hispanic men have a more difficult time finding jobs than white men. Some become so discouraged they give up, dropping out of the labor force entirely.

Labor force participation rates vary by race and Hispanic origin

(percent of men aged 35 to 54 in the labor force by race and Hispanic origin, 1998)

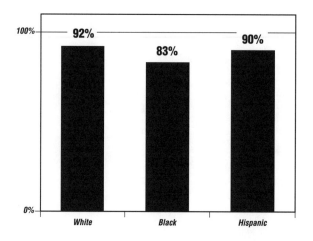

Employment Status of Men Aged 35 to 54 by Race and Hispanic Origin, 1998

(number and percent of men aged 16 or older and aged 35 to 54 in the civilian labor force by race, Hispanic origin, and employment status, 1998; numbers in thousands)

| | civilian noninstitutional population | civilian labor force | | | unemployed | |
		total	percent of population	employed	number	percent of labor force
White men	**83,352**	**63,034**	**75.6%**	**60,604**	**2,431**	**3.9%**
Total aged 35 to 54	32,710	30,160	92.2	29,376	783	2.6
Aged 35 to 44	18,310	17,157	93.7	16,715	441	2.6
Aged 45 to 54	14,400	13,003	90.3	12,661	342	2.6
Aged 35 to 39	9,269	8,719	94.1	8,492	227	2.6
Aged 40 to 44	9,041	8,438	93.3	8,223	215	2.5
Aged 45 to 49	7,840	7,198	91.8	7,013	185	2.6
Aged 50 to 54	6,561	5,805	88.5	5,649	157	2.7
Black men	**10,927**	**7,542**	**69.0**	**6,871**	**671**	**8.9**
Total aged 35 to 54	4,202	3,485	82.9	3,292	193	5.5
Aged 35 to 44	2,520	2,142	85.0	2,008	133	6.2
Aged 45 to 54	1,682	1,343	79.9	1,284	60	4.4
Aged 35 to 39	1,293	1,106	85.5	1,034	72	6.5
Aged 40 to 44	1,227	1,036	84.5	974	62	5.9
Aged 45 to 49	989	818	82.7	780	39	4.7
Aged 50 to 54	693	525	75.8	504	21	4.0
Hispanic men*	**10,734**	**8,571**	**79.8**	**8,018**	**552**	**5.2**
Total aged 35 to 54	3,719	3,337	89.7	3,192	146	4.4
Aged 35 to 44	2,377	2,173	91.4	2,077	97	4.5
Aged 45 to 54	1,342	1,164	86.7	1,115	49	4.2

* Employment status by detailed age group is not available for Hispanics.
Source: Bureau of Labor Statistics, Employment and Earnings, *January 1999*

Hispanic Women Have the Lowest Participation Rate

But the majority are in the labor force.

Two out of three Hispanic women aged 35 to 54 are in the labor force, significantly below the rate for white and black women in the age group. Among white women aged 35 to 54, 77 percent are in the labor force. Among blacks, the rate is an even higher 78 percent.

Black women aged 35 to 44 are more likely to work than their white counterparts, and the labor force participation rate exceeds 80 percent among blacks aged 40 to 44. But in the 45-to-54 age group, the labor force participation rate of black women falls below that of white women; only 69 percent of black women aged 50 to 54 are in the labor force compared with 74 percent of their white counterparts.

◆ Hispanic women aged 35 to 54 are less likely to work than black and white women in the age group because their families are larger and they are busy raising children.

Black women are most likely to work

(percent of women aged 35 to 54 in the labor force by race and Hispanic origin, 1998)

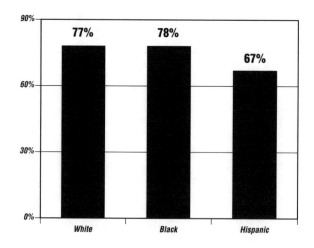

Employment Status of Women Aged 35 to 54 by Race and Hispanic Origin, 1998

(number and percent of women aged 16 or older and aged 35 to 54 in the civilian labor force by race, Hispanic origin, and employment status, 1998; numbers in thousands)

	civilian noninstitutional population	civilian labor force total	percent of population	employed	unemployed number	percent of labor force
White women	**88,126**	**52,380**	**59.4%**	**50,327**	**2,053**	**3.9%**
Total aged 35 to 54	33,032	25,343	76.7	24,605	739	2.9
Aged 35 to 44	18,300	14,064	76.9	13,604	460	3.3
Aged 45 to 54	14,732	11,279	76.6	11,001	279	2.5
Aged 35 to 39	9,248	6,970	75.4	6,728	242	3.5
Aged 40 to 44	9,052	7,094	78.4	6,876	218	3.1
Aged 45 to 49	7,955	6,291	79.1	6,133	158	2.5
Aged 50 to 54	6,777	4,988	73.6	4,867	120	2.4
Black women	**13,446**	**8,441**	**62.8**	**7,685**	**756**	**9.0**
Total aged 35 to 54	5,044	3,910	77.5	3,685	225	5.8
Aged 35 to 44	2,991	2,390	79.9	2,230	160	6.7
Aged 45 to 54	2,053	1,520	74.0	1,455	65	4.3
Aged 35 to 39	1,547	1,222	79.0	1,127	95	7.8
Aged 40 to 44	1,444	1,167	80.9	1,103	65	5.5
Aged 45 to 49	1,191	922	77.4	877	45	4.9
Aged 50 to 54	862	598	69.4	578	20	3.3
Hispanic women*	**10,335**	**5,746**	**55.6**	**5,273**	**473**	**8.2**
Total aged 35 to 54	3,692	2,460	66.6	2,307	154	6.3
Aged 35 to 44	2,259	1,533	67.9	1,428	106	6.9
Aged 45 to 54	1,433	927	64.7	879	48	5.1

* Employment status by detailed age group is not available for Hispanics.
Source: Bureau of Labor Statistics, Employment and Earnings, *January 1999*

Most Couples Are Dual-Earners

Seven out of 10 couples aged 35 to 54 are dual-earners.

In more than 18 million of the nation's 26 million middle-aged married couples both partners work—71 percent of couples in the 35-to-54 age group. In fewer than 6 million couples with the householder aged 35 to 54 (23 percent) only the husband is in the labor force.

The largest share of middle-aged couples in which only the husband works is in the 35-to-39 age group, at 26 percent. Many wives in their late thirties are at home caring for children. The dual-earner share of middle-aged couples is smallest in the 50-to-54 age group, at 68 percent. In 1998, this age group had not yet entirely filled with baby boomers (the oldest of whom turned 52 in that year). As boomers age, the two-earner share of couples in the 50-to-54 age group will surpass 70 percent.

♦ Neither husband nor wife specializes in household management in dual-earner couples. Consequently, they spend less money than their single-earner counterparts on household products purchased most often by housewives—such as cleaning supplies.

Dual-Income Couples Aged 35 to 54, 1998

(number and percent distribution of total married couples and couples headed by people aged 35 to 54 by labor force status of husband and wife, 1998; numbers in thousands)

	total couples	husband and wife in labor force	husband only in labor force	wife only in labor force	husband and wife not in labor force
Total couples	54,317	30,591	11,582	3,087	9,057
Total aged 35 to 54	25,914	18,479	5,874	971	591
Aged 35 to 39	6,941	4,861	1,822	161	98
Aged 40 to 44	7,239	5,250	1,600	255	134
Aged 45 to 49	6,239	4,619	1,251	252	117
Aged 50 to 54	5,495	3,749	1,201	303	242
Total couples	**100.0%**	**56.3%**	**21.3%**	**5.7%**	**16.7%**
Total aged 35 to 54	100.0	71.3	22.7	3.7	2.3
Aged 35 to 39	100.0	70.0	26.2	2.3	1.4
Aged 40 to 44	100.0	72.5	22.1	3.5	1.9
Aged 45 to 49	100.0	74.0	20.1	4.0	1.9
Aged 50 to 54	100.0	68.2	21.9	5.5	4.4

Source: Bureau of the Census, detailed tables from Household and Family Characteristics: March 1998, *Current Population Reports, P20-515, 1998; calculations by New Strategist*

Workers Aged 35 to 54 Dominate the Labor Force

Nearly half the nation's workers are aged 35 to 54.

Among the 131 million employed Americans in 1998, 64 million were between the ages of 35 and 54—or 49 percent of the total. The percentage in the 35-to-54 age group exceeds 50 percent in many occupations. Middle-aged workers account for 58 percent of managers, for example, including 60 percent of educational administrators and 65 percent of managers in health and medicine. The age group accounts for 55 percent of professional specialty workers, including 59 percent of physicians and 62 percent of registered nurses. Behind this dominance is the fact that people aged 35 to 54 are at the height of their careers. While only 30 percent of all employed Americans are managers or professionals, the proportion reaches a peak of 36 percent among people aged 45 to 54.

Middle-aged workers are least likely to be found in the lowest-paid occupations. They account for only 23 percent of cashiers, for example, and for only 39 percent of construction laborers. These occupations tend to attract young adults who are just starting out in the labor force.

◆ Because 35-to-54-year-olds are at the height of their career, they are enjoying peak earnings. Baby boomers now hold many of the nation's top jobs.

Occupations of Workers Aged 35 to 54, 1998

(number of employed workers aged 16 or older and aged 35 to 54 by occupation, 1998; numbers in thousands)

	total	aged 35 to 54		
		total	35 to 44	45 to 54
Total workers	**131,463**	**63,865**	**36,278**	**27,587**
Managerial and professional specialty	38,937	21,929	11,906	10,023
Executive, administrative, and managerial	19,054	11,024	5,996	5,028
Professional specialty	19,883	10,905	5,910	4,995
Technical, sales, and administrative support	38,521	17,508	9,903	7,605
Technicians and related support	4,261	2,159	1,324	835
Sales	15,850	6,543	3,722	2,821
Administrative support, including clerical	18,410	8,806	4,856	3,950
Service	17,836	7,053	4,147	2,906
Private household	847	355	193	162
Protective services	2,417	1,124	660	464
Other services	14,572	5,575	3,295	2,280
Precision production, craft, and repair	14,411	7,700	4,644	3,056
Mechanics and repairers	4,786	2,608	1,548	1,060
Construction trades	5,594	2,843	1,772	1,071
Extractive occupations	125	79	48	31
Precision production	3,907	2,171	1,277	894
Operators, fabricators, and laborers	18,256	8,253	4,867	3,386
Machine operators, assemblers, and inspectors	7,791	3,782	2,229	1,553
Transport and material moving	5,363	2,733	1,548	1,185
Handlers, equipment cleaners, helpers, and laborers	5,102	1,738	1,090	648
Farming, forestry, and fishing	3,502	1,421	811	610
Farm operators and managers	1,187	547	270	277
Other agricultural and related occupations	2,171	800	497	303
Forestry and logging	91	44	28	16
Fishing, hunting, and trapping	53	30	16	14

Source: Bureau of Labor Statistics, unpublished data from the 1998 Current Population Survey

Distribution of Workers Aged 35 to 54 by Occupation, 1998

(percent distribution of employed people aged 16 or older and aged 35 to 54 by occupation, 1998)

	total	aged 35 to 54 total	35 to 44	45 to 54
Total workers	**100.0%**	**100.0%**	**100.0%**	**100.0%**
Managerial and professional specialty	29.6	34.3	32.8	36.3
Executive, administrative, and managerial	14.5	17.3	16.5	18.2
Professional specialty	15.1	17.1	16.3	18.1
Technical, sales, and administrative support	29.3	27.4	27.3	27.6
Technicians and related support	3.2	3.4	3.6	3.0
Sales	12.1	10.2	10.3	10.2
Administrative support, including clerical	14.0	13.8	13.4	14.3
Service	13.6	11.0	11.4	10.5
Private household	0.6	0.6	0.5	0.6
Protective services	1.8	1.8	1.8	1.7
Other services	11.1	8.7	9.1	8.3
Precision production, craft, and repair	11.0	12.1	12.8	11.1
Mechanics and repairers	3.6	4.1	4.3	3.8
Construction trades	4.3	4.5	4.9	3.9
Extractive occupations	0.1	0.1	0.1	0.1
Precision production	3.0	3.4	3.5	3.2
Operators, fabricators, and laborers	13.9	12.9	13.4	12.3
Machine operators, assemblers, and inspectors	5.9	5.9	6.1	5.6
Transport and material moving	4.1	4.3	4.3	4.3
Handlers, equipment cleaners, helpers, and laborers	3.9	2.7	3.0	2.3
Farming, forestry, and fishing	2.7	2.2	2.2	2.2
Farm operators and managers	0.9	0.9	0.7	1.0
Other agricultural and related occupations	1.7	1.3	1.4	1.1
Forestry and logging	0.1	0.1	0.1	0.1
Fishing, hunting, and trapping	0.0	0.0	0.0	0.1

Source: Bureau of Labor Statistics, unpublished data from the 1998 Current Population Survey; calculations by New Strategist

Share of Workers Aged 35 to 54 by Occupation, 1998

(employed persons aged 35 to 54 as a percent of total employed people aged 16 or older by occupation, 1998)

	total	aged 35 to 54		
		total	*35 to 44*	*45 to 54*
Total workers	**100.0%**	**48.6%**	**27.6%**	**21.0%**
Managerial and professional specialty	100.0	56.3	30.6	25.7
Executive, administrative, and managerial	100.0	57.9	31.5	26.4
Professional specialty	100.0	54.8	29.7	25.1
Technical, sales, and administrative support	100.0	45.5	25.7	19.7
Technicians and related support	100.0	50.7	31.1	19.6
Sales	100.0	41.3	23.5	17.8
Administrative support, including clerical	100.0	47.8	26.4	21.5
Service	100.0	39.5	23.3	16.3
Private household	100.0	41.9	22.8	19.1
Protective services	100.0	46.5	27.3	19.2
Other services	100.0	38.3	22.6	15.6
Precision production, craft, and repair	100.0	53.4	32.2	21.2
Mechanics and repairers	100.0	54.5	32.3	22.1
Construction trades	100.0	50.8	31.7	19.1
Extractive occupations	100.0	63.2	38.4	24.8
Precision production	100.0	55.6	32.7	22.9
Operators, fabricators, and laborers	100.0	45.2	26.7	18.5
Machine operators, assemblers, and inspectors	100.0	48.5	28.6	19.9
Transport and material moving	100.0	51.0	28.9	22.1
Handlers, equipment cleaners, helpers, and laborers	100.0	34.1	21.4	12.7
Farming, forestry, and fishing	100.0	40.6	23.2	17.4
Farm operators and managers	100.0	46.1	22.7	23.3
Other agricultural and related occupations	100.0	36.8	22.9	14.0
Forestry and logging	100.0	48.4	30.8	17.6
Fishing, hunting, and trapping	100.0	56.6	30.2	26.4

Source: Bureau of Labor Statistics, unpublished data from the 1998 Current Population Survey; calculations by New Strategist

Workers Aged 35 to 54 by Detailed Occupation, 1998

(number of employed workers aged 16 or older and number and percent aged 35 to 54 by selected detailed occupation; 1998; numbers in thousands)

	total workers	aged 35 to 54 number	aged 35 to 54 percent of total
Total workers	**131,463**	**63,865**	**48.6%**
Legislators, chief exec., and gen. admin., public admin.	28	13	46.4
Officials and administrators, public admin.	630	410	65.1
Financial managers	705	419	59.4
Managers, marketing, advertising, public relations	772	458	59.3
Administrators, education	752	458	60.9
Managers, medicine and health	725	473	65.2
Architects	158	91	57.6
Engineers	2,052	1,140	55.6
Computer system analysts and scientists	1,471	790	53.7
Natural scientists	519	275	53.0
Physicians	740	436	58.9
Registered nurses	2,032	1,256	61.8
Teachers, postsecondary	919	440	47.9
Teachers, except postsecondary	4,962	2,732	55.1
Psychologists	232	138	59.5
Clergy	325	175	53.8
Lawyers	912	539	59.1
Authors	130	73	56.2
Designers	692	350	50.6
Actors and directors	130	59	45.4
Editors and reporters	274	63	23.0
Public relations specialists	170	93	54.7
Airplane pilots and navigators	113	74	65.5
Computer programmers	613	314	51.2
Insurance sales	592	337	56.9
Real estate sales	749	397	53.0
Securities and financial service sales	477	223	46.8
Advertising sales	186	80	43.0
Sales workers, motor vehicles and boats	309	150	48.5
Sales workers, apparel	447	89	19.9
Cashiers	3,025	702	23.2
Secretaries	2,914	1,543	53.0

(continued)

(continued from previous page)

	total workers	aged 35 to 54	
		number	percent of total
Receptionists	1,006	353	35.1%
File clerks	348	113	32.5
Bookkeepers	1,726	874	50.6
Telephone operators	159	74	46.5
Bank tellers	416	149	35.8
Teachers' aides	633	378	59.7
Firefighters	250	154	61.6
Police and detectives	1,062	509	47.9
Waiters and waitresses	1,379	313	22.7
Cooks	2,135	688	32.2
Nursing aides	1,913	880	46.0
Janitors and cleaners	2,233	1,074	48.1
Barbers	66	18	27.3
Hairdressers and cosmetologists	763	341	44.7
Automobile mechanics	877	413	47.1
Carpenters	1,346	653	48.5
Electricians	806	410	50.9
Plumbers	531	282	53.1
Machinists	535	293	54.8
Tailors	50	17	34.0
Shoe repairers	16	7	43.8
Machine operators, assemblers, and inspectors	7,791	3,782	48.5
Truck drivers	3,012	1,527	50.7
Bus drivers	471	271	57.5
Taxicab drivers	273	123	45.1
Construction laborers	821	318	38.7
Garbage collectors	44	22	50.0
Farm operators and managers	1,187	547	46.1
Farm workers	835	277	33.2
Groundskeepers and gardeners	924	337	36.5

Source: Bureau of Labor Statistics, unpublished tables from the 1998 Current Population Survey; calculations by New Strategist

Boomers Are Less Likely to Be Part-Time Workers

Men and women aged 35 to 54 are less likely than the average worker to hold part-time jobs.

Fewer than 4 percent of working men aged 35 to 54 have part-time jobs, a share well below the 11 percent of all working men who work part-time. Among working women aged 35 to 54, 20 percent work part-time—well below the 26 percent share among all working women.

Because there are so many people aged 35 to 54, however, the age group accounts for a significant share of part-time workers—particularly among women. The 6 million women aged 35 to 54 who work part-time account for 38 percent of the 16 million women who work part-time. Boomer women account for an even larger share—the 53 percent majority—of women who work full-time, while boomer men account for 52 percent of men with full-time jobs.

◆ Most men and women aged 35 to 54 are in the labor force, and most of those with jobs work full-time. This busy lifestyle guarantees that boomers need convenience and want simplicity when purchasing products and services.

Full-Time and Part-Time Workers Aged 35 to 54 by Sex, 1998

(number and percent distribution of employed people aged 16 or older and aged 35 to 54 by full- and part-time employment status, by sex, 1998; numbers in thousands)

	men total	men full-time	men part-time	women total	women full-time	women part-time
NUMBER						
Total employed	**70,693**	**63,189**	**7,504**	**60,771**	**45,014**	**15,757**
Total aged 35 to 54	34,177	32,916	1,261	29,687	23,724	5,963
Aged 35 to 44	19,633	18,953	680	16,644	13,101	3,543
Aged 45 to 54	14,544	13,963	581	13,043	10,623	2,420
PERCENT DISTRIBUTION BY EMPLOYMENT STATUS						
Total employed	**100.0%**	**89.4%**	**10.6%**	**100.0%**	**74.1%**	**25.9%**
Total aged 35 to 54	100.0	96.3	3.7	100.0	79.9	20.1
Aged 35 to 44	100.0	96.5	3.5	100.0	78.7	21.3
Aged 45 to 54	100.0	96.0	4.0	100.0	81.4	18.6
PERCENT DISTRIBUTION BY AGE						
Total employed	**100.0%**	**100.0%**	**100.0%**	**100.0%**	**100.0%**	**100.0%**
Total aged 35 to 54	48.3	52.1	16.8	48.9	52.7	37.8
Aged 35 to 44	27.8	30.0	9.1	27.4	29.1	22.5
Aged 45 to 54	20.6	22.1	7.7	21.5	23.6	15.4

Source: Bureau of Labor Statistics, unpublished data from the 1998 Current Population Survey; calculations by New Strategist

Few Boomers Are Self-Employed

But 35-to-54-year-olds are more likely to be self-employed than the average worker.

Despite all the talk about our entrepreneurial economy, few Americans are self-employed. Only 7 percent of the nation's nonagricultural workers were self-employed in 1998. Among 35-to-54-year-olds, a slightly higher 8 percent were self-employed. This age group accounts for 57 percent of the nation's self-employed.

Men are more likely to be self-employed than women. Among 35-to-54-year-old workers in 1998, 9 percent of men and 7 percent of women were self-employed. Among the middle-aged, those most likely to be self-employed are men aged 45 to 54, 11 percent of whom work for themselves.

◆ The statistics on the next page count as self-employed only those who are self-employed on their primary job, and exclude all those who run a business on the side. Because of this limitation, the numbers presented here are a conservative estimate of the nation's self-employed.

Self-Employed Workers Aged 35 to 54 by Sex, 1998

(number of employed nonagricultural workers aged 16 or older and aged 35 to 54, number and percent whose longest job in 1998 was self-employment, and percent of total self-employed accounted for by age group, by sex, 1998; numbers in thousands)

	total workers	self-employed		percent of total self-employed
		number	percent	
Total workers	**128,084**	**8,962**	**7.0%**	**100.0%**
Total aged 35 to 54	62,477	5,113	8.2	57.1
Aged 35 to 44	35,486	2,710	7.6	30.2
Aged 45 to 54	26,991	2,403	8.9	26.8
Total working men	**68,139**	**5,480**	**8.0**	**100.0**
Total aged 35 to 54	33,158	3,116	9.4	56.9
Aged 35 to 44	19,034	1,612	8.5	29.4
Aged 45 to 54	14,124	1,504	10.6	27.4
Total working women	**59,945**	**3,482**	**5.8**	**100.0**
Total aged 35 to 54	29,319	1,997	6.8	57.4
Aged 35 to 44	16,452	1,098	6.7	31.5
Aged 45 to 54	12,867	899	7.0	25.8

Source: Bureau of Labor Statistics, Employment and Earnings, *January 1999; calculations by New Strategist*

Job Tenure of Men Is Down

Men aged 45 to 54 experienced the biggest decline.

Job tenure is on the decline for middle-aged men, while it is rising for women. Working men aged 45 to 54 had been with their current employer a median of 9.4 years in 1998, down from 12.8 years in 1983—a loss of more than three years in job tenure. Working men aged 35 to 44 saw their median job tenure decline nearly two years, falling from 7.3 to 5.5 years between 1983 and 1998.

The median job tenure of women aged 35 to 54 has increased slightly, rising less than one year between 1983 and 1998. Women aged 35 to 44 had been with their current employer a median of 4.5 years in 1998, while those aged 45 to 54 had been with their employer a median of 7.2 years.

◆ The job tenure of men aged 35 to 54 has fallen during the past 15 years for two reasons: more job hopping by independent-minded boomers, and widespread layoffs during the recession of the early 1990s.

◆ The job tenure of women aged 35 to 54 has been increasing as career-oriented boomer women have replaced just-a-job women in the age group.

Job Tenure of People Aged 35 to 54 by Sex, 1983 and 1998

(median number of years workers aged 16 or older and aged 35 to 54 have been with their current employer by sex and age, 1983 and 1998; change in years, 1983–98)

	1998	1983	change in years 1983–98
Total workers	**3.6**	**3.5**	**0.1**
Aged 35 to 44	5.0	5.2	–0.2
Aged 45 to 54	8.1	9.5	–1.4
Total working men	**3.8**	**4.1**	**–0.3**
Aged 35 to 44	5.5	7.3	–1.8
Aged 45 to 54	9.4	12.8	–3.4
Total working women	**3.4**	**3.1**	**0.3**
Aged 35 to 44	4.5	4.1	0.4
Aged 45 to 54	7.2	6.3	0.9

Source: Bureau of Labor Statistics, Internet web site <http://www.bls.gov/news.release/tenure.t01.htm>; calculations by New Strategist

Independent Contracting Appeals to Many

More than 1 in 10 workers aged 35 to 54 is in an alternative work arrangement, most often as independent contractor.

Among the 61 million workers aged 35 to 54 in 1997, more than 6 million were in alternative work arrangements. The Bureau of Labor Statistics defines alternative workers as independent contractors, on-call workers (such as substitute teachers), temporary-help agency workers, and people who work for contract firms (such as lawn or janitorial service companies).

The most popular alternative work arrangement is independent contracting. One in 10 working men aged 35 to 54 is an independent contractor. The proportion is smaller among women in the age group—fewer than 6 percent are independent contractors. Slightly more than 1 percent of working men and women aged 35 to 54 are on-call workers, while slightly fewer than 1 percent are temps or work for contract firms.

Most independent contractors (84 percent) prefer their alternative work arrangement to a more traditional job, according to Bureau of Labor Statistics surveys. In contrast, most workers in other types of alternative work would prefer traditional employment.

♦ The proportion of workers who are independent contractors increases with age. As the baby-boom generation enters its fifties and sixties, the number of independent contractors should surge.

Workers Aged 35 to 54 in Alternative Work Arrangements, 1997

(number of workers aged 16 or older and aged 35 to 54, and number and percent employed in alternative work arrangements, by sex, 1997; numbers in thousands)

		alternative workers				
	total	total	independent contractors	on-call workers	temporary-help agency workers	workers provided by contract firms
Total employed	126,742	12,561	8,456	1,996	1,300	809
Total aged 35 to 54	61,428	6,521	4,868	796	490	367
Aged 35 to 44	35,282	3,670	2,631	508	279	252
Aged 45 to 54	26,146	2,851	2,237	288	211	115
Total men	67,931	7,758	5,633	979	581	565
Total aged 35 to 54	32,740	4,051	3,249	379	171	252
Aged 35 to 44	18,965	2,263	1,754	241	90	178
Aged 45 to 54	13,775	1,788	1,495	138	81	74
Total women	58,811	4,804	2,824	1,017	719	244
Total aged 35 to 54	28,688	2,470	1,619	417	319	115
Aged 35 to 44	16,317	1,407	877	267	189	74
Aged 45 to 54	12,371	1,063	742	150	130	41
Total employed	100.0%	9.9%	6.7%	1.6%	1.0%	0.6%
Total aged 35 to 54	100.0	10.6	7.9	1.3	0.8	0.6
Aged 35 to 44	100.0	10.4	7.5	1.4	0.8	0.7
Aged 45 to 54	100.0	10.9	8.6	1.1	0.8	0.4
Total men	100.0	11.4	8.3	1.4	0.9	0.8
Total aged 35 to 54	100.0	12.4	9.9	1.2	0.5	0.8
Aged 35 to 44	100.0	11.9	9.2	1.3	0.5	0.9
Aged 45 to 54	100.0	13.0	10.9	1.0	0.6	0.5
Total women	100.0	8.2	4.8	1.7	1.2	0.4
Total aged 35 to 54	100.0	8.6	5.6	1.5	1.1	0.4
Aged 35 to 44	100.0	8.6	5.4	1.6	1.2	0.5
Aged 45 to 54	100.0	8.6	6.0	1.2	1.1	0.3

Note: Independent contractors are workers who obtain customers on their own to provide a product or service, including the self-employed. On-call workers are in a pool of workers who are called to work only as needed, such as substitute teachers and construction workers supplied by a union hiring hall. Temporary-help agency workers are those who said they are paid by a temporary-help agency. Workers provided by contract firms are those employed by a company that provides employees or their services to others under contract, such as security, landscaping, and computer programming.
Source: Bureau of Labor Statistics, Contingent and Alternative Employment Arrangements, *February 1997, Internet web site <http://stats.bls.gov/newsrels.htm>; calculations by New Strategist*

More People Are Working at Home

Computers, the Internet, and e-mail allow more people to work from home, and most of them are baby boomers.

Between 1991 and 1997, the number of wage and salary workers paid to work at home rose from 1.9 million to 3.6 million, according to the Bureau of Labor Statistics. The technological revolution of the 1990s—particularly the explosion in Internet access and use—is allowing a growing number of people to avoid the commute to the office. Not only does this practice save employers overhead costs, but it gives workers much more flexibility in their schedules.

Overall, 3 percent of wage and salary workers are paid to work at home. The 54 percent majority are aged 35 to 54. The number of wage and salary workers who are paid to work at home nearly equals the number of home-based self-employed. Among the self-employed who work at home, the 57 percent majority are aged 35 to 54. Outnumbering both groups are wage and salary workers who work at home but are not paid for doing so. Unpaid home workers numbered 11 million in 1997, with 60 percent aged 35 to 54.

♦ The number of workers paid to work at home will grow rapidly in the years ahead as technology continues to improve and employers wake up to the advantages of home-based work.

Boomers account for the majority of those who work at home

(35-to-54-year-olds as a share of people who work at home, by type of home work, 1998)

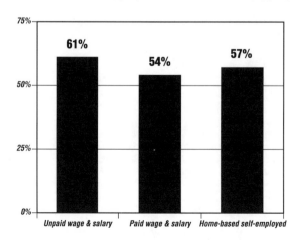

People Who Work at Home by Age, 1997

(number and percent distribution of workers aged 16 or older in nonagricultural industries by work-at-home status for primary job, by age, 1997; numbers in thousands)

	total workers	working at home total	wage and salary unpaid	wage and salary paid	home-based self-employed
NUMBER					
Total workers	**121,629**	**18,836**	**11,067**	**3,644**	**4,125**
Under age 35	47,899	5,127	3,142	1,173	812
Aged 35 to 54	59,203	11,084	6,734	1,982	2,368
Aged 35 to 44	33,944	6,015	3,548	1,181	1,286
Aged 45 to 54	25,259	5,069	3,186	801	1,082
Aged 55 or older	14,526	2,714	1,281	488	945
PERCENT DISTRIBUTION BY AGE					
Total workers	**100.0%**	**100.0%**	**100.0%**	**100.0%**	**100.0%**
Under age 35	39.4	27.2	28.4	32.2	19.7
Aged 35 to 54	48.7	58.8	60.8	54.4	57.4
Aged 35 to 44	27.9	31.9	32.1	32.4	31.2
Aged 45 to 54	20.8	26.9	28.8	22.0	26.2
Aged 55 or older	11.9	14.4	11.6	13.4	22.9
PERCENT DISTRIBUTION BY WORK STATUS					
Total workers	**100.0%**	**15.5%**	**9.1%**	**3.0%**	**3.4%**
Under age 35	100.0	10.7	6.6	2.4	1.7
Aged 35 to 54	100.0	18.7	11.4	3.3	4.0
Aged 35 to 44	100.0	17.7	10.5	3.5	3.8
Aged 45 to 54	100.0	20.1	12.6	3.2	4.3
Aged 55 or older	100.0	18.7	8.8	3.4	6.5

Source: Bureau of Labor Statistics, Work at Home in 1997, *USDL 98-93, Internet web site <http://stats.bls .gov/>; calculations by New Strategist*

Fewer Men Aged 35 to 44 in Labor Force of 2006

But the number of working men aged 45 to 54 will grow rapidly.

Between 1996 and 2006, the number of workers aged 45 to 54 will grow rapidly. While the labor force as a whole is projected to grow 11 percent during those years, the number of working men aged 45 to 54 will expand 29 percent. The number of working women in the age group will grow an even greater 38 percent. In contrast, the number of men aged 35 to 44 in the labor force will fall 6 percent between 1996 and 2006, while the number of working women in the age group will grow just 0.1 percent.

The Bureau of Labor Statistics projects that women's labor force participation rate will top 80 percent in the 35-to-44 age group by 2006. In contrast, the participation rate of men aged 35 to 44 is projected to drop nearly 2 percentage points. By 2006, the gap between the labor force participation rates of men and women aged 45 to 54 will stand at less than 8 percentage points.

♦ The rapid rise in the number of older workers will focus attention on the problem of age discrimination in the workplace.

Divergent trends in age of workers

(percent change in number of workers aged 35 to 44 and 45 to 54, by sex, 1996–2006)

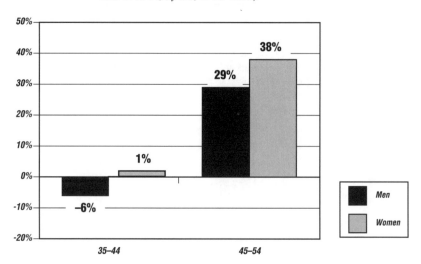

Projections of the Labor Force Aged 35 to 54 by Sex, 1996 to 2006

(number and percent of people aged 16 or older and aged 35 to 54 in the civilian labor force by sex; 1996 and 2006; percent change in number and percentage point change in participation rate 1996–2006; numbers in thousands)

	number			participation rate		
	1996	*2006*	*percent change 1996–2006*	*1996*	*2006*	*percentage point change 1996–2006*
Total labor force	**133,943**	**148,847**	**11.1%**	**66.8%**	**67.1%**	**0.3**
Total men in labor force	**72,087**	**78,226**	**8.5**	**74.9**	**73.1**	**–1.8**
Total aged 35 to 54	33,569	36,439	8.5	91.0	89.2	–1.8
Aged 35 to 44	19,602	18,478	–5.7	92.4	90.7	–1.7
Aged 45 to 54	13,967	17,961	28.6	89.1	87.7	–1.4
Total women in labor force	**61,857**	**70,620**	**14.2**	**59.3**	**61.4**	**2.1**
Total aged 35 to 54	29,384	34,173	16.3	76.6	80.0	3.4
Aged 35 to 44	16,954	16,977	0.1	77.5	80.2	2.7
Aged 45 to 54	12,430	17,196	38.3	75.4	79.9	4.5

Source: Bureau of Labor Statistics, Internet web site <http://www.bls.gov/>; calculations by New Strategist

6

Living Arrangements

◆ Most households headed by 35-to-54-year-olds are married couples.

◆ Household size peaks in the 35-to-44 age group, at more than three persons per household, on average.

◆ Half the households headed by boomers include children under age 18, but 61 percent include children of any age.

◆ Although boomers typically have small families, a substantial 25 percent of married couples aged 35 to 39 have three or more children under age 18 at home.

◆ A significant 10 percent of boomers live alone, 12 percent of men and 9 percent of women.

◆ Of the households headed by a black householder aged 35 to 54, only 36 percent are married couples. The comparable figures are 61 percent for Hispanics and 63 percent for whites.

◆ In the 35-to-54 age group, black householders outnumber Hispanic ones by 1.8 million, but Hispanic married couples outnumber black couples by nearly 300,000.

Most Boomer Households Are Headed by Married Couples

Households vary little by type within the 35-to-54 age group.

In middle-age, the lifestyles of the baby-boom generation are more alike than they have ever been. Sixty percent of households headed by people aged 35 to 54 are married couples, and the proportion barely changes by age. Female-headed families comprise only 14 percent of households headed by 35-to-54-year-olds, ranging from a high of 15 percent among 35-to-39-year-olds to a low of 10 percent among 50-to-54-year-olds. Families headed by men are a tiny fraction of boomer households, accounting for just 4 percent.

Nineteen percent of households headed by 35-to-54-year-olds are people who live alone. In the age group, there are more men (4.6 million) than women (3.6 million) who live alone.

◆ Single women begin to outnumber single men in the 50-to-54 age group. As boomers age into their sixties, women will increasingly outnumber men among those who live alone due to men's higher mortality rate.

Couples far surpass female-headed families

(the five most common types of households among householders aged 35 to 54, in percent, 1998)

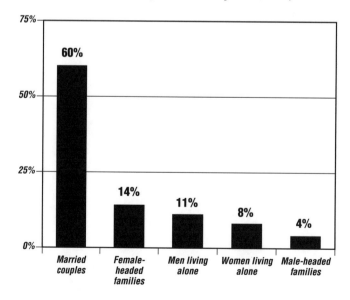

Households Headed by People Aged 35 to 54 by Household Type, 1998: Total Households

(number and percent distribution of total households and households headed by people aged 35 to 54, by household type; numbers in thousands, 1998)

| | | | aged 35 to 54 | | | | | |
| | | | aged 35 to 44 | | | aged 45 to 54 | | |
	total	*total*	*total*	*35 to 39*	*40 to 44*	*total*	*45 to 49*	*50 to 54*
Total households	102,528	43,490	23,943	11,838	12,105	19,547	10,601	8,946
Family households	70,880	33,566	18,872	9,252	9,620	14,694	8,011	6,684
Married couples	54,317	25,914	14,180	6,941	7,239	11,734	6,239	5,495
Female householder, no spouse present	12,652	5,897	3,637	1,818	1,819	2,260	1,367	893
Male householder, no spouse present	3,911	1,755	1,055	493	562	700	405	296
Nonfamily households	31,648	9,925	5,072	2,587	2,485	4,853	2,590	2,263
Female householder	17,516	4,284	1,863	971	892	2,421	1,197	1,224
Living alone	15,317	3,607	1,498	772	727	2,109	1,036	1,072
Male householder	14,133	5,640	3,208	1,615	1,593	2,432	1,393	1,038
Living alone	11,010	4,566	2,555	1,251	1,304	2,011	1,157	855
Total households	100.0%	100.0%	100.0%	100.0%	100.0%	100.0%	100.0%	100.0%
Family households	69.1	77.2	78.8	78.2	79.5	75.2	75.6	74.7
Married couples	53.0	59.6	59.2	58.6	59.8	60.0	58.9	61.4
Female householder, no spouse present	12.3	13.6	15.2	15.4	15.0	11.6	12.9	10.0
Male householder, no spouse present	3.8	4.0	4.4	4.2	4.6	3.6	3.8	3.3
Nonfamily households	30.9	22.8	21.2	21.9	20.5	24.8	24.4	25.3
Female householder	17.1	9.9	7.8	8.2	7.4	12.4	11.3	13.7
Living alone	14.9	8.3	6.3	6.5	6.0	10.8	9.8	12.0
Male householder	13.8	13.0	13.4	13.6	13.2	12.4	13.1	11.6
Living alone	10.7	10.5	10.7	10.6	10.8	10.3	10.9	9.6

Source: Bureau of the Census, unpublished data from the 1998 Current Population Survey, Internet web site <http://www.bls.census.gov/cps>; calculations by New Strategist

Couples Dominate White and Hispanic Households

But only 36 percent of black households are headed by married couples.

Married couples are by far the dominant household type among white and Hispanic households headed by 35-to-54-year-olds, accounting for 61 percent of Hispanic and 63 percent of white households. While married couples account for the largest share of households among blacks aged 35 to 54 as well, they surpass female-headed families by fewer than 200,000. Thirty-two percent of black householders aged 35 to 54 are women who head families without a spouse. The comparable figures for Hispanics and whites are 20 percent and 11 percent, respectively.

Hispanic householders aged 35 to 54 are least likely to live alone. Only 11 percent of Hispanic householders in the age group live by themselves. In contrast, 18 percent of white householders and 25 percent of black householders live by themselves.

The composition of white and Hispanic households varies little by age within the 35-to-54 age group, but black households vary greatly. Among black householders aged 35 to 39, for example, only 8 percent are women who live alone. This figure rises to 20 percent in the 50-to-54 age group.

◆ While the white and Hispanic household markets are dominated by married couples, the black household market is highly segmented.

Households Headed by People Aged 35 to 54 by Household Type, 1998: Black Households

(number and percent distribution of total black households and black households headed by people aged 35 to 54, by household type; numbers in thousands, 1997)

| | | aged 35 to 54 | | | | | | |
| | | | aged 35 to 44 | | | aged 45 to 54 | | |
	total	*total*	*total*	*35 to 39*	*40 to 44*	*total*	*45 to 49*	*50 to 54*
Total black households	**12,474**	**5,467**	**3,096**	**1,608**	**1,489**	**2,371**	**1,393**	**979**
Family households	**8,409**	**3,946**	**2,352**	**1,258**	**1,094**	**1,594**	**970**	**623**
Married couples	3,921	1,950	1,066	538	528	884	520	363
Female householder,								
no spouse present	3,926	1,753	1,146	654	492	607	393	214
Male householder,								
no spouse present	562	243	140	66	74	103	57	46
Nonfamily households	**4,066**	**1,522**	**744**	**350**	**394**	**778**	**422**	**356**
Female householder	2,190	705	302	140	162	403	192	211
Living alone	1,982	646	267	124	143	379	187	192
Male householder	1,876	817	442	210	232	375	230	145
Living alone	1,594	709	366	175	191	343	213	130
Total black households	**100.0%**	**100.0%**	**100.0%**	**100.0%**	**100.0%**	**100.0%**	**100.0%**	**100.0%**
Family households	**67.4**	**72.2**	**76.0**	**78.2**	**73.5**	**67.2**	**69.6**	**63.6**
Married couples	31.4	35.7	34.4	33.5	35.5	37.3	37.3	37.1
Female householder,								
no spouse present	31.5	32.1	37.0	40.7	33.0	25.6	28.2	21.9
Male householder,								
no spouse present	4.5	4.4	4.5	4.1	5.0	4.3	4.1	4.7
Nonfamily households	**32.6**	**27.8**	**24.0**	**21.8**	**26.5**	**32.8**	**30.3**	**36.4**
Female householder	17.6	12.9	9.8	8.7	10.9	17.0	13.8	21.6
Living alone	15.9	11.8	8.6	7.7	9.6	16.0	13.4	19.6
Male householder	15.0	14.9	14.3	13.1	15.6	15.8	16.5	14.8
Living alone	12.8	13.0	11.8	10.9	12.8	14.5	15.3	13.3

Source: Bureau of the Census, unpublished data from the 1998 Current Population Survey, Internet web site <http://www.bls.census.gov/cps>; calculations by New Strategist

Households Headed by People Aged 35 to 54 by Household Type, 1998: Hispanic Households

(number and percent distribution of total Hispanic households and Hispanic households headed by people aged 35 to 54, by household type; numbers in thousands, 1997)

		aged 35 to 54						
			aged 35 to 44			aged 45 to 54		
	total	*total*	*total*	*35 to 39*	*40 to 44*	*total*	*45 to 49*	*50 to 54*
Total Hispanic households	**8,590**	**3,702**	**2,316**	**1,198**	**1,119**	**1,386**	**782**	**605**
Family households	**6,961**	**3,168**	**2,002**	**1,029**	**973**	**1,166**	**659**	**507**
Married couples	4,804	2,239	1,427	729	698	812	445	367
Female householder,								
no spouse present	1,612	745	461	241	220	284	171	113
Male householder,								
no spouse present	545	184	114	59	55	70	43	27
Nonfamily households	**1,629**	**534**	**314**	**169**	**145**	**220**	**123**	**98**
Female householder	754	188	93	48	45	95	47	49
Living alone	617	146	71	37	34	75	39	35
Male householder	875	346	221	121	100	125	76	49
Living alone	623	253	159	86	73	94	60	35
Total Hispanic households	**100.0%**	**100.0%**	**100.0%**	**100.0%**	**100.0%**	**100.0%**	**100.0%**	**100.0%**
Family households	**81.0**	**85.6**	**86.4**	**85.9**	**87.0**	**84.1**	**84.3**	**83.8**
Married couples	55.9	60.5	61.6	60.9	62.4	58.6	56.9	60.7
Female householder,								
no spouse present	18.8	20.1	19.9	20.1	19.7	20.5	21.9	18.7
Male householder,								
no spouse present	6.3	5.0	4.9	4.9	4.9	5.1	5.5	4.5
Nonfamily households	**19.0**	**14.4**	**13.6**	**14.1**	**13.0**	**15.9**	**15.7**	**16.2**
Female householder	8.8	5.1	4.0	4.0	4.0	6.9	6.0	8.1
Living alone	7.2	3.9	3.1	3.1	3.0	5.4	5.0	5.8
Male householder	10.2	9.3	9.5	10.1	8.9	9.0	9.7	8.1
Living alone	7.3	6.8	6.9	7.2	6.5	6.8	7.7	5.8

Source: Bureau of the Census, unpublished data from the 1998 Current Population Survey, Internet web site <http://www.bls.census.gov/cps>; calculations by New Strategist

Households Headed by People Aged 35 to 54 by Household Type, 1998: White Households

(number and percent distribution of total white households and white households headed by people aged 35 to 54, by household type; numbers in thousands, 1997)

| | | aged 35 to 54 | | | | | | |
| | | | aged 35 to 44 | | | aged 45 to 54 | | |
	total	*total*	*total*	*35 to 39*	*40 to 44*	*total*	*45 to 49*	*50 to 54*
Total white households	**86,106**	**36,161**	**19,761**	**9,699**	**10,062**	**16,400**	**8,816**	**7,583**
Family households	**59,511**	**28,057**	**15,603**	**7,557**	**8,046**	**12,454**	**6,719**	**5,735**
Married couples	48,066	22,706	12,382	6,067	6,315	10,324	5,461	4,863
Female householder,								
no spouse present	8,308	3,922	2,371	1,108	1,263	1,551	923	628
Male householder,								
no spouse present	3,137	1,430	851	382	468	579	335	243
Nonfamily households	**26,596**	**8,103**	**4,158**	**2,142**	**2,016**	**3,945**	**2,097**	**1,848**
Female householder	14,871	3,444	1,491	802	690	1,953	959	994
Living alone	12,980	2,846	1,179	620	559	1,667	805	862
Male householder	11,725	4,659	2,667	1,340	1,326	1,992	1,138	854
Living alone	9,018	3,726	2,113	1,028	1,084	1,613	922	691
Total white households	**100.0%**	**100.0%**	**100.0%**	**100.0%**	**100.0%**	**100.0%**	**100.0%**	**100.0%**
Family households	**69.1**	**77.6**	**79.0**	**77.9**	**80.0**	**75.9**	**76.2**	**75.6**
Married couples	55.8	62.8	62.7	62.6	62.8	63.0	61.9	64.1
Female householder,								
no spouse present	9.6	10.8	12.0	11.4	12.6	9.5	10.5	8.3
Male householder,								
no spouse present	3.6	4.0	4.3	3.9	4.7	3.5	3.8	3.2
Nonfamily households	**30.9**	**22.4**	**21.0**	**22.1**	**20.0**	**24.1**	**23.8**	**24.4**
Female householder	17.3	9.5	7.5	8.3	6.9	11.9	10.9	13.1
Living alone	15.1	7.9	6.0	6.4	5.6	10.2	9.1	11.4
Male householder	13.6	12.9	13.5	13.8	13.2	12.1	12.9	11.3
Living alone	10.5	10.3	10.7	10.6	10.8	9.8	10.5	9.1

Source: Bureau of the Census, unpublished data from the 1998 Current Population Survey, Internet web site <http://www.bls.census.gov/cps>; calculations by New Strategist

Baby-Boom Households Are Crowded

Household size peaks in the 35-to-39 age group.

The number of people in the average American household has been declining for decades as families have fewer children and more people live by themselves. In 1998, the average American household was home to 2.62 people.

Households headed by 35-to-39-year-olds are the largest, with 3.29 people on average. Households headed by 40-to-44-year-olds also average more than three people. Household size peaks in middle-age because most people in their thirties and forties are married and many have children in their home. Overall, households headed by 35-to-54-year-olds had an average of 3.05 people in 1998.

Among households headed by 35-to-44-year-olds, the most common household size is four people, accounting for more than one in four households in the age group. Among 45-to-54-year-olds, two-person households are most common as children have grown up and left home.

◆ The number of people living in the average American household will continue to shrink as boomers age into their fifties and sixties.

Most boomer households have three or more people

(percent distribution of households headed by people aged 35 to 54 by household size, 1998)

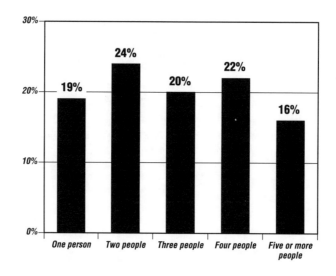

Households Headed by People Aged 35 to 54 by Size, 1998

(number and percent distribution of households headed by people aged 35 to 54, by size, 1998; numbers in thousands)

	total	aged 35 to 54 total	aged 35 to 44 total	35 to 39	40 to 44	45 to 54
Total households	**102,528**	**43,490**	**23,943**	**11,838**	**12,105**	**19,547**
One person	26,327	8,174	4,054	2,023	2,031	4,120
Two people	32,965	10,249	4,284	1,955	2,329	5,965
Three people	17,331	8,731	4,609	2,210	2,399	4,122
Four people	15,358	9,605	6,392	3,278	3,114	3,213
Five people	7,048	4,566	3,128	1,619	1,509	1,438
Six people	2,232	1,380	963	481	482	417
Seven or more people	1,267	786	514	274	240	272
Total households	**100.0%**	**100.0%**	**100.0%**	**100.0%**	**100.0%**	**100.0%**
One person	25.7	18.8	16.9	17.1	16.8	21.1
Two people	32.2	23.6	17.9	16.5	19.2	30.5
Three people	16.9	20.1	19.2	18.7	19.8	21.1
Four people	15.0	22.1	26.7	27.7	25.7	16.4
Five people	6.9	10.5	13.1	13.7	12.5	7.4
Six people	2.2	3.2	4.0	4.1	4.0	2.1
Seven or more people	1.2	1.8	2.1	2.3	2.0	1.4
Average number of people per household	2.62	3.05	3.26	3.29	3.23	2.80

Source: Bureau of the Census, detailed tables from Household and Family Characteristics: March 1998, *Current Population Reports, P20-515, 1998; calculations by New Strategist*

Half the Boomer Households Include Children under Age 18

Those most likely to have children under age 18 at home are householders aged 35 to 39.

The lifestyles of boomers revolve around their children. Fifty percent of householders aged 35 to 54 have children under age 18 living in their home, ranging from a high of 67 percent among 35-to-39-year-olds to a low of 21 percent among 50-to-54-year-olds. The majority of boomer couples have children under age 18 at home, as do most male and female family householders.

Hispanic householders aged 35 to 54 are much more likely to have children under age 18 at home than white or black householders in the age group. Sixty-three percent of Hispanic householders aged 35 to 54 have children at home compared with 46 percent of black and 50 percent of white householders in the age group. Even among Hispanic householders aged 45 to 49, the majority have children under age 18 at home. Hispanics tend to have larger families than whites or blacks, extending their childrearing years into older ages.

◆ To attract boomers, marketers must make their products and services appealing to parents.

Hispanics are much more likely to have children under age 18 at home

(percent of households headed by people aged 35 to 54 with children under age 18, by race and Hispanic origin, 1998)

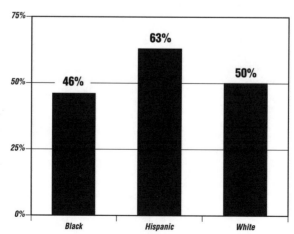

Householders Aged 35 to 54 by Type of Household and Presence of Children, 1998: Total Households

(number and percent of total households and households headed by people aged 35 to 54 by household type and presence of own children under age 18 at home, 1998; numbers in thousands)

		with own children under age 18	
	total	*number*	*percent*
Total households	**102,528**	**34,760**	**33.9%**
Total aged 35 to 54	43,490	21,578	49.6
Aged 35 to 39	11,838	7,984	67.4
Aged 40 to 44	12,105	7,345	60.7
Aged 45 to 49	10,601	4,377	41.3
Aged 50 to 54	8,946	1,872	20.9
Married couples	**54,317**	**25,269**	**46.5**
Total aged 35 to 54	25,914	16,526	63.8
Aged 35 to 39	6,941	5,967	86.0
Aged 40 to 44	7,239	5,625	77.7
Aged 45 to 49	6,239	3,406	54.6
Aged 50 to 54	5,495	1,528	27.8
Female householder, no spouse present	**12,652**	**7,693**	**60.8**
Total aged 35 to 54	5,897	4,007	67.9
Aged 35 to 39	1,818	1,684	92.6
Aged 40 to 44	1,819	1,357	74.6
Aged 45 to 49	1,367	740	54.1
Aged 50 to 54	893	226	25.3
Male householder, no spouse present	**3,911**	**1,798**	**46.0**
Total aged 35 to 54	1,756	1,043	59.4
Aged 35 to 39	493	332	67.3
Aged 40 to 44	562	362	64.4
Aged 45 to 49	405	231	57.0
Aged 50 to 54	296	118	39.9

Source: Bureau of the Census, detailed tables from Household and Family Characteristics: March 1998; Current Population Reports, P20-515, 1998; calculations by New Strategist

Householders Aged 35 to 54 by Type of Household and Presence of Children, 1998: Black Households

(number and percent of total black households and black households headed by people aged 35 to 54 by household type and presence of own children under age 18 at home, 1998; numbers in thousands)

| | total | with own children under age 18 | |
		number	percent
Total black households	**12,474**	**4,847**	**38.9%**
Total aged 35 to 54	5,467	2,526	46.2
Aged 35 to 39	1,608	1,104	68.7
Aged 40 to 44	1,489	757	50.8
Aged 45 to 49	1,393	498	35.8
Aged 50 to 54	979	167	17.1
Married couples	**3,921**	**2,055**	**52.4**
Total aged 35 to 54	1,949	1,254	64.3
Aged 35 to 39	538	480	89.2
Aged 40 to 44	528	395	74.8
Aged 45 to 49	520	274	52.7
Aged 50 to 54	363	105	28.9
Female householder, no spouse present	**3,926**	**2,569**	**65.4**
Total aged 35 to 54	1,753	1,160	66.2
Aged 35 to 39	654	594	90.8
Aged 40 to 44	492	329	66.9
Aged 45 to 49	393	193	49.1
Aged 50 to 54	214	44	20.6
Male householder, no spouse present	**562**	**223**	**39.7**
Total aged 35 to 54	243	110	45.3
Aged 35 to 39	66	29	43.9
Aged 40 to 44	74	33	44.6
Aged 45 to 49	57	30	52.6
Aged 50 to 54	46	18	39.1

Source: Bureau of the Census, detailed tables from Household and Family Characteristics: March 1998; *Current Population Reports, P20-515, 1998; calculations by New Strategist*

Householders Aged 35 to 54 by Type of Household and Presence of Children, 1998: Hispanic Households

(number and percent of total Hispanic households and Hispanic households headed by people aged 35 to 54 by household type and presence of own children under age 18 at home, 1998; numbers in thousands)

	total	with own children under age 18	
		number	percent
Total Hispanic households	**8,590**	**4,475**	**52.1%**
Total aged 35 to 54	3,702	2,328	62.9
Aged 35 to 39	1,198	914	76.3
Aged 40 to 44	1,119	797	71.2
Aged 45 to 49	782	418	53.5
Aged 50 to 54	605	199	32.9
Married couples	**4,804**	**3,121**	**65.0**
Total aged 35 to 54	2,239	1,690	75.5
Aged 35 to 39	729	659	90.4
Aged 40 to 44	698	590	84.5
Aged 45 to 49	445	301	67.6
Aged 50 to 54	367	140	38.1
Female householder, no spouse present	**1,612**	**1,121**	**69.5**
Total aged 35 to 54	745	544	73.0
Aged 35 to 39	241	229	95.0
Aged 40 to 44	220	174	79.1
Aged 45 to 49	171	96	56.1
Aged 50 to 54	113	45	39.8
Male householder, no spouse present	**545**	**233**	**42.8**
Total aged 35 to 54	184	94	51.1
Aged 35 to 39	59	26	44.1
Aged 40 to 44	55	33	60.0
Aged 45 to 49	43	21	48.8
Aged 50 to 54	27	14	51.9

Source: Bureau of the Census, detailed tables from Household and Family Characteristics: March 1998; *Current Population Reports, P20-515, 1998; calculations by New Strategist*

Householders Aged 35 to 54 by Type of Household and Presence of Children, 1998: White Households

(number and percent of total white households and white households headed by people aged 35 to 54 by household type and presence of own children under age 18 at home, 1998; numbers in thousands)

	total	with own children under age 18 number	percent
Total white households	**86,106**	**28,336**	**32.9%**
Total aged 35 to 54	36,161	17,969	49.7
Aged 35 to 39	9,699	6,534	67.4
Aged 40 to 44	10,062	6,222	61.8
Aged 45 to 49	8,816	3,654	41.4
Aged 50 to 54	7,583	1,559	20.6
Married couples	**48,066**	**21,910**	**45.6**
Total aged 35 to 54	22,706	14,353	63.2
Aged 35 to 39	6,067	5,206	85.8
Aged 40 to 44	6,315	4,920	77.9
Aged 45 to 49	5,461	2,936	53.8
Aged 50 to 54	4,863	1,291	26.5
Female householder, no spouse present	**8,308**	**4,912**	**59.1**
Total aged 35 to 54	3,922	2,722	69.4
Aged 35 to 39	1,108	1,053	95.0
Aged 40 to 44	1,263	981	77.7
Aged 45 to 49	923	519	56.2
Aged 50 to 54	628	169	26.9
Male householder, no spouse present	**3,137**	**1,514**	**48.3**
Total aged 35 to 54	1,428	895	62.7
Aged 35 to 39	382	275	72.0
Aged 40 to 44	468	321	68.6
Aged 45 to 49	335	199	59.4
Aged 50 to 54	243	100	41.2

Source: Bureau of the Census, detailed tables from Household and Family Characteristics: March 1998; *Current Population Reports, P20-515, 1998; calculations by New Strategist*

Many Boomers Have Grown Children at Home

Even among boomers aged 45 to 54, the majority have children at home.

Although just one-half of householders aged 35 to 54 have children under age 18 living in their home, the 61 percent majority have children of any age at home.

The proportion of householders with children of any age at home remains above 50 percent even in the 45-to-54 age group. While only 32 percent of householders in this age group have children under age 18 at home, the 52 percent majority have children of any age living with them.

The children of boomers are well beyond infancy. Only 2 percent of households headed by 35-to-54-year-olds have children under age 1 in their home. Preschoolers are also uncommon in boomer homes, with only 14 percent of householders aged 35 to 54 having children under age 6 at home. This figure ranges from 31 percent among householders aged 35 to 39 to just 4 percent among those aged 50 to 54. Most householders aged 35 to 44 have school-aged children, however, as do 30 percent of those aged 50 to 54.

♦ As the proportion of young adults who live at home rises, parenting duties are extending into later life. Boomers in their late forties and early fifties may no longer need baby sitters, but they aren't entirely free to do as they please.

Boomer lives revolve around children

(percent of households headed by people aged 35 to 54 with children at home, by age of child, 1998)

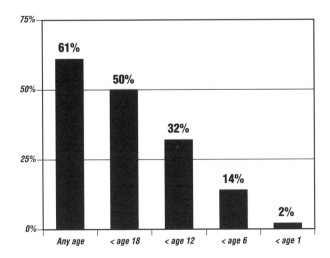

Households Headed by People Aged 35 to 54 by Presence and Age of Children at Home, 1998

(number and percent distribution of total households and households headed by people aged 35 to 54, by presence and age of own children at home, 1998; numbers in thousands)

	total	aged 35 to 54			
		total	*35 to 39*	*40 to 44*	*45 to 54*
Total households	**102,528**	**43,490**	**11,838**	**12,105**	**19,547**
With own children					
of any age	**44,979**	**26,497**	**8,153**	**8,257**	**10,087**
Under age 25	40,006	25,595	8,143	8,217	9,235
Under age 18	34,760	21,578	7,984	7,345	6,249
Under age 12	26,030	13,849	6,576	4,654	2,619
Under age 6	15,532	6,072	3,644	1,730	698
Under age 3	8,927	2,813	1,830	675	308
Under age 1	3,160	833	563	192	78
Aged 6 to 17	26,298	19,131	6,472	6,739	5,920
Total households	**100.0%**	**100.0%**	**100.0%**	**100.0%**	**100.0%**
With own children					
of any age	**43.9**	**60.9**	**68.9**	**68.2**	**51.6**
Under age 25	39.0	58.9	68.8	67.9	47.2
Under age 18	33.9	49.6	67.4	60.7	32.0
Under age 12	25.4	31.8	55.5	38.4	13.4
Under age 6	15.1	14.0	30.8	14.3	3.6
Under age 3	8.7	6.5	15.5	5.6	1.6
Under age 1	3.1	1.9	4.8	1.6	0.4
Aged 6 to 17	25.6	44.0	54.7	55.7	30.3

Source: Bureau of the Census, detailed tables from Household and Family Characteristics: March 1998; *Current Population Reports, P20-515, 1998; calculations by New Strategist*

Most Couples Have at Least Two Children

Three children are common among 35-to-39-year-olds.

Although most boomers typically have small families, a significant proportion have three or more children. Two out of three couples aged 35 to 39 have at least two children under age 18 at home. Those with three children at home are more numerous (25 percent) than those with only one child (22 percent). Only 14 percent of 35-to-39-year-olds do not have any children under age 18 at home.

Over half the couples aged 40 to 44 have two or more children under age 18 at home, with the largest share having two (34 percent). A 42 percent minority of couples aged 45 to 54 have children under age 18 at home. Those with children at home are most likely to have only one child living with them.

♦ As boomers age into their fifties, many will become empty-nesters. Expect to see boomers break out of their cocoons and spend more time having fun.

Married Couples Aged 35 to 54 by Presence and Number of Children, 1998

(number and percent distribution of total married couples and couples headed by 35-to-54-year-olds, by presence and number of own children under age 18 at home, 1998; numbers in thousands)

	total	35 to 54	35 to 39	40 to 44	45 to 54
Total married couples	**54,317**	**25,914**	**6,941**	**7,239**	**11,734**
Without own children <18	29,048	9,387	974	1,614	6,799
With own children <18	25,269	16,527	5,967	5,625	4,935
One	9,507	5,961	1,495	1,885	2,581
Two	10,241	6,874	2,758	2,426	1,690
Three or more	5,521	3,692	1,714	1,315	663
Total married couples	**100.0%**	**100.0%**	**100.0%**	**100.0%**	**100.0%**
Without own children <18	53.5	36.2	14.0	22.3	57.9
With own children <18	46.5	63.8	86.0	77.7	42.1
One	17.5	23.0	21.5	26.0	22.0
Two	18.9	26.5	39.7	33.5	14.0
Three or more	10.2	14.2	24.7	18.2	5.7

Source: Bureau of the Census, detailed tables from Household and Family Characteristics: March 1998, *Current Population Reports, P20-515, 1998; calculations by New Strategist*

Single-Parent Families Are Small

One child is most common for both female- and male-headed single-parent families.

Among 35-to-54-year-olds, most single-parent families are the result of divorce. Following a divorce, people are not likely to have additional children until they remarry. Consequently, middle-aged men and women who head families by themselves have fewer children than married couples do. While 41 percent of couples aged 35 to 54 have two or more children under age 18 at home, only 32 percent of female-headed families in the age group have that many children. The proportion is an even smaller 24 percent among male-headed families.

More than 90 percent of female family heads aged 35 to 39 have children under age 18 living with them, as do 75 percent of those aged 40 to 44. Male family heads aged 35 to 44 are much less likely to be raising children than their female counterparts. Only about two-thirds of those aged 35 to 44 have children under age 18. But male family heads aged 45 to 54 are more likely than their female counterparts to have children under age 18 at home, 50 versus 43 percent. Male and female family heads who do not have children under age 18 at home have other relatives living with them, such as adult children, siblings, or elderly parents.

♦ The lifestyles of male and female family householders in the 35-to-44 age group differ from those of their counterparts aged 45 to 54. Single parents dominate the younger group, while adult interests and activities rule among the older group.

Female-Headed Families Aged 35 to 54 by Presence and Number of Children, 1998

(number and percent distribution of total female-headed families and families headed by 35-to-54-year-old females, by presence and number of own children under age 18 at home, 1998; numbers in thousands)

	total	35 to 54	35 to 39	40 to 44	45 to 5
Total female-headed families	**12,652**	**5,897**	**1,818**	**1,819**	**2,260**
Without own children <18	4,960	1,889	133	462	1,294
With own children <18	7,693	4,007	1,684	1,357	966
One	3,739	2,129	645	772	712
Two	2,425	1,219	642	399	178
Three or more	1,529	657	397	185	75
Total female-headed families	**100.0%**	**100.0%**	**100.0%**	**100.0%**	**100.0%**
Without own children <18	39.2	32.0	7.3	25.4	57.3
With own children <18	60.8	67.9	92.6	74.6	42.7
One	29.6	36.1	35.5	42.4	31.5
Two	19.2	20.7	35.3	21.9	7.9
Three or more	12.1	11.1	21.8	10.2	3.3

Source: Bureau of the Census, detailed tables from Household and Family Characteristics: March 1998, *Current Population Reports, P20-515, 1998; calculations by New Strategist*

Male-Headed Families Aged 35 to 54 by Presence and Number of Children at Home, 1998

(number and percent distribution of total male-headed families and families headed by males aged 35 to 55, by presence and number of own children under age 18 at home, 1998; numbers in thousands)

	total	35 to 54	35 to 39	40 to 44	45 to 54
Total male-headed families	**3,911**	**1,755**	**493**	**562**	**700**
Without own children <18	2,113	713	161	200	352
With own children <18	1,798	1,043	332	362	349
One	1,117	618	181	199	238
Two	456	288	101	107	80
Three or more	225	138	50	57	31
Total male-headed families	**100.0%**	**100.0%**	**100.0%**	**100.0%**	**100.0%**
Without own children <18	54.0	40.6	32.7	35.6	50.3
With own children <18	46.0	59.4	67.3	64.4	49.9
One	28.6	35.2	36.7	35.4	34.0
Two	11.7	16.4	20.5	19.0	11.4
Three or more	5.8	7.9	10.1	10.1	4.4

Source: Bureau of the Census, detailed tables from Household and Family Characteristics: March 1998; *Current Population Reports, P20-515, 1998; calculations by New Strategist*

Few Boomers Live Alone

Trends in lone living diverge for men and women in the 35-to-54 age group.

People aged 35 to 54 are less likely to live alone than those in any other age group. Among boomers, 12 percent of men and 9 percent of women live alone. The proportion of women who live alone bottoms out in the 40-to-44 age group at 6.6 percent. For men that proportion is lowest in the 35-to-39 age group at 11.1 percent.

Lone living becomes more common among women as they age from their mid-thirties to their mid-fifties, rising from 7 to 14 percent as marriages dissolve due to divorce or death. In contrast, lone living becomes less common among men as they age into their fifties. These trends continue into old age, when women are far more likely to live alone than men.

Although middle-aged Americans are not likely to live alone, lone living is somewhat more common among 35-to-54-year-olds today than it was a quarter-century ago. In 1970, 7 percent of 35-to-54-year-olds lived by themselves; today, 10 percent do.

◆ Although few people aged 35 to 54 live alone, those who do comprise a significant share of the boomer market. With 12 percent of boomer men and 9 percent of boomer women living alone, marketers cannot ignore these consumers.

People Aged 35 to 54 Who Live Alone, 1998

(number and percent of people aged 15 or older and people 35 to 54 who live alone by sex, 1998; numbers in thousands)

	total	living alone number	living alone percent
Total people	**209,291**	**26,327**	**12.6%**
Total aged 35 to 54	**78,520**	**8,174**	**10.4**
Aged 35 to 44	44,462	4,054	9.1
Aged 45 to 54	34,058	4,120	12.1
Aged 35 to 39	22,691	2,023	8.9
Aged 40 to 44	21,771	2,031	9.3
Aged 45 to 49	18,634	2,193	11.8
Aged 50 to 54	15,424	1,927	12.5
Total men	**101,123**	**11,010**	**10.9**
Total aged 35 to 54	**38,654**	**4,567**	**11.8**
Aged 35 to 44	22,055	2,555	11.6
Aged 45 to 54	16,599	2,012	12.1
Aged 35 to 39	11,299	1,251	11.1
Aged 40 to 44	10,756	1,304	12.1
Aged 45 to 49	9,116	1,157	12.7
Aged 50 to 54	7,483	855	11.4
Total women	**108,168**	**15,317**	**14.2**
Total aged 35 to 54	**39,866**	**3,607**	**9.0**
Aged 35 to 44	22,407	1,499	6.7
Aged 45 to 54	17,459	2,108	12.1
Aged 35 to 39	11,392	772	6.8
Aged 40 to 44	11,015	727	6.6
Aged 45 to 49	9,518	1,036	10.9
Aged 50 to 54	7,941	1,072	13.5

Source: Bureau of the Census, unpublished tables from the 1998 Current Population Survey, Internet web site <http://www.bls.census.gov/cps>; calculations by New Strategist

Most Boomer Men Live with a Spouse

Living alone is the second most common living arrangement among men aged 35 to 54.

By the time men reach their mid-thirties, most are married. Among men aged 35 to 39, fully 62 percent live with a spouse. The proportion rises to 67 percent among those aged 40 to 44 and to 72 percent among men aged 45 to 54.

Six percent of men aged 35 to 54 still live with their parents, double the figure for their female counterparts and surpassing the proportion of men who head families without a spouse.

Nineteen percent of men aged 35 to 54 live alone or with nonrelatives. Overall, about one in eight boomer men lives alone, a proportion that does not vary much by age. The percentage of men who live with nonrelatives declines in middle-age, from nearly 10 percent of 35-to-39-year-olds to 6 percent of 45-to-54-year-olds.

◆ Men are far more likely than women to live with their parents as young adults, and the tendency continues through middle-age.

Living Arrangements of Men Aged 35 to 54, 1998

(number and percent distribution of total men and men aged 35 to 54 by living arrangement, 1998; numbers in thousands)

		aged 35 to 54			
	total	*total*	*35 to 39*	*40 to 44*	*45 to 54*
Total men	**101,123**	**38,653**	**11,299**	**10,756**	**16,598**
Living with spouse	55,304	26,245	7,056	7,174	12,015
Other family householder	3,911	1,755	493	562	700
Living with parents	18,421	2,243	1,073	687	483
Other family member	3,678	1,009	352	279	378
Living alone	11,010	4,566	1,251	1,304	2,011
Living with nonrelatives	8,799	2,835	1,074	749	1,012
Total men	**100.0%**	**100.0%**	**100.0%**	**100.0%**	**100.0%**
Living with spouse	54.7	67.9	62.4	66.7	72.4
Other family householder	3.9	4.5	4.4	5.2	4.2
Living with parents	18.2	5.8	9.5	6.4	2.9
Other family member	3.6	2.6	3.1	2.6	2.3
Living alone	10.9	11.8	11.1	12.1	12.1
Living with nonrelatives	8.7	7.3	9.5	7.0	6.1

Source: Bureau of the Census, Marital Status and Living Arrangements: March 1998, *Current Population Reports, P20-514, 1998; and unpublished tables from the 1998 Current Population Survey, Internet web site <http://www.bls.census.gov/cps>; calculations by New Strategist*

Living Arrangements of Boomer Women Vary Little by Age

Two out of three live with a spouse.

Boomer women are about as likely as boomer men to live with a spouse, but they are more likely than men to head family households without a spouse. Fifteen percent of women aged 35 to 54 are family heads, about three times the proportion of their male counterparts.

Few middle-aged women still live with their parents. In every age group, the share of women who live in their parents' home is about half that of men. While boomer women are less likely than men to live alone, they become increasingly more likely to do so with age. The proportion rises from fewer than 7 percent of women aged 35 to 44 to 12 percent of women aged 45 to 54.

♦ As boomer women age into their sixties and beyond, a growing proportion will live alone. Eventually, lone living will become their dominant living arrangement.

Living Arrangements of Women Aged 35 to 54, 1998

(number and percent distribution of total women and women aged 35 to 54 by living arrangement, 1998; numbers in thousands)

	total	aged 35 to 54			
		total	35 to 39	40 to 44	45 to 54
Total women	**108,168**	**39,866**	**11,392**	**11,015**	**17,459**
Living with spouse	55,304	26,497	7,517	7,434	11,546
Other family householder	12,652	5,897	1,818	1,819	2,260
Living with parents	14,224	1,129	458	304	367
Other family member	4,116	919	256	222	441
Living alone	15,317	3,608	772	727	2,109
Living with nonrelatives	6,555	1,817	571	510	736
Total women	**100.0%**	**100.0%**	**100.0%**	**100.0%**	**100.0%**
Living with spouse	51.1	66.5	66.0	67.5	66.1
Other family householder	11.7	14.8	16.0	16.5	12.9
Living with parents	13.1	2.8	4.0	2.8	2.1
Other family member	3.8	2.3	2.2	2.0	2.5
Living alone	14.2	9.1	6.8	6.6	12.1
Living with nonrelatives	6.1	4.6	5.0	4.6	4.2

Source: Bureau of the Census, Marital Status and Living Arrangements: March 1998, *Current Population Reports, P20-514, 1998; and unpublished tables from the 1998 Current Population Survey, Internet web site <http://www.bls.census.gov/cps>; calculations by New Strategist*

Most Boomers Are Married

More than 70 percent of 35-to-54-year-olds are married.

In middle-age, most people are married. The married proportion rises steadily for men through middle-age, from 67 percent among 35-to-39-year-olds to 76 percent of 45-to-54-year-olds. For women, the married proportion peaks in the 40-to-44 age group at 73 percent.

Twenty-two percent of men aged 35 to 39 have not married, a proportion that falls to just 9 percent by the 45-to-54 age group. Among women, the never-married share drops from 14 percent among 35-to-39-year-olds to just 7 percent among 45-to-54-year-olds.

The proportion of boomers who are currently divorced is a substantial 13 percent among men and 16 percent among women. But at least 30 percent of boomers have ever experienced divorce.

Widowhood among mid-life men is rare. But a significant 4 percent of women in the 45-to-54 age group are widows, reflecting men's higher mortality rate.

♦ The boomer market is a couples' market, although many husbands and wives are in their second or even third marriages.

Marital statuses of boomer men and women are similar

(percent distribution of people aged 35 to 54 by marital status and sex, 1998)

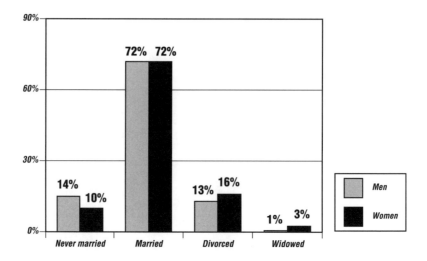

Marital Status of People Aged 35 to 54 by Sex, 1998: Total

(number and percent distribution of total people aged 15 or older and people aged 35 to 54 by sex and marital status, 1998; numbers in thousands)

	total	35 to 54	35 to 39	40 to 44	45 to 54
Total men	**101,123**	**38,653**	**11,299**	**10,756**	**16,598**
Never married	31,591	5,601	2,444	1,676	1,481
Married	58,633	27,896	7,598	7,633	12,665
Divorced	8,331	4,913	1,213	1,397	2,303
Widowed	2,569	244	44	50	150
Total women	**108,168**	**39,866**	**11,392**	**11,015**	**17,459**
Never married	26,713	3,984	1,626	1,095	1,263
Married	59,333	28,506	8,145	8,016	12,345
Divorced	11,093	6,376	1,484	1,738	3,154
Widowed	11,029	1,001	138	166	697
Total men	**100.0%**	**100.0%**	**100.0%**	**100.0%**	**100.0%**
Never married	31.2	14.5	21.6	15.6	8.9
Married	58.0	72.2	67.2	71.0	76.3
Divorced	8.2	12.7	10.7	13.0	13.9
Widowed	2.5	0.6	0.4	0.5	0.9
Total women	**100.0**	**100.0**	**100.0**	**100.0**	**100.0**
Never married	24.7	10.0	14.3	9.9	7.2
Married	54.9	71.5	71.5	72.8	70.7
Divorced	10.3	16.0	13.0	15.8	18.1
Widowed	10.2	2.5	1.2	1.5	4.0

Source: Bureau of the Census, Marital Status and Living Arrangements: March 1998, *Current Population Reports, P20-514, 1998; calculations by New Strategist*

Black Boomers Most Likely to Be Single

More than one in four blacks aged 35 to 54 has never married.

The marital status of the middle-aged differs sharply by race. Among men and women aged 35 to 54, about three out four whites and Hispanics are currently married. But among blacks of that age, only 57 percent of men and 51 percent of women are married.

Behind the lower marriage rate of blacks is their growing propensity to postpone marriage altogether. In the 35-to-39 age group, fully 40 percent of black men and 34 percent of black women have never married. In contrast, the proportions of never-married white men and women in the age group are 19 and 11 percent, respectively.

Blacks are also more likely to be currently divorced than whites or Hispanics. Among women aged 35 to 54, 21 percent of blacks are currently divorced, versus 16 percent of whites and 14 percent of Hispanics.

Widowhood is more common for black and Hispanic women than for white women. In the 45-to-54 age group, 6 percent of both black and Hispanic women are widows compared with fewer than 4 percent of white women.

◆ Among blacks, the boomer market is highly segmented. While the majority of middle-aged blacks are married, the never-married and the divorced represent substantial shares of the market.

Marital Status of People Aged 35 to 54 by Sex, 1998: Blacks

(number and percent distribution of total blacks aged 15 or older and blacks aged 35 to 54 by sex and marital status, 1998; numbers in thousands)

	total	35 to 54	35 to 39	40 to 44	45 to 54
Total black men	11,283	4,153	1,306	1,211	1,636
Never married	5,191	1,164	519	391	254
Married	4,675	2,355	671	639	1,045
Divorced	1,035	590	114	172	304
Widowed	382	43	3	9	34
Total black women	13,715	5,010	1,545	1,437	2,028
Never married	5,689	1,203	530	365	308
Married	4,983	2,543	732	755	1,056
Divorced	1,673	1,055	245	273	537
Widowed	1,370	208	37	44	127
Total black men	100.0%	100.0%	100.0%	100.0%	100.0%
Never married	46.0	28.0	39.7	32.3	15.5
Married	41.4	56.7	51.4	52.8	63.9
Divorced	9.2	14.2	8.7	14.2	18.6
Widowed	3.4	1.0	0.2	0.7	2.1
Total black women	100.0	100.0	100.0	100.0	100.0
Never married	41.5	24.0	34.3	25.4	15.2
Married	36.3	50.8	47.4	52.5	52.1
Divorced	12.2	21.1	15.9	19.0	26.5
Widowed	10.0	4.2	2.4	3.1	6.3

Source: Bureau of the Census, Marital Status and Living Arrangements: March 1998, *Current Population Reports, P20-514, 1998; calculations by New Strategist*

Marital Status of People Aged 35 to 54 by Sex, 1998: Hispanics

(number and percent distribution of total Hispanics aged 15 or older and Hispanics aged 35 to 54 by sex and marital status, 1998; numbers in thousands)

	total	35 to 54	35 to 39	40 to 44	45 to 54
Total Hispanic men	**10,944**	**3,686**	**1,339**	**1,025**	**1,322**
Never married	4,370	647	358	130	159
Married	5,797	2,625	854	768	1,003
Divorced	647	400	120	126	154
Widowed	131	16	7	2	7
Total Hispanic women	**10,485**	**3,618**	**1,166**	**1,075**	**1,377**
Never married	3,072	356	154	91	111
Married	5,911	2,663	862	814	987
Divorced	885	490	134	153	203
Widowed	617	109	16	17	76
Total Hispanic men	**100.0%**	**100.0%**	**100.0%**	**100.0%**	**100.0%**
Never married	39.9	17.6	26.7	12.7	12.0
Married	53.0	71.2	63.8	74.9	75.9
Divorced	5.9	10.9	9.0	12.3	11.6
Widowed	1.2	0.4	0.5	0.2	0.5
Total Hispanic women	**100.0**	**100.0**	**100.0**	**100.0**	**100.0**
Never married	29.3	9.8	13.2	8.5	8.1
Married	56.4	73.6	73.9	75.7	71.7
Divorced	8.4	13.5	11.5	14.2	14.7
Widowed	5.9	3.0	1.4	1.6	5.5

Source: Bureau of the Census, Marital Status and Living Arrangements: March 1998, *Current Population Reports, P20–514, 1998; calculations by New Strategist*

Marital Status of People Aged 35 to 54 by Sex, 1998: Whites

(number and percent distribution of total whites aged 15 or older and whites aged 35 to 54 by sex and marital status, 1998; numbers in thousands)

	total	35 to 54	35 to 39	40 to 44	45 to 54
Total white men	**85,219**	**32,748**	**9,434**	**9,030**	**14,284**
Never married	24,775	4,244	1,807	1,238	1,199
Married	51,299	24,144	6,551	6,558	11,035
Divorced	7,038	4,175	1,041	1,194	1,940
Widowed	2,106	187	36	41	110
Total white women	**89,489**	**32,859**	**9,263**	**9,009**	**14,587**
Never married	19,614	2,590	1,011	684	895
Married	51,410	24,399	6,966	6,800	10,633
Divorced	9,115	5,140	1,189	1,412	2,539
Widowed	9,351	728	96	112	520
Total white men	**100.0%**	**100.0%**	**100.0%**	**100.0%**	**100.0%**
Never married	29.1	13.0	19.2	13.7	8.4
Married	60.2	73.7	69.4	72.6	77.3
Divorced	8.3	12.7	11.0	13.2	13.6
Widowed	2.5	0.6	0.4	0.5	0.8
Total white women	**100.0**	**100.0**	**100.0**	**100.0**	**100.0**
Never married	21.9	7.9	10.9	7.6	6.1
Married	57.4	74.3	75.2	75.5	72.9
Divorced	10.2	15.6	12.8	15.7	17.4
Widowed	10.4	2.2	1.0	1.2	3.6

Source: Bureau of the Census, Marital Status and Living Arrangements: March 1998, *Current Population Reports, P20-514, 1998; calculations by New Strategist*

7

Population

◆ With the baby-boom generation spanning the ages of 35 to 53 in 1999, it now almost entirely fills the 35-to-54 age group. Consequently, little additional growth is forecast for the middle-aged population.

◆ While the oldest boomers receive a lot of media attention as they enter each new lifestage, most boomers are still younger than age 45.

◆ Although people aged 35 to 54 are less diverse than younger generations, one in four is an ethnic or racial minority—a share too large to ignore.

◆ In all but one state, there will be fewer 35-to-44-year-olds in 2005 than there are today. The exception is Utah, where the number of 35-to-44-year-olds will increase 1 percent between 2000 and 2005.

◆ The number of 45-to-54-year-olds will expand in every state between 2000 and 2005, with the greatest growth (22 percent) projected for Nevada.

◆ While people aged 35 to 54 dominate most markets, they account for just 22 percent of all movers.

Thirty Percent of Americans Are between 35 and 54 Years Old

The 35-to-54 age group includes more than 80 million people.

The numbers of men and women aged 35 to 54 are almost equal—40 million men and 41 million women in 1999. But within the age group, women begin to outnumber men by a significant margin among those in their fifties. Behind the growing numerical superiority of women is their sturdier biology. Women may get sick more often than men, but men are more likely to die of their illnesses than women.

In the 35-to-39 age group, women outnumber men by only 85,000. But in the 50-to-54 age group, there are 456,000 more women than men. The gap continues to widen as people age into their sixties and beyond because men's mortality rate is higher than women's.

◆ Most men and women aged 35 to 54 are married and have children at home. This makes them a family-oriented market.

◆ In the 50-to-54 age group, the lifestyles of women and men begin to diverge as more women live alone.

Population Aged 35 to 54 by Sex, 1999

(number of total people and people aged 35 to 54 by sex, and sex ratio by age, 1999; numbers in thousands)

	total	men	women	males per 100 females
Total people	**272,330**	**133,039**	**139,291**	**96**
Total aged 35 to 54	**80,379**	**39,611**	**40,748**	**97**
Aged 35 to 44	44,662	37,400	38,523	97
Aged 45 to 54	35,717	35,204	36,305	97
Aged 35 to 39	22,492	11,204	11,289	99
Aged 40 to 44	22,168	10,961	11,188	98
Aged 45 to 49	19,295	9,464	9,832	96
Aged 50 to 54	16,422	7,983	8,439	95
Aged 35	4,436	2,211	2,225	99
Aged 36	4,414	2,196	2,218	99
Aged 37	4,543	2,262	2,281	99
Aged 38	4,295	2,113	2,162	98
Aged 39	4,805	2,401	2,404	100
Aged 40	4,592	2,280	2,312	99
Aged 41	4,497	2,228	2,269	98
Aged 42	4,466	2,213	2,253	98
Aged 43	4,250	2,091	2,158	97
Aged 44	4,364	2,169	2,195	99
Aged 45	4,150	2,046	2,105	97
Aged 46	3,917	1,923	1,994	96
Aged 47	3,876	1,897	1,979	96
Aged 48	3,522	1,718	1,803	95
Aged 49	3,831	1,880	1,951	96
Aged 50	3,640	1,775	1,865	95
Aged 51	3,496	1,703	1,793	95
Aged 52	3,727	1,817	1,910	95
Aged 53	2,727	1,319	1,408	94
Aged 54	2,831	1,369	1,463	94

Source: Bureau of the Census, Population Projections of the United States, by Age, Sex, Race, and Hispanic Origin: 1995 to 2050, *Current Population Reports, P25-1130, 1996; calculations by New Strategist*

Number of 35-to-54-Year-Olds Will Rise to 84 Million by 2005

The percentage of Americans in this age group has never been higher than it is today.

The baby-boom generation, aged 35 to 53 in 1999, almost entirely fills the 35-to-54 age group. Today, there are 32 million more people aged 35 to 54 than in 1980, when the middle-aged share of the population hit its 20th-century low. Never before has the number of middle-aged Americans expanded so furiously—and the gain is not over yet. In the next six years, the number of 35-to-54-year-olds will grow another 3 million to reach 84 million in 2005.

Within the 35-to-54 age group, the growth rate will vary dramatically. Between 1999 and 2005, the number of people aged 35 to 39 will fall 12 percent as boomers age out of this segment. In contrast, the number of people aged 50 to 54 will surge 19 percent as boomers entirely fill this segment.

◆ While the oldest baby boomers turn 53 in 1999, most boomers are still younger than age 45.

◆ The median age of the baby boom, which stands at 44 in 1999, is the best predictor of boomer wants and needs. This is the age marketers should target if they want to appeal to the largest number of boomers.

Biggest growth for older ages

(percent change in number of people aged 35 to 54 by age, 1999–2005)

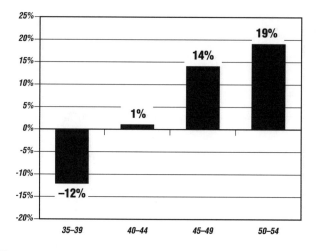

Population Aged 35 to 54, 1999 to 2005

(number of total people and people aged 35 to 54, 1999–2005; numerical and percent change, 1999–2005; numbers in thousands)

	1999	2000	2005	change, 1999–2005 number	change, 1999–2005 percent
Total people	**272,330**	**274,634**	**285,981**	**13,651**	**5.0%**
Total aged 35 to 54	**80,377**	**81,689**	**83,671**	**3,294**	**4.1**
Aged 35 to 44	44,660	44,659	42,165	–2,495	–5.6
Aged 45 to 54	35,717	37,030	41,506	5,789	16.2
Aged 35 to 39	22,492	22,180	19,802	–2,690	–12.0
Aged 40 to 44	22,168	22,479	22,363	195	0.9
Aged 45 to 49	19,295	19,806	21,988	2,693	14.0
Aged 50 to 54	16,422	17,224	19,518	3,096	18.9
Aged 35	4,436	4,288	4,077	–359	–8.1
Aged 36	4,414	4,350	3,884	–530	–12.0
Aged 37	4,543	4,469	3,873	–670	–14.7
Aged 38	4,295	4,290	3,723	–572	–13.3
Aged 39	4,805	4,783	4,246	–559	–11.6
Aged 40	4,592	4,667	4,351	–241	–5.2
Aged 41	4,497	4,494	4,403	–94	–2.1
Aged 42	4,466	4,488	4,458	–8	–0.2
Aged 43	4,250	4,424	4,491	241	5.7
Aged 44	4,364	4,407	4,660	296	6.8
Aged 45	4,150	4,268	4,578	428	10.3
Aged 46	3,917	4,034	4,379	462	11.8
Aged 47	3,876	3,958	4,431	555	14.3
Aged 48	3,522	3,681	4,185	663	18.8
Aged 49	3,831	3,864	4,414	583	15.2
Aged 50	3,640	3,721	4,245	605	16.6
Aged 51	3,496	3,504	3,974	478	13.7
Aged 52	3,727	3,476	3,837	110	3.0
Aged 53	2,727	3,754	3,785	1,058	38.8
Aged 54	2,831	2,769	3,678	847	29.9

Source: Bureau of the Census, Population Projections of the United States, by Age, Sex, Race, and Hispanic Origin: 1995 to 2050, *Current Population Reports, P25-1130, 1996; calculations by New Strategist*

The Middle-Aged Are Less Diverse Than Young Adults

Three out of four 35-to-54-year-olds are non-Hispanic whites.

America's children and young adults are much more racially and ethnically diverse than boomers and older Americans. Among boomers, however, diversity differs by age.

Overall, 75 percent of 35-to-54-year-olds are non-Hispanic whites, but this proportion is lowest (72 percent) among 35-to-39-year-olds and highest (79 percent) among 50-to-54-year-olds. The Hispanic share is greatest among 35-to-39-year-olds (11 percent) and lowest among 50-to-54-year-olds (7.5 percent).

Blacks are the largest minority among boomers. Eleven percent of 35-to-54-year-olds are non-Hispanic blacks. The black share of the middle-aged ranges from a high of 12 percent among 35-to-39-year-olds to a low of 10 percent among 50-to-54-year-olds. Non-Hispanic Asians account for 3.8 percent of 35-to-54-year-olds, while Native Americans are just 0.7 percent.

◆ Although people aged 35 to 54 are less diverse than younger Americans, nearly one in four is an ethnic or racial minority—a share too large to ignore.

◆ In some metropolitan areas, the minority share of 35-to-54-year-olds is much greater than the national figures. Local and regional marketers need to consider the ethnic and racial composition of the middle-aged on a market-by-market basis.

Non-Hispanics Aged 35 to 54 by Race, 1999

(number and percent distribution of total people and non-Hispanics aged 35 to 54 by race, 1999; numbers in thousands)

	total	non-Hispanic					Hispanic
		total	white	black	Asian	Native American	
Total people	**272,330**	**241,869**	**196,441**	**33,180**	**10,219**	**2,029**	**30,461**
Total aged 35 to 54	**80,377**	**72,839**	**60,237**	**9,057**	**3,022**	**523**	**7,540**
Aged 35 to 44	44,660	39,995	32,631	5,317	1,747	300	4,666
Aged 45 to 54	35,717	32,844	27,606	3,740	1,275	223	2,874
Aged 35 to 39	22,492	19,947	16,165	2,725	903	154	2,545
Aged 40 to 44	22,168	20,048	16,466	2,592	844	146	2,121
Aged 45 to 49	19,295	17,661	14,696	2,128	713	124	1,634
Aged 50 to 54	16,422	15,183	12,910	1,612	562	99	1,240
Total people	**100.0%**	**88.8%**	**72.1%**	**12.2%**	**3.8%**	**0.7%**	**11.2%**
Total aged 35 to 54	**100.0**	**90.6**	**74.9**	**11.3**	**3.8**	**0.7**	**9.4**
Aged 35 to 44	100.0	89.6	73.1	11.9	3.9	0.7	10.4
Aged 45 to 54	100.0	92.0	77.3	10.5	3.6	0.6	8.0
Aged 35 to 39	100.0	88.7	71.9	12.1	4.0	0.7	11.3
Aged 40 to 44	100.0	90.4	74.3	11.7	3.8	0.7	9.6
Aged 45 to 49	100.0	91.5	76.2	11.0	3.7	0.6	8.5
Aged 50 to 54	100.0	92.5	78.6	9.8	3.4	0.6	7.6

Source: Bureau of the Census, Population Projections of the United States, by Age, Sex, Race, and Hispanic Origin: 1995 to 2050, *Current Population Reports, P25-1130, 1996; calculations by New Strategist*

Hispanics Aged 35 to 54 by Race, 1999

(number and percent distribution of total people and Hispanics aged 35 to 54 by race, 1999; numbers in thousands)

	total	Hispanic total	white	black	Asian	Native American	non-Hispanic
Total people	**272,330**	**30,461**	**27,662**	**1,816**	**642**	**340**	**241,869**
Total aged 35 to 54	**80,377**	**7,540**	**6,832**	**466**	**159**	**83**	**72,837**
Aged 35 to 44	44,660	4,666	4,226	290	98	52	39,994
Aged 45 to 54	35,717	2,874	2,606	176	61	31	32,843
Aged 35 to 39	22,492	2,545	2,308	156	53	28	19,947
Aged 40 to 44	22,168	2,121	1,918	134	45	24	20,047
Aged 45 to 49	19,295	1,634	1,479	102	35	18	17,661
Aged 50 to 54	16,422	1,240	1,127	74	26	13	15,182
Total people	**100.0%**	**11.2%**	**10.2%**	**0.7%**	**0.2%**	**0.1%**	**88.8%**
Total aged 35 to 54	**100.0**	**9.4**	**8.5**	**0.6**	**0.2**	**0.1**	**90.6**
Aged 35 to 44	100.0	10.4	9.5	0.6	0.2	0.1	89.6
Aged 45 to 54	100.0	8.0	7.3	0.5	0.2	0.1	92.0
Aged 35 to 39	100.0	11.3	10.3	0.7	0.2	0.1	88.7
Aged 40 to 44	100.0	9.6	8.7	0.6	0.2	0.1	90.4
Aged 45 to 49	100.0	8.5	7.7	0.5	0.2	0.1	91.5
Aged 50 to 54	100.0	7.6	6.9	0.5	0.2	0.1	92.4

Source: Bureau of the Census, Population Projections of the United States, by Age, Sex, Race, and Hispanic Origin: 1995 to 2050, *Current Population Reports, P25-1130, 1996; calculations by New Strategist*

Lopsided Growth Projected for 35-to-54-Year-Olds

In every region, the number of 35-to-44-year-olds will decline while the number of 45-to-54-year-olds grows.

The number of 35-to-54-year-olds is projected to grow only 2 percent between 2000 and 2005 now that the baby-boom generation has entirely filled the age group. This stability masks sharp differences in growth by age, however. The number of 35-to-44-year-olds should decline 6 percent nationally, while the number of 45-to-54-year-olds is projected to grow 12 percent.

This pattern of growth will be the same in all regions and divisions, with only the scale of gain or loss differing. In the West North Central division, the number of people aged 35 to 44 will fall 9 percent compared with a 4 percent decline in the Mountain and Pacific divisions. The number of people aged 45 to 54 will grow only 9 percent in the Middle Atlantic states, but 15 percent in the Mountain states.

♦ Unlike the older market, the middle-aged are almost evenly split between men and women in every region of the country.

West should see biggest gain

(percent change in number of people aged 35 to 54 by region, 2000–2005)

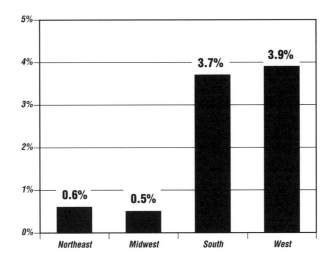

Population Aged 35 to 54 by Region, Division, and Sex, 2000

(number of total people and people aged 35 to 54 by region, division, and sex; women's share of people aged 35 to 54 by region and division, 2000; numbers in thousands)

	total	men	women	percent women
UNITED STATES, TOTAL	**274,634**	**134,181**	**140,453**	**51.1%**
Total aged 35 to 54	**81,689**	**40,273**	**41,416**	**50.7**
Aged 35 to 44	44,659	22,181	22,478	50.3
Aged 45 to 54	37,030	18,092	18,938	51.1
NORTHEAST, TOTAL	**52,107**	**25,180**	**26,927**	**51.7**
Total aged 35 to 54	**15,835**	**7,728**	**8,107**	**51.2**
Aged 35 to 44	8,673	4,276	4,397	50.7
Aged 45 to 54	7,162	3,452	3,710	51.8
New England, total	**13,581**	**6,599**	**6,982**	**51.4**
Total aged 35 to 54	**4,224**	**2,081**	**2,143**	**50.7**
Aged 35 to 44	2,336	1,157	1,179	50.5
Aged 45 to 54	1,888	924	964	51.1
Middle Atlantic, total	**38,526**	**18,581**	**19,945**	**51.8**
Total aged 35 to 54	**11,612**	**5,648**	**5,964**	**51.4**
Aged 35 to 44	6,338	3,120	3,218	50.8
Aged 45 to 54	5,274	2,528	2,746	52.1
MIDWEST, TOTAL	**63,502**	**30,970**	**32,532**	**51.2**
Total aged 35 to 54	**18,836**	**9,299**	**9,537**	**50.6**
Aged 35 to 44	10,246	5,089	5,157	50.3
Aged 45 to 54	8,590	4,210	4,380	51.0
East North Central, total	**44,419**	**21,631**	**22,788**	**51.3**
Total aged 35 to 54	**13,242**	**6,514**	**6,728**	**50.8**
Aged 35 to 44	7,209	3,568	3,641	50.5
Aged 45 to 54	6,033	2,946	3,087	51.2
West North Central, total	**19,082**	**9,338**	**9,744**	**51.1**
Total aged 35 to 54	**5,594**	**2,785**	**2,809**	**50.2**
Aged 35 to 44	3,037	1,521	1,516	49.9
Aged 45 to 54	2,557	1,264	1,293	50.6

(continued)

(continued from previous page)

	total	men	women	percent women
SOUTH, TOTAL	**97,613**	**47,462**	**50,151**	**51.4%**
Total aged 35 to 54	**28,888**	**14,162**	**14,726**	**51.0**
Aged 35 to 44	15,713	7,753	7,960	50.7
Aged 45 to 54	13,175	6,409	6,766	51.4
South Atlantic, total	**50,147**	**24,341**	**25,806**	**51.5**
Total aged 35 to 54	**15,140**	**7,411**	**7,729**	**51.1**
Aged 35 to 44	8,267	4,072	4,195	50.7
Aged 45 to 54	6,873	3,339	3,534	51.4
East South Central, total	**16,918**	**8,164**	**8,754**	**51.7**
Total aged 35 to 54	**5,009**	**2,439**	**2,570**	**51.3**
Aged 35 to 44	2,671	1,305	1,366	51.1
Aged 45 to 54	2,338	1,134	1,204	51.5
West South Central, total	**30,548**	**14,957**	**15,591**	**51.0**
Total aged 35 to 54	**8,739**	**4,312**	**4,427**	**50.7**
Aged 35 to 44	4,775	2,376	2,399	50.2
Aged 45 to 54	3,964	1,936	2,028	51.2
WEST, TOTAL	**61,413**	**30,570**	**30,843**	**50.2**
Total aged 35 to 54	**18,130**	**9,083**	**9,047**	**49.9**
Aged 35 to 44	10,027	5,063	4,964	49.5
Aged 45 to 54	8,103	4,020	4,083	50.4
Mountain, total	**17,725**	**8,797**	**8,928**	**50.4**
Total aged 35 to 54	**5,143**	**2,575**	**2,568**	**49.9**
Aged 35 to 44	2,765	1,391	1,374	49.7
Aged 45 to 54	2,378	1,184	1,194	50.2
Pacific, total	**43,687**	**21,772**	**21,915**	**50.2**
Total aged 35 to 54	**12,987**	**6,509**	**6,478**	**49.9**
Aged 35 to 44	7,262	3,672	3,590	49.4
Aged 45 to 54	5,725	2,837	2,888	50.4

Source: Bureau of the Census, Population Projections for States by Age, Sex, Race and Hispanic Origin: 1995 to 2025, *PPL-47, 1996; calculations by New Strategist*

Population Aged 35 to 54
by Region and Division, 2000 and 2005

(number of total people and people aged 35 to 54 by region and division, 2000 and 2005; percent change, 2000–2005; numbers in thousands)

	2000	2005	percent change 2000–2005
UNITED STATES, TOTAL	**274,634**	**285,981**	**4.1%**
Total aged 35 to 54	**81,689**	**83,672**	**2.4**
Aged 35 to 44	44,659	42,165	–5.6
Aged 45 to 54	37,030	41,507	12.1
NORTHEAST, TOTAL	**52,107**	**52,767**	**1.3**
Total aged 35 to 54	**15,835**	**15,933**	**0.6**
Aged 35 to 44	8,673	8,092	–6.7
Aged 45 to 54	7,162	7,841	9.5
New England, total	**13,581**	**13,843**	**1.9**
Total aged 35 to 54	**4,224**	**4,294**	**1.7**
Aged 35 to 44	2,336	2,200	–5.8
Aged 45 to 54	1,888	2,094	10.9
Middle Atlantic, total	**38,526**	**38,923**	**1.0**
Total aged 35 to 54	**11,612**	**11,639**	**0.2**
Aged 35 to 44	6,338	5,892	–7.0
Aged 45 to 54	5,274	5,747	9.0
MIDWEST, TOTAL	**63,502**	**64,825**	**2.1**
Total aged 35 to 54	**18,836**	**18,924**	**0.5**
Aged 35 to 44	10,246	9,407	–8.2
Aged 45 to 54	8,590	9,517	10.8
East North Central, total	**44,419**	**45,151**	**1.6**
Total aged 35 to 54	**13,242**	**13,274**	**0.2**
Aged 35 to 44	7,209	6,631	–8.0
Aged 45 to 54	6,033	6,643	10.1
West North Central, total	**19,082**	**19,673**	**3.1**
Total aged 35 to 54	**5,594**	**5,651**	**1.0**
Aged 35 to 44	3,037	2,776	–8.6
Aged 45 to 54	2,557	2,875	12.4

(continued)

(continued from previous page)

	2000	2005	percent change 2000–2005
SOUTH, TOTAL	**97,613**	**102,788**	**5.3%**
Total aged 35 to 54	**28,888**	**29,969**	**3.7**
Aged 35 to 44	15,713	15,015	–4.4
Aged 45 to 54	13,175	14,954	13.5
South Atlantic, total	**50,147**	**52,921**	**5.5**
Total aged 35 to 54	**15,140**	**15,821**	**4.5**
Aged 35 to 44	8,267	7,966	–3.6
Aged 45 to 54	6,873	7,855	14.3
East South Central, total	**16,918**	**17,604**	**4.1**
Total aged 35 to 54	**5,009**	**5,173**	**3.3**
Aged 35 to 44	2,671	2,557	–4.3
Aged 45 to 54	2,338	2,616	11.9
West South Central, total	**30,548**	**32,263**	**5.6**
Total aged 35 to 54	**8,739**	**8,975**	**2.7**
Aged 35 to 44	4,775	4,492	–5.9
Aged 45 to 54	3,964	4,483	13.1
WEST, TOTAL	**61,413**	**65,603**	**6.8**
Total aged 35 to 54	**18,130**	**18,845**	**3.9**
Aged 35 to 44	10,027	9,651	–3.7
Aged 45 to 54	8,103	9,194	13.5
Mountain, total	**17,725**	**19,249**	**8.6**
Total aged 35 to 54	**5,143**	**5,402**	**5.0**
Aged 35 to 44	2,765	2,662	–3.7
Aged 45 to 54	2,378	2,740	15.2
Pacific, total	**43,687**	**46,354**	**6.1**
Total aged 35 to 54	**12,987**	**13,442**	**3.5**
Aged 35 to 44	7,262	6,988	–3.8
Aged 45 to 54	5,725	6,454	12.7

Source: Bureau of the Census, Population Projections for States by Age, Sex, Race and Hispanic Origin: 1995 to 2025, *PPL-47, 1996; calculations by New Strategist*

Some States Will See No Growth in Middle-Aged

But in Nevada the number of 35-to-54-year-olds will grow 10 percent between 2000 and 2005.

Now that the baby-boom generation has entirely filled the 35-to-54 age group, only the states that attract domestic migrants will see a significant rise in their middle-aged populations during the next five years. Nevada, for example, which is the nation's fastest-growing state because of migration, will see a 10 percent increase in 35-to-54-year-olds between 2000 and 2005. In contrast, the number of people in that age group is projected to decline in Alaska, Iowa, New York, North Dakota, Ohio, West Virginia, and the District of Columbia during those years.

In all but one state, there will be fewer 35-to-44-year-olds in 2005 than in 2000. The only exception is Utah, where the age group will grow 1 percent. In every state, the number of 45-to-54-year-olds will expand. The greatest gain is projected for Nevada, where the number of people in that age group will increase 22 percent. Eighteen percent gains are projected for Arizona and Florida.

♦ In every state, the aging of the baby-boom generation will have an impact on marketers. As boomers move out of the 35-to-44 age group, their wants and needs will shift from caring for children to doing more for themselves.

Nevada to see biggest increase

(percent change in number of people aged 35 to 54 for the five states with the biggest projected gain, 2000–2005)

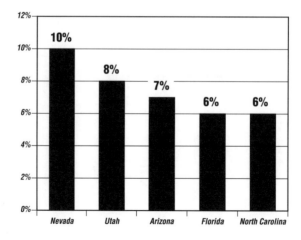

Population Aged 35 to 54 by State and Sex, 2000

(number of total people and people aged 35 to 54 by state and sex, women's share of people aged 35 to 54 by state; 2000; numbers in thousands)

	total	men	women	percent women
United States, total	**274,634**	**134,181**	**140,453**	**51.1%**
Total aged 35 to 54	**81,689**	**40,273**	**41,416**	**50.7**
Aged 35 to 44	44,659	22,181	22,478	50.3
Aged 45 to 54	37,030	18,092	18,938	51.1
Alabama, total	**4,451**	**2,140**	**2,311**	**51.9**
Total aged 35 to 54	**1,306**	**634**	**672**	**51.5**
Aged 35 to 44	694	338	356	51.3
Aged 45 to 54	612	296	316	51.6
Alaska, total	**653**	**339**	**314**	**48.1**
Total aged 35 to 54	**204**	**108**	**96**	**47.1**
Aged 35 to 44	112	59	53	47.3
Aged 45 to 54	92	49	43	46.7
Arizona, total	**4,798**	**2,368**	**2,430**	**50.6**
Total aged 35 to 54	**1,342**	**669**	**673**	**50.1**
Aged 35 to 44	731	368	363	49.7
Aged 45 to 54	611	301	310	50.7
Arkansas, total	**2,631**	**1,270**	**1,361**	**51.7**
Total aged 35 to 54	**749**	**365**	**384**	**51.3**
Aged 35 to 44	392	192	200	51.0
Aged 45 to 54	357	173	184	51.5
California, total	**32,521**	**16,216**	**16,305**	**50.1**
Total aged 35 to 54	**9,505**	**4,758**	**4,747**	**49.9**
Aged 35 to 44	5,411	2,740	2,671	49.4
Aged 45 to 54	4,094	2,018	2,076	50.7
Colorado, total	**4,168**	**2,066**	**2,102**	**50.4**
Total aged 35 to 54	**1,321**	**662**	**659**	**49.9**
Aged 35 to 44	711	358	353	49.6
Aged 45 to 54	610	304	306	50.2

(continued)

(continued from previous page)

	total	men	women	percent women
Connecticut, total	**3,284**	**1,596**	**1,688**	**51.4%**
Total aged 35 to 54	**1,026**	**504**	**522**	**50.9**
Aged 35 to 44	569	282	287	50.4
Aged 45 to 54	457	222	235	51.4
Delaware, total	**768**	**375**	**393**	**51.2**
Total aged 35 to 54	**233**	**115**	**118**	**50.6**
Aged 35 to 44	131	65	66	50.4
Aged 45 to 54	102	50	52	51.0
District of Columbia, total	**523**	**246**	**277**	**53.0**
Total aged 35 to 54	**151**	**71**	**80**	**53.0**
Aged 35 to 44	83	40	43	51.8
Aged 45 to 54	68	31	37	54.4
Florida, total	**15,233**	**7,367**	**7,866**	**51.6**
Total aged 35 to 54	**4,373**	**2,146**	**2,227**	**50.9**
Aged 35 to 44	2,353	1,166	1,187	50.4
Aged 45 to 54	2,020	980	1,040	51.5
Georgia, total	**7,875**	**3,831**	**4,044**	**51.4**
Total aged 35 to 54	**2,431**	**1,186**	**1,245**	**51.2**
Aged 35 to 44	1,360	666	694	51.0
Aged 45 to 54	1,071	520	551	51.4
Hawaii, total	**1,257**	**633**	**624**	**49.6**
Total aged 35 to 54	**370**	**188**	**182**	**49.2**
Aged 35 to 44	200	103	97	48.5
Aged 45 to 54	170	85	85	50.0
Idaho, total	**1,347**	**672**	**675**	**50.1**
Total aged 35 to 54	**373**	**188**	**185**	**49.6**
Aged 35 to 44	195	98	97	49.7
Aged 45 to 54	178	90	88	49.4
Illinois, total	**12,051**	**5,878**	**6,173**	**51.2**
Total aged 35 to 54	**3,578**	**1,758**	**1,820**	**50.9**
Aged 35 to 44	1,984	984	1,000	50.4
Aged 45 to 54	1,594	774	820	51.4

(continued)

(continued from previous page)

	total	men	women	percent women
Indiana, total	**6,045**	**2,945**	**3,100**	**51.3%**
Total aged 35 to 54	**1,797**	**886**	**911**	**50.7**
Aged 35 to 44	970	481	489	50.4
Aged 45 to 54	827	405	422	51.0
Iowa, total	**2,900**	**1,413**	**1,487**	**51.3**
Total aged 35 to 54	**831**	**415**	**416**	**50.1**
Aged 35 to 44	436	219	217	49.8
Aged 45 to 54	395	196	199	50.4
Kansas, total	**2,668**	**1,314**	**1,354**	**50.7**
Total aged 35 to 54	**773**	**388**	**385**	**49.8**
Aged 35 to 44	420	212	208	49.5
Aged 45 to 54	353	176	177	50.1
Kentucky, total	**3,995**	**1,940**	**2,055**	**51.4**
Total aged 35 to 54	**1,204**	**590**	**614**	**51.0**
Aged 35 to 44	640	315	325	50.8
Aged 45 to 54	564	275	289	51.2
Louisiana, total	**4,425**	**2,131**	**2,294**	**51.8**
Total aged 35 to 54	**1,246**	**603**	**643**	**51.6**
Aged 35 to 44	667	325	342	51.3
Aged 45 to 54	579	278	301	52.0
Maine, total	**1,259**	**614**	**645**	**51.2**
Total aged 35 to 54	**407**	**202**	**205**	**50.4**
Aged 35 to 44	215	106	109	50.7
Aged 45 to 54	192	96	96	50.0
Maryland, total	**5,275**	**2,563**	**2,712**	**51.4**
Total aged 35 to 54	**1,710**	**831**	**879**	**51.4**
Aged 35 to 44	967	472	495	51.2
Aged 45 to 54	743	359	384	51.7
Massachusetts, total	**6,199**	**3,001**	**3,198**	**51.6**
Total aged 35 to 54	**1,897**	**931**	**966**	**50.9**
Aged 35 to 44	1,058	524	534	50.5
Aged 45 to 54	839	407	432	51.5

(continued)

(continued from previous page)

	total	men	women	percent women
Michigan, total	**9,679**	**4,714**	**4,965**	**51.3%**
Total aged 35 to 54	**2,912**	**1,429**	**1,483**	**50.9**
Aged 35 to 44	1,581	778	803	50.8
Aged 45 to 54	1,331	651	680	51.1
Minnesota, total	**4,830**	**2,378**	**2,452**	**50.8**
Total aged 35 to 54	**1,473**	**739**	**734**	**49.8**
Aged 35 to 44	815	411	404	49.6
Aged 45 to 54	658	328	330	50.2
Mississippi, total	**2,816**	**1,351**	**1,465**	**52.0**
Total aged 35 to 54	**777**	**375**	**402**	**51.7**
Aged 35 to 44	417	202	215	51.6
Aged 45 to 54	360	173	187	51.9
Missouri, total	**5,540**	**2,685**	**2,855**	**51.5**
Total aged 35 to 54	**1,634**	**800**	**834**	**51.0**
Aged 35 to 44	892	440	452	50.7
Aged 45 to 54	742	360	382	51.5
Montana, total	**950**	**471**	**479**	**50.4**
Total aged 35 to 54	**283**	**143**	**140**	**49.5**
Aged 35 to 44	142	71	71	50.0
Aged 45 to 54	141	72	69	48.9
Nebraska, total	**1,705**	**835**	**870**	**51.0**
Total aged 35 to 54	**486**	**242**	**244**	**50.2**
Aged 35 to 44	261	130	131	50.2
Aged 45 to 54	225	112	113	50.2
Nevada, total	**1,871**	**942**	**929**	**49.7**
Total aged 35 to 54	**600**	**305**	**295**	**49.2**
Aged 35 to 44	324	166	158	48.8
Aged 45 to 54	276	139	137	49.6
New Hampshire, total	**1,224**	**602**	**622**	**50.8**
Total aged 35 to 54	**401**	**201**	**200**	**49.9**
Aged 35 to 44	226	113	113	50.0
Aged 45 to 54	175	88	87	49.7

(continued)

(continued from previous page)

	total	men	women	percent women
New Jersey, total	**8,178**	**3,963**	**4,215**	**51.5%**
Total aged 35 to 54	**2,548**	**1,242**	**1,306**	**51.3**
Aged 35 to 44	1,417	698	719	50.7
Aged 45 to 54	1,131	544	587	51.9
New Mexico, total	**1,860**	**917**	**943**	**50.7**
Total aged 35 to 54	**534**	**264**	**270**	**50.6**
Aged 35 to 44	289	144	145	50.2
Aged 45 to 54	245	120	125	51.0
New York, total	**18,146**	**8,740**	**9,406**	**51.8**
Total aged 35 to 54	**5,422**	**2,618**	**2,804**	**51.7**
Aged 35 to 44	2,977	1,459	1,518	51.0
Aged 45 to 54	2,445	1,159	1,286	52.6
North Carolina, total	**7,777**	**3,776**	**4,001**	**51.4**
Total aged 35 to 54	**2,338**	**1,145**	**1,193**	**51.0**
Aged 35 to 44	1,266	624	642	50.7
Aged 45 to 54	1,072	521	551	51.4
North Dakota, total	**662**	**329**	**333**	**50.3**
Total aged 35 to 54	**182**	**93**	**89**	**48.9**
Aged 35 to 44	96	49	47	49.0
Aged 45 to 54	86	44	42	48.8
Ohio, total	**11,319**	**5,480**	**5,839**	**51.6**
Total aged 35 to 54	**3,370**	**1,648**	**1,722**	**51.1**
Aged 35 to 44	1,815	894	921	50.7
Aged 45 to 54	1,555	754	801	51.5
Oklahoma, total	**3,373**	**1,648**	**1,725**	**51.1**
Total aged 35 to 54	**955**	**471**	**484**	**50.7**
Aged 35 to 44	503	251	252	50.1
Aged 45 to 54	452	220	232	51.3
Oregon, total	**3,397**	**1,674**	**1,723**	**50.7**
Total aged 35 to 54	**1,050**	**524**	**526**	**50.1**
Aged 35 to 44	536	267	269	50.2
Aged 45 to 54	514	257	257	50.0

(continued)

(continued from previous page)

	total	men	women	percent women
Pennsylvania, total	**12,202**	**5,879**	**6,323**	**51.8%**
Total aged 35 to 54	**3,640**	**1,786**	**1,854**	**50.9**
Aged 35 to 44	1,943	962	981	50.5
Aged 45 to 54	1,697	824	873	51.4
Rhode Island, total	**998**	**482**	**516**	**51.7**
Total aged 35 to 54	**296**	**146**	**150**	**50.7**
Aged 35 to 44	163	81	82	50.3
Aged 45 to 54	133	65	68	51.1
South Carolina, total	**3,858**	**1,863**	**1,995**	**51.7**
Total aged 35 to 54	**1,154**	**562**	**592**	**51.3**
Aged 35 to 44	616	301	315	51.1
Aged 45 to 54	538	261	277	51.5
South Dakota, total	**777**	**383**	**394**	**50.7**
Total aged 35 to 54	**215**	**109**	**106**	**49.3**
Aged 35 to 44	115	58	57	49.6
Aged 45 to 54	100	51	49	49.0
Tennessee, total	**5,657**	**2,734**	**2,923**	**51.7**
Total aged 35 to 54	**1,721**	**839**	**882**	**51.2**
Aged 35 to 44	920	449	471	51.2
Aged 45 to 54	801	390	411	51.3
Texas, total	**20,119**	**9,908**	**10,211**	**50.8**
Total aged 35 to 54	**5,789**	**2,874**	**2,915**	**50.4**
Aged 35 to 44	3,214	1,610	1,604	49.9
Aged 45 to 54	2,575	1,264	1,311	50.9
Utah, total	**2,207**	**1,099**	**1,108**	**50.2**
Total aged 35 to 54	**533**	**266**	**267**	**50.1**
Aged 35 to 44	293	147	146	49.8
Aged 45 to 54	240	119	121	50.4
Vermont, total	**617**	**304**	**313**	**50.7**
Total aged 35 to 54	**197**	**98**	**99**	**50.3**
Aged 35 to 44	104	51	53	51.0
Aged 45 to 54	93	47	46	49.5

(continued)

(continued from previous page)

	total	men	women	percent women
Virginia, total	**6,997**	**3,433**	**3,564**	**50.9%**
Total aged 35 to 54	**2,205**	**1,088**	**1,117**	**50.7**
Aged 35 to 44	1,222	606	616	50.4
Aged 45 to 54	983	482	501	51.0
Washington, total	**5,858**	**2,909**	**2,949**	**50.3**
Total aged 35 to 54	**1,858**	**931**	**927**	**49.9**
Aged 35 to 44	1,003	503	500	49.9
Aged 45 to 54	855	428	427	49.9
West Virginia, total	**1,841**	**886**	**955**	**51.9**
Total aged 35 to 54	**546**	**269**	**277**	**50.7**
Aged 35 to 44	269	132	137	50.9
Aged 45 to 54	277	137	140	50.5
Wisconsin, total	**5,326**	**2,616**	**2,710**	**50.9**
Total aged 35 to 54	**1,585**	**792**	**793**	**50.0**
Aged 35 to 44	859	431	428	49.8
Aged 45 to 54	726	361	365	50.3
Wyoming, total	**525**	**263**	**262**	**49.9**
Total aged 35 to 54	**155**	**79**	**76**	**49.0**
Aged 35 to 44	79	40	39	49.4
Aged 45 to 54	76	39	37	48.7

Source: Bureau of the Census, Population Projections for States by Age, Sex, Race and Hispanic Origin: 1995 to 2025, *PPL-47, 1996; calculations by New Strategist*

Population Aged 35 to 54 by State, 2000 and 2005

(number of total people and people aged 35 to 54 by state, 2000 and 2005; numbers in thousands)

	2000	2005	percent change 2000–2005
United States, total	**274,634**	**285,981**	**4.1%**
Total aged 35 to 54	**81,689**	**83,672**	**2.4**
Aged 35 to 44	44,659	42,165	−5.6
Aged 45 to 54	37,030	41,507	12.1
Alabama, total	**4,451**	**4,631**	**4.0**
Total aged 35 to 54	**1,306**	**1,352**	**3.5**
Aged 35 to 44	694	666	−4.0
Aged 45 to 54	612	686	12.1
Alaska, total	**653**	**700**	**7.2**
Total aged 35 to 54	**204**	**201**	**−1.5**
Aged 35 to 44	112	102	−8.9
Aged 45 to 54	92	99	7.6
Arizona, total	**4,798**	**5,230**	**9.0**
Total aged 35 to 54	**1,342**	**1,434**	**6.9**
Aged 35 to 44	731	713	−2.5
Aged 45 to 54	**611**	**721**	**18.0**
Arkansas, total	**2,631**	**2,750**	**4.5**
Total aged 35 to 54	**749**	**773**	**3.2**
Aged 35 to 44	392	371	−5.4
Aged 45 to 54	357	402	12.6
California, total	**32,521**	**34,441**	**5.9**
Total aged 35 to 54	**9,505**	**9,880**	**3.9**
Aged 35 to 44	5,411	5,240	−3.2
Aged 45 to 54	4,094	4,640	13.3
Colorado, total	**4,168**	**4,468**	**7.2**
Total aged 35 to 54	**1,321**	**1,342**	**1.6**
Aged 35 to 44	711	664	−6.6
Aged 45 to 54	610	678	11.1
Connecticut, total	**3,284**	**3,317**	**1.0**
Total aged 35 to 54	**1,026**	**1,029**	**0.3**
Aged 35 to 44	569	526	−7.6
Aged 45 to 54	457	503	10.1

(continued)

(continued from previous page)

	2000	2005	percent change 2000–2005
Delaware, total	**768**	**800**	**4.2%**
Total aged 35 to 54	**233**	**245**	**5.2**
Aged 35 to 44	131	127	−3.1
Aged 45 to 54	102	118	15.7
District of Columbia, total	**523**	**529**	**1.1**
Total aged 35 to 54	**151**	**146**	**−3.3**
Aged 35 to 44	83	76	−8.4
Aged 45 to 54	68	70	2.9
Florida, total	**15,233**	**16,279**	**6.9**
Total aged 35 to 54	**4,373**	**4,630**	**5.9**
Aged 35 to 44	2,353	2,256	−4.1
Aged 45 to 54	2,020	2,374	17.5
Georgia, total	**7,875**	**8,413**	**6.8**
Total aged 35 to 54	**2,431**	**2,562**	**5.4**
Aged 35 to 44	1,360	1,326	−2.5
Aged 45 to 54	1,071	1,236	15.4
Hawaii, total	**1,257**	**1,342**	**6.8**
Total aged 35 to 54	**370**	**376**	**1.6**
Aged 35 to 44	200	191	−4.5
Aged 45 to 54	170	185	8.8
Idaho, total	**1,347**	**1,480**	**9.9**
Total aged 35 to 54	**373**	**394**	**5.6**
Aged 35 to 44	195	190	−2.6
Aged 45 to 54	178	204	14.6
Illinois, total	**12,051**	**12,266**	**1.8**
Total aged 35 to 54	**3,578**	**3,590**	**0.3**
Aged 35 to 44	1,984	1,830	−7.8
Aged 45 to 54	1,594	1,760	10.4
Indiana, total	**6,045**	**6,215**	**2.8**
Total aged 35 to 54	**1,797**	**1,826**	**1.6**
Aged 35 to 44	970	909	−6.3
Aged 45 to 54	827	917	10.9
Iowa, total	**2,900**	**2,941**	**1.4**
Total aged 35 to 54	**831**	**828**	**−0.4**
Aged 35 to 44	436	399	−8.5
Aged 45 to 54	395	429	8.6

(continued)

(continued from previous page)

	2000	2005	percent change 2000–2005
Kansas, total	**2,668**	**2,761**	**3.5%**
Total aged 35 to 54	**773**	**784**	**1.4**
Aged 35 to 44	420	389	–7.4
Aged 45 to 54	353	395	11.9
Kentucky, total	**3,995**	**4,098**	**2.6**
Total aged 35 to 54	**1,204**	**1,222**	**1.5**
Aged 35 to 44	640	600	–6.3
Aged 45 to 54	564	622	10.3
Louisiana, total	**4,425**	**4,535**	**2.5**
Total aged 35 to 54	**1,246**	**1,246**	**0.0**
Aged 35 to 44	667	612	–8.2
Aged 45 to 54	579	634	9.5
Maine, total	**1,259**	**1,285**	**2.1**
Total aged 35 to 54	**407**	**408**	**0.2**
Aged 35 to 44	215	194	–9.8
Aged 45 to 54	192	214	11.5
Maryland, total	**5,275**	**5,467**	**3.6**
Total aged 35 to 54	**1,710**	**1,750**	**2.3**
Aged 35 to 44	967	909	–6.0
Aged 45 to 54	743	841	13.2
Massachusetts, total	**6,199**	**6,310**	**1.8**
Total aged 35 to 54	**1,897**	**1,939**	**2.2**
Aged 35 to 44	1,058	1,016	–4.0
Aged 45 to 54	839	923	10.0
Michigan, total	**9,679**	**9,763**	**0.9**
Total aged 35 to 54	**2,912**	**2,898**	**–0.5**
Aged 35 to 44	1,581	1,442	–8.8
Aged 45 to 54	1,331	1,456	9.4
Minnesota, total	**4,830**	**5,005**	**3.6**
Total aged 35 to 54	**1,473**	**1,491**	**1.2**
Aged 35 to 44	815	739	–9.3
Aged 45 to 54	658	752	14.3
Mississippi, total	**2,816**	**2,908**	**3.3**
Total aged 35 to 54	**777**	**805**	**3.6**
Aged 35 to 44	417	401	–3.8
Aged 45 to 54	360	404	12.2

(continued)

(continued from previous page)

	2000	2005	percent change 2000–2005
Missouri, total	**5,540**	**5,718**	**3.2%**
Total aged 35 to 54	**1,634**	**1,662**	**1.7**
Aged 35 to 44	892	820	–8.1
Aged 45 to 54	742	842	13.5
Montana, total	**950**	**1,006**	**5.9**
Total aged 35 to 54	**283**	**283**	**0.0**
Aged 35 to 44	142	129	–9.2
Aged 45 to 54	141	154	9.2
Nebraska, total	**1,705**	**1,761**	**3.3**
Total aged 35 to 54	**486**	**486**	**0.0**
Aged 35 to 44	261	238	–8.8
Aged 45 to 54	225	248	10.2
Nevada, total	**1,871**	**2,070**	**10.6**
Total aged 35 to 54	**600**	**658**	**9.7**
Aged 35 to 44	324	320	–1.2
Aged 45 to 54	276	338	22.5
New Hampshire, total	**1,224**	**1,281**	**4.7**
Total aged 35 to 54	**401**	**414**	**3.2**
Aged 35 to 44	226	210	–7.1
Aged 45 to 54	175	204	16.6
New Jersey, total	**8,178**	**8,392**	**2.6**
Total aged 35 to 54	**2,548**	**2,592**	**1.7**
Aged 35 to 44	1,417	1,330	–6.1
Aged 45 to 54	1,131	1,262	11.6
New Mexico, total	**1,860**	**2,016**	**8.4**
Total aged 35 to 54	**534**	**556**	**4.1**
Aged 35 to 44	289	277	–4.2
Aged 45 to 54	245	279	13.9
New York, total	**18,146**	**18,250**	**0.6**
Total aged 35 to 54	**5,422**	**5,401**	**–0.4**
Aged 35 to 44	2,977	2,775	–6.8
Aged 45 to 54	2,445	2,626	7.4
North Carolina, total	**7,777**	**8,227**	**5.8**
Total aged 35 to 54	**2,338**	**2,477**	**5.9**
Aged 35 to 44	1,266	1,251	–1.2
Aged 45 to 54	1,072	1,226	14.4

(continued)

(continued from previous page)

	2000	2005	percent change 2000–2005
North Dakota, total	**662**	**677**	**2.3%**
Total aged 35 to 54	**182**	**180**	**−1.1**
Aged 35 to 44	96	86	−10.4
Aged 45 to 54	86	94	9.3
Ohio, total	**11,319**	**11,428**	**1.0**
Total aged 35 to 54	**3,370**	**3,351**	**−0.6**
Aged 35 to 44	1,815	1,657	−8.7
Aged 45 to 54	1,555	1,694	8.9
Oklahoma, total	**3,373**	**3,491**	**3.5**
Total aged 35 to 54	**955**	**959**	**0.4**
Aged 35 to 44	503	458	−8.9
Aged 45 to 54	452	501	10.8
Oregon, total	**3,397**	**3,613**	**6.4**
Total aged 35 to 54	**1,050**	**1,065**	**1.4**
Aged 35 to 44	536	507	−5.4
Aged 45 to 54	514	558	8.6
Pennsylvania, total	**12,202**	**12,281**	**0.6**
Total aged 35 to 54	**3,640**	**3,647**	**0.2**
Aged 35 to 44	1,943	1,787	−8.0
Aged 45 to 54	1,697	1,860	9.6
Rhode Island, total	**998**	**1,012**	**1.4**
Total aged 35 to 54	**296**	**306**	**3.4**
Aged 35 to 44	163	157	−3.7
Aged 45 to 54	133	149	12.0
South Carolina, total	**3,858**	**4,033**	**4.5**
Total aged 35 to 54	**1,154**	**1,195**	**3.6**
Aged 35 to 44	616	595	−3.4
Aged 45 to 54	538	600	11.5
South Dakota, total	**777**	**810**	**4.2**
Total aged 35 to 54	**215**	**220**	**2.3**
Aged 35 to 44	115	106	−7.8
Aged 45 to 54	100	114	14.0
Tennessee, total	**5,657**	**5,966**	**5.5**
Total aged 35 to 54	**1,721**	**1,794**	**4.2**
Aged 35 to 44	920	891	−3.2
Aged 45 to 54	801	903	12.7

(continued)

(continued from previous page)

	2000	2005	percent change 2000–2005
Texas, total	**20,119**	**21,487**	**6.8%**
Total aged 35 to 54	**5,789**	**5,998**	**3.6**
Aged 35 to 44	3,214	3,052	–5.0
Aged 45 to 54	2,575	2,946	14.4
Utah, total	**2,207**	**2,411**	**9.2**
Total aged 35 to 54	**533**	**577**	**8.3**
Aged 35 to 44	293	297	1.4
Aged 45 to 54	240	280	16.7
Vermont, total	**617**	**638**	**3.4**
Total aged 35 to 54	**197**	**200**	**1.5**
Aged 35 to 44	104	98	–5.8
Aged 45 to 54	93	102	9.7
Virginia, total	**6,997**	**7,324**	**4.7**
Total aged 35 to 54	**2,205**	**2,285**	**3.6**
Aged 35 to 44	1,222	1,181	–3.4
Aged 45 to 54	983	1,104	12.3
Washington, total	**5,858**	**6,258**	**6.8**
Total aged 35 to 54	**1,858**	**1,920**	**3.3**
Aged 35 to 44	1,003	949	–5.4
Aged 45 to 54	855	971	13.6
West Virginia, total	**1,841**	**1,849**	**0.4**
Total aged 35 to 54	**546**	**531**	**–2.7**
Aged 35 to 44	269	245	–8.9
Aged 45 to 54	277	286	3.2
Wisconsin, total	**5,326**	**5,479**	**2.9**
Total aged 35 to 54	**1,585**	**1,608**	**1.5**
Aged 35 to 44	859	793	–7.7
Aged 45 to 54	726	815	12.3
Wyoming, total	**525**	**568**	**8.2**
Total aged 35 to 54	**155**	**157**	**1.3**
Aged 35 to 44	79	72	–8.9
Aged 45 to 54	76	85	11.8

Source: Bureau of the Census, Population Projections for States by Age, Sex, Race and Hispanic Origin: 1995 to 2025, *PPL-47, 1996; calculations by New Strategist*

Some States Are Much More Diverse Than Others

In most states, younger boomers are more diverse than their older counterparts.

Racial and ethnic diversity is much greater among children and young adults than it is among the elderly. People aged 35 to 54 straddle these two extremes. By state, the youngest boomers typically are more diverse than the state population as a whole, while older boomers are less diverse. In the nation's largest state, California, a 48 percent minority of the total population is non-Hispanic white versus the 54 percent majority of 35-to-54-year-olds. But only 48 percent of 35-to-39-year-olds in the state are non-Hispanic white compared to 60 percent of 50-to-54-year-olds.

This pattern occurs in state after state. In Florida, 68 percent of the total population is non-Hispanic white compared to 70 percent of 35-to-54-year-olds. But while 74 percent of Floridians aged 50 to 54 are non-Hispanic white, the proportion is just 66 percent among 35-to-39-year-olds.

Overall, at least one in four 35-to-54-year-olds is a minority in sixteen states (as well as the District of Columbia), including some of the biggest such as California, Florida, New Jersey, New York, and Texas. Conversely, more than 90 percent of boomers are non-Hispanic white in 14 states, including Minnesota, Montana, and New Hampshire.

♦ While the diversity of boomers is significant, it pales in comparison to the multicultural world in which their children are growing up. Marketers who want to appeal to boomer families should send a message of inclusiveness.

State Populations Aged 35 to 54 by Race and Hispanic Origin, 2000

(number and percent distribution of total people and people aged 35 to 54 by race and Hispanic origin, 2000)

| | | non-Hispanic | | | | | non-Hispanic | | | | |
	total	white	black	Native American	Asian	Hispanic	white	black	Native American	Asian	Hispanic
Alabama, total	**4,450,583**	**3,231,301**	**1,133,242**	**17,243**	**32,502**	**36,295**	**72.6%**	**25.5%**	**0.4%**	**0.7%**	**0.8%**
Total, aged 35 to 54	**1,305,800**	**979,083**	**301,075**	**5,398**	**10,147**	**10,097**	**75.0**	**23.1**	**0.4**	**0.8**	**0.8**
Aged 35–39	340,054	250,716	81,647	1,261	3,116	3,314	73.7	24.0	0.4	0.9	1.0
Aged 40–44	353,717	260,722	85,867	1,500	2,779	2,849	73.7	24.3	0.4	0.8	0.8
Aged 45–49	322,623	240,987	75,721	1,422	2,266	2,227	74.7	23.5	0.4	0.7	0.7
Aged 50–54	289,406	226,658	57,840	1,215	1,986	1,707	78.3	20.0	0.4	0.7	0.6
Alaska, total	**653,293**	**461,334**	**26,766**	**90,940**	**44,412**	**29,841**	**70.6**	**4.1**	**13.9**	**6.8**	**4.6**
Total, aged 35 to 54	**204,103**	**156,038**	**7,273**	**21,129**	**12,219**	**7,444**	**76.5**	**3.6**	**10.4**	**6.0**	**3.6**
Aged 35–39	54,528	39,525	2,617	5,978	3,739	2,669	72.5	4.8	11.0	6.9	4.9
Aged 40–44	57,305	43,234	2,306	6,096	3,477	2,192	75.4	4.0	10.6	6.1	3.8
Aged 45–49	51,996	40,817	1,504	5,244	2,864	1,567	78.5	2.9	10.1	5.5	3.0
Aged 50–54	40,274	32,462	846	3,811	2,139	1,016	80.6	2.1	9.5	5.3	2.5
Arizona, total	**4,797,526**	**3,253,086**	**150,088**	**232,236**	**91,649**	**1,070,467**	**67.8**	**3.1**	**4.8**	**1.9**	**22.3**
Total, aged 35 to 54	**1,341,894**	**972,534**	**42,538**	**49,895**	**27,311**	**249,616**	**72.5**	**3.2**	**3.7**	**2.0**	**18.6**
Aged 35–39	364,240	246,829	12,715	15,759	8,245	80,692	67.8	3.5	4.3	2.3	22.2
Aged 40–44	366,428	262,062	12,450	14,187	7,558	70,171	71.5	3.4	3.9	2.1	19.2
Aged 45–49	323,667	240,436	9,890	11,258	6,280	55,803	74.3	3.1	3.5	1.9	17.2
Aged 50–54	287,559	223,207	7,483	8,691	5,228	42,950	77.6	2.6	3.0	1.8	14.9

(continued)

(continued from previous page)

		non-Hispanic					non-Hispanic				
	total	white	black	Native American	Asian	Hispanic	white	black	Native American	Asian	Hispanic
Arkansas, total	**2,631,383**	**2,154,759**	**407,431**	**15,187**	**18,604**	**35,402**	**81.9%**	**15.5%**	**0.6%**	**0.7%**	**1.3%**
Total, aged 35 to 54	**749,025**	**627,696**	**102,430**	**4,329**	**5,553**	**9,017**	**83.8**	**13.7**	**0.6**	**0.7**	**1.2**
Aged 35–39	192,491	158,512	28,276	1,142	1,607	2,954	82.3	14.7	0.6	0.8	1.5
Aged 40–44	199,202	164,881	29,073	1,202	1,488	2,558	82.8	14.6	0.6	0.7	1.3
Aged 45–49	184,809	154,658	25,732	1,045	1,306	2,068	83.7	13.9	0.6	0.7	1.1
Aged 50–54	172,523	149,645	19,349	940	1,152	1,437	86.7	11.2	0.5	0.7	0.8
California, total	**32,521,102**	**15,561,848**	**2,137,541**	**169,997**	**4,005,991**	**10,645,725**	**47.9**	**6.6**	**0.5**	**12.3**	**32.7**
Total, aged 35 to 54	**9,505,000**	**5,093,789**	**639,580**	**52,991**	**1,164,669**	**2,553,971**	**53.6**	**6.7**	**0.6**	**12.3**	**26.9**
Aged 35–39	2,767,355	1,326,853	194,607	14,838	334,072	896,985	47.9	7.0	0.5	12.1	32.4
Aged 40–44	2,643,848	1,390,974	184,790	14,481	325,090	728,513	52.6	7.0	0.5	12.3	27.6
Aged 45–49	2,233,806	1,253,034	146,959	12,784	280,287	540,742	56.1	6.6	0.6	12.5	24.2
Aged 50–54	1,859,991	1,122,928	113,224	10,888	225,220	387,731	60.4	6.1	0.6	12.1	20.8
Colorado, total	**4,168,224**	**3,267,777**	**178,393**	**30,168**	**97,742**	**594,144**	**78.4**	**4.3**	**0.7**	**2.3**	**14.3**
Total, aged 35 to 54	**1,321,210**	**1,077,190**	**52,189**	**8,626**	**28,061**	**155,144**	**81.5**	**4.0**	**0.7**	**2.1**	**11.7**
Aged 35–39	344,842	270,247	15,874	2,518	8,551	47,652	78.4	4.6	0.7	2.5	13.8
Aged 40–44	366,471	297,048	15,522	2,381	7,971	43,549	81.1	4.2	0.6	2.2	11.9
Aged 45–49	329,394	273,123	12,055	2,137	6,449	35,630	82.9	3.7	0.6	2.0	10.8
Aged 50–54	280,503	236,772	8,738	1,590	5,090	28,313	84.4	3.1	0.6	1.8	10.1

(continued)

(continued from previous page)

	total	non-Hispanic					non-Hispanic				
		white	black	Native American	Asian	Hispanic	white	black	Native American	Asian	Hispanic
Connecticut, total	**3,284,142**	**2,622,264**	**292,778**	**5,759**	**76,019**	**287,322**	**79.8%**	**8.9%**	**0.2%**	**2.3%**	**8.7%**
Total, aged 35 to 54	**1,025,844**	**844,473**	**81,268**	**1,872**	**23,603**	**74,628**	**82.3**	**7.9**	**0.2**	**2.3**	**7.3**
Aged 35–39	283,431	222,921	26,010	558	7,795	26,147	78.7	9.2	0.2	2.8	9.2
Aged 40–44	285,602	234,885	22,516	530	6,642	21,029	82.2	7.9	0.2	2.3	7.4
Aged 45–49	242,742	203,802	17,855	456	5,118	15,511	84.0	7.4	0.2	2.1	6.4
Aged 50–54	214,069	182,865	14,887	328	4,048	11,941	85.4	7.0	0.2	1.9	5.6
Delaware, total	**767,559**	**582,611**	**142,599**	**2,079**	**14,887**	**25,383**	**75.9**	**18.6**	**0.3**	**1.9**	**3.3**
Total, aged 35 to 54	**232,994**	**180,539**	**40,502**	**720**	**4,675**	**6,558**	**77.5**	**17.4**	**0.3**	**2.0**	**2.8**
Aged 35–39	65,704	49,510	12,276	203	1,393	2,322	75.4	18.7	0.3	2.1	3.5
Aged 40–44	65,649	50,792	11,449	193	1,305	1,910	77.4	17.4	0.3	2.0	2.9
Aged 45–49	54,359	42,477	9,293	166	1,082	1,341	78.1	17.1	0.3	2.0	2.5
Aged 50–54	47,282	37,760	7,484	158	895	985	79.9	15.8	0.3	1.9	2.1
District of Columbia, total	**523,328**	**152,409**	**315,434**	**851**	**13,845**	**40,789**	**29.1**	**60.3**	**0.2**	**2.6**	**7.8**
Total, aged 35 to 54	**151,105**	**47,545**	**88,509**	**233**	**4,038**	**10,780**	**31.5**	**58.6**	**0.2**	**2.7**	**7.1**
Aged 35–39	43,074	14,007	24,166	58	1,252	3,591	32.5	56.1	0.1	2.9	8.3
Aged 40–44	39,794	12,158	23,556	56	1,106	2,918	30.6	59.2	0.1	2.8	7.3
Aged 45–49	36,164	10,797	21,988	64	904	2,411	29.9	60.8	0.2	2.5	6.7
Aged 50–54	32,073	10,583	18,799	55	776	1,860	33.0	58.6	0.2	2.4	5.8

(continued)

(continued from previous page)

		non-Hispanic					non-Hispanic				
	total	white	black	Native American	Asian	Hispanic	white	black	Native American	Asian	Hispanic
Florida, total	**15,233,224**	**10,404,927**	**2,159,717**	**38,913**	**238,797**	**2,390,870**	**68.3%**	**14.2%**	**0.3%**	**1.6%**	**15.7%**
Total, aged 35 to 54	**4,372,805**	**3,040,087**	**568,671**	**12,883**	**77,437**	**673,727**	**69.5**	**13.0**	**0.3**	**1.8**	**15.4**
Aged 35–39	1,168,543	769,988	166,607	3,268	21,066	207,614	65.9	14.3	0.3	1.8	17.8
Aged 40–44	1,184,518	814,452	162,805	3,539	21,139	182,583	68.8	13.7	0.3	1.8	15.4
Aged 45–49	1,058,456	748,042	134,910	3,242	18,815	153,447	70.7	12.7	0.3	1.8	14.5
Aged 50–54	961,288	707,605	104,349	2,834	16,417	130,083	73.6	10.9	0.3	1.7	13.5
Georgia, total	**7,874,792**	**5,269,997**	**2,262,068**	**15,340**	**137,045**	**190,342**	**66.9**	**28.7**	**0.2**	**1.7**	**2.4**
Total, aged 35 to 54	**2,430,411**	**1,686,192**	**643,649**	**5,196**	**43,646**	**51,728**	**69.4**	**26.5**	**0.2**	**1.8**	**2.1**
Aged 35–39	690,535	460,607	196,899	1,436	13,132	18,461	66.7	28.5	0.2	1.9	2.7
Aged 40–44	669,259	456,188	183,955	1,436	12,532	15,148	68.2	27.5	0.2	1.9	2.3
Aged 45–49	571,972	400,208	149,646	1,266	10,128	10,724	70.0	26.2	0.2	1.8	1.9
Aged 50–54	498,645	369,189	113,149	1,058	7,854	7,395	74.0	22.7	0.2	1.6	1.5
Hawaii, total	**1,257,404**	**362,790**	**26,579**	**4,624**	**755,738**	**107,673**	**28.9**	**2.1**	**0.4**	**60.1**	**8.6**
Total, aged 35 to 54	**369,499**	**123,338**	**6,943**	**1,485**	**211,849**	**25,884**	**33.4**	**1.9**	**0.4**	**57.3**	**7.0**
Aged 35–39	98,753	33,115	2,904	413	54,162	8,159	33.5	2.9	0.4	54.8	8.3
Aged 40–44	100,958	32,987	2,111	407	57,962	7,491	32.7	2.1	0.4	57.4	7.4
Aged 45–49	91,047	30,002	1,177	368	53,514	5,986	33.0	1.3	0.4	58.8	6.6
Aged 50–54	78,741	27,234	751	297	46,211	4,248	34.6	1.0	0.4	58.7	5.4

(continued)

(continued from previous page)

		non-Hispanic					non-Hispanic				
	total	white	black	Native American	Asian	Hispanic	white	black	Native American	Asian	Hispanic
Idaho, total	**1,346,506**	**1,211,465**	**6,101**	**17,747**	**14,834**	**96,359**	**90.0%**	**0.5%**	**1.3%**	**1.1%**	**7.2%**
Total, aged 35 to 54	**373,351**	**341,619**	**1,689**	**4,422**	**3,936**	**21,685**	**91.5**	**0.5**	**1.2**	**1.1**	**5.8**
Aged 35–39	93,641	82,987	573	1,284	1,235	7,562	88.6	0.6	1.4	1.3	8.1
Aged 40–44	101,561	92,542	500	1,221	1,079	6,219	91.1	0.5	1.2	1.1	6.1
Aged 45–49	94,845	87,929	384	1,071	928	4,533	92.7	0.4	1.1	1.0	4.8
Aged 50–54	83,304	78,161	232	846	694	3,371	93.8	0.3	1.0	0.8	4.0
Illinois, total	**12,050,818**	**8,553,616**	**1,812,651**	**18,191**	**398,270**	**1,268,090**	**71.0**	**15.0**	**0.2**	**3.3**	**10.5**
Total, aged 35 to 54	**3,578,038**	**2,659,879**	**480,698**	**5,679**	**119,487**	**312,295**	**74.3**	**13.4**	**0.2**	**3.3**	**8.7**
Aged 35–39	991,821	710,364	138,089	1,548	35,105	106,715	71.6	13.9	0.2	3.5	10.8
Aged 40–44	992,089	731,944	137,370	1,583	32,230	88,962	73.8	13.8	0.2	3.2	9.0
Aged 45–49	859,503	648,386	114,373	1,368	28,408	66,968	75.4	13.3	0.2	3.3	7.8
Aged 50–54	734,625	569,185	90,866	1,180	23,744	49,650	77.5	12.4	0.2	3.2	6.8
Indiana, total	**6,044,528**	**5,337,906**	**494,936**	**13,378**	**57,857**	**140,451**	**88.3**	**8.2**	**0.2**	**1.0**	**2.3**
Total, aged 35 to 54	**1,796,459**	**1,605,380**	**133,248**	**4,131**	**17,265**	**36,435**	**89.4**	**7.4**	**0.2**	**1.0**	**2.0**
Aged 35–39	474,315	418,527	37,554	1,090	5,604	11,540	88.2	7.9	0.2	1.2	2.4
Aged 40–44	495,538	440,491	38,598	1,172	4,857	10,420	88.9	7.8	0.2	1.0	2.1
Aged 45–49	442,902	397,444	32,420	1,030	3,774	8,234	89.7	7.3	0.2	0.9	1.9
Aged 50–54	383,704	348,918	24,676	839	3,030	6,241	90.9	6.4	0.2	0.8	1.6

(continued)

(continued from previous page)

	total	white	black	Native American	Asian	Hispanic	non-Hispanic white	black	Native American	Asian	Hispanic
Iowa, total	**2,899,829**	**2,736,647**	**60,432**	**8,072**	**41,610**	**53,068**	**94.4%**	**2.1%**	**0.3%**	**1.4%**	**1.8%**
Total, aged 35 to 54	**830,513**	**790,791**	**14,924**	**2,043**	**10,265**	**12,490**	**95.2**	**1.8**	**0.2**	**1.2**	**1.5**
Aged 35–39	208,553	195,230	4,656	573	3,722	4,372	93.6	2.2	0.3	1.8	2.1
Aged 40–44	227,317	216,043	4,239	581	2,834	3,620	95.0	1.9	0.3	1.2	1.6
Aged 45–49	211,726	203,128	3,405	477	2,158	2,558	95.9	1.6	0.2	1.0	1.2
Aged 50–54	182,917	176,390	2,624	412	1,551	1,940	96.4	1.4	0.2	0.8	1.1
Kansas, total	**2,668,263**	**2,292,993**	**166,801**	**22,701**	**47,339**	**138,429**	**85.9**	**6.3**	**0.9**	**1.8**	**5.2**
Total, aged 35 to 54	**772,819**	**676,534**	**44,505**	**5,895**	**12,421**	**33,464**	**87.5**	**5.8**	**0.8**	**1.6**	**4.3**
Aged 35–39	205,331	174,543	13,746	1,619	3,999	11,424	85.0	6.7	0.8	1.9	5.6
Aged 40–44	214,660	186,793	13,315	1,660	3,356	9,536	87.0	6.2	0.8	1.6	4.4
Aged 45–49	191,279	169,656	10,064	1,531	2,856	7,172	88.7	5.3	0.8	1.5	3.7
Aged 50–54	161,549	145,542	7,380	1,085	2,210	5,332	90.1	4.6	0.7	1.4	3.3
Kentucky, total	**3,994,566**	**3,643,538**	**284,955**	**6,293**	**27,201**	**32,579**	**91.2**	**7.1**	**0.2**	**0.7**	**0.8**
Total, aged 35 to 54	**1,204,454**	**1,104,884**	**79,669**	**2,038**	**8,814**	**9,049**	**91.7**	**6.6**	**0.2**	**0.7**	**0.8**
Aged 35–39	313,886	285,330	22,380	535	2,630	3,011	90.9	7.1	0.2	0.8	1.0
Aged 40–44	326,197	297,294	23,380	567	2,435	2,521	91.1	7.2	0.2	0.7	0.8
Aged 45–49	296,557	272,844	19,228	500	2,032	1,953	92.0	6.5	0.2	0.7	0.7
Aged 50–54	267,814	249,416	14,681	436	1,717	1,564	93.1	5.5	0.2	0.6	0.6

(continued)

(continued from previous page)

		non-Hispanic					non-Hispanic			
	total	white	black	Native American	Asian	Hispanic	white	black	Native American	Asian	Hispanic
Louisiana, total	**4,424,618**	**2,791,582**	**1,438,366**	**17,941**	**57,812**	**118,917**	**63.1%**	**32.5%**	**0.4%**	**1.3%**	**2.7%**
Total, aged 35 to 54	**1,245,904**	**830,630**	**361,775**	**4,853**	**15,972**	**32,674**	**66.7**	**29.0**	**0.4**	**1.3**	**2.6**
Aged 35–39	323,962	209,536	98,797	1,295	4,623	9,711	64.7	30.5	0.4	1.4	3.0
Aged 40–44	342,693	226,065	102,055	1,276	4,368	8,929	66.0	29.8	0.4	1.3	2.6
Aged 45–49	310,803	207,935	90,068	1,205	3,905	7,690	66.9	29.0	0.4	1.3	2.5
Aged 50–54	268,446	187,094	70,855	1,077	3,076	6,344	69.7	26.4	0.4	1.1	2.4
Maine, total	**1,259,170**	**1,230,020**	**4,517**	**5,768**	**9,451**	**9,414**	**97.7**	**0.4**	**0.5**	**0.8**	**0.7**
Total, aged 35 to 54	**406,462**	**397,803**	**1,384**	**1,781**	**2,885**	**2,609**	**97.9**	**0.3**	**0.4**	**0.7**	**0.6**
Aged 35–39	103,318	100,636	451	499	845	887	97.4	0.4	0.5	0.8	0.9
Aged 40–44	111,567	109,077	387	522	845	736	97.8	0.3	0.5	0.8	0.7
Aged 45–49	101,833	99,815	323	406	707	582	98.0	0.3	0.4	0.7	0.6
Aged 50–54	89,744	88,275	223	354	488	404	98.4	0.2	0.4	0.5	0.5
Maryland, total	**5,274,608**	**3,370,473**	**1,462,797**	**13,474**	**212,224**	**215,640**	**63.9**	**27.7**	**0.3**	**4.0**	**4.1**
Total, aged 35 to 54	**1,710,047**	**1,110,009**	**464,216**	**4,464**	**68,453**	**62,905**	**64.9**	**27.1**	**0.3**	**4.0**	**3.7**
Aged 35–39	492,921	305,648	142,422	1,340	20,930	22,581	62.0	28.9	0.3	4.2	4.6
Aged 40–44	474,450	305,370	131,282	1,192	18,753	17,853	64.4	27.7	0.3	4.0	3.8
Aged 45–49	399,759	264,263	105,733	1,050	15,658	13,055	66.1	26.4	0.3	3.9	3.3
Aged 50–54	342,917	234,728	84,779	882	13,112	9,416	68.5	24.7	0.3	3.8	2.7

(continued)

(continued from previous page)

		non-Hispanic						non-Hispanic			
	total	white	black	Native American	Asian	Hispanic	white	black	Native American	Asian	Hispanic
Massachusetts, total	**6,198,746**	**5,182,035**	**331,601**	**10,336**	**238,368**	**436,406**	**83.6%**	**5.3%**	**0.2%**	**3.8%**	**7.0%**
Total, aged 35 to 54	**1,897,225**	**1,634,225**	**90,125**	**3,015**	**66,305**	**103,555**	**86.1**	**4.8**	**0.2**	**3.5**	**5.5**
Aged 35–39	538,531	449,562	28,447	846	22,101	37,575	83.5	5.3	0.2	4.1	7.0
Aged 40–44	519,199	444,717	25,359	805	19,033	29,285	85.7	4.9	0.2	3.7	5.6
Aged 45–49	446,144	389,833	20,052	747	14,380	21,132	87.4	4.5	0.2	3.2	4.7
Aged 50–54	393,351	350,113	16,267	617	10,791	15,563	89.0	4.1	0.2	2.7	4.0
Michigan, total	**9,678,943**	**7,789,804**	**1,417,504**	**55,157**	**156,781**	**259,697**	**80.5**	**14.6**	**0.6**	**1.6**	**2.7**
Total, aged 35 to 54	**2,911,863**	**2,402,710**	**381,158**	**15,942**	**47,029**	**65,024**	**82.5**	**13.1**	**0.5**	**1.6**	**2.2**
Aged 35–39	770,883	627,013	103,443	4,547	14,937	20,943	81.3	13.4	0.6	1.9	2.7
Aged 40–44	810,040	666,975	107,391	4,412	12,888	18,374	82.3	13.3	0.5	1.6	2.3
Aged 45–49	717,428	594,960	93,507	3,848	10,460	14,653	82.9	13.0	0.5	1.5	2.0
Aged 50–54	613,512	513,762	76,817	3,135	8,744	11,054	83.7	12.5	0.5	1.4	1.8
Minnesota, total	**4,829,798**	**4,387,552**	**151,933**	**60,493**	**135,380**	**94,440**	**90.8**	**3.1**	**1.3**	**2.8**	**2.0**
Total, aged 35 to 54	**1,473,194**	**1,369,371**	**39,129**	**14,042**	**28,554**	**22,098**	**93.0**	**2.7**	**1.0**	**1.9**	**1.5**
Aged 35–39	402,325	366,607	13,426	4,433	9,751	8,108	91.1	3.3	1.1	2.4	2.0
Aged 40–44	413,172	383,183	11,694	4,090	7,947	6,258	92.7	2.8	1.0	1.9	1.5
Aged 45–49	358,940	336,723	8,355	3,135	6,193	4,534	93.8	2.3	0.9	1.7	1.3
Aged 50–54	298,757	282,858	5,654	2,384	4,663	3,198	94.7	1.9	0.8	1.6	1.1

(continued)

(continued from previous page)

		non-Hispanic						non-Hispanic			
	total	white	black	Native American	Asian	Hispanic	white	black	Native American	Asian	Hispanic
Mississippi, total	**2,815,743**	**1,754,438**	**1,009,938**	**8,649**	**19,946**	**22,772**	**62.3%**	**35.9%**	**0.3%**	**0.7%**	**0.8%**
Total, aged 35 to 54	**777,260**	**515,958**	**247,400**	**2,169**	**5,811**	**5,922**	**66.4**	**31.8**	**0.3**	**0.7**	**0.8**
Aged 35–39	204,216	131,926	67,875	582	1,835	1,998	64.6	33.2	0.3	0.9	1.0
Aged 40–44	212,611	137,528	71,313	547	1,585	1,638	64.7	33.5	0.3	0.7	0.8
Aged 45–49	191,488	126,618	61,731	536	1,348	1,255	66.1	32.2	0.3	0.7	0.7
Aged 50–54	168,945	119,886	46,481	504	1,043	1,031	71.0	27.5	0.3	0.6	0.6
Missouri, total	**5,540,378**	**4,745,409**	**621,746**	**22,207**	**61,038**	**89,978**	**85.7**	**11.2**	**0.4**	**1.1**	**1.6**
Total, aged 35 to 54	**1,633,965**	**1,420,161**	**165,997**	**6,526**	**17,750**	**23,531**	**86.9**	**10.2**	**0.4**	**1.1**	**1.4**
Aged 35–39	438,944	375,546	48,058	1,766	5,707	7,867	85.6	10.9	0.4	1.3	1.8
Aged 40–44	453,504	391,900	48,373	1,786	4,748	6,697	86.4	10.7	0.4	1.0	1.5
Aged 45–49	395,363	345,989	38,830	1,623	3,923	4,998	87.5	9.8	0.4	1.0	1.3
Aged 50–54	346,154	306,726	30,736	1,351	3,372	3,969	88.6	8.9	0.4	1.0	1.1
Montana, total	**949,657**	**860,423**	**3,469**	**58,124**	**7,172**	**20,469**	**90.6**	**0.4**	**6.1**	**0.8**	**2.2**
Total, aged 35 to 54	**283,271**	**262,149**	**901**	**13,205**	**1,930**	**5,086**	**92.5**	**0.3**	**4.7**	**0.7**	**1.8**
Aged 35–39	65,647	59,203	322	3,850	649	1,623	90.2	0.5	5.9	1.0	2.5
Aged 40–44	76,701	70,755	279	3,776	499	1,392	92.2	0.4	4.9	0.7	1.8
Aged 45–49	74,502	69,591	201	3,086	458	1,166	93.4	0.3	4.1	0.6	1.6
Aged 50–54	66,421	62,600	99	2,493	324	905	94.2	0.1	3.8	0.5	1.4

(continued)

(continued from previous page)

		non-Hispanic					non-Hispanic				
	total	white	black	Native American	Asian	Hispanic	white	black	Native American	Asian	Hispanic
Nebraska, total	**1,705,467**	**1,539,408**	**69,984**	**14,222**	**21,711**	**60,142**	**90.3%**	**4.1%**	**0.8%**	**1.3%**	**3.5%**
Total, aged 35 to 54	**486,679**	**446,506**	**17,796**	**2,979**	**5,546**	**13,852**	**91.7**	**3.7**	**0.6**	**1.1**	**2.8**
Aged 35–39	127,158	114,192	5,509	894	1,901	4,662	89.8	4.3	0.7	1.5	3.7
Aged 40–44	134,240	122,500	5,271	847	1,580	4,042	91.3	3.9	0.6	1.2	3.0
Aged 45–49	121,604	112,754	4,034	677	1,119	3,020	92.7	3.3	0.6	0.9	2.5
Aged 50–54	103,677	97,060	2,982	561	946	2,128	93.6	2.9	0.5	0.9	2.1
Nevada, total	**1,871,299**	**1,365,753**	**127,830**	**24,867**	**76,899**	**275,950**	**73.0**	**6.8**	**1.3**	**4.1**	**14.7**
Total, aged 35 to 54	**600,150**	**457,221**	**37,962**	**7,560**	**24,294**	**73,113**	**76.2**	**6.3**	**1.3**	**4.0**	**12.2**
Aged 35–39	161,713	116,414	11,406	2,165	6,529	25,199	72.0	7.1	1.3	4.0	15.6
Aged 40–44	162,522	122,633	10,860	2,072	6,628	20,329	75.5	6.7	1.3	4.1	12.5
Aged 45–49	145,671	113,510	8,846	1,794	5,863	15,658	77.9	6.1	1.2	4.0	10.7
Aged 50–54	130,244	104,664	6,850	1,529	5,274	11,927	80.4	5.3	1.2	4.0	9.2
New Hampshire, total	**1,224,230**	**1,183,300**	**7,215**	**2,345**	**14,213**	**17,157**	**96.7**	**0.6**	**0.2**	**1.2**	**1.4**
Total, aged 35 to 54	**400,960**	**388,920**	**2,140**	**708**	**4,432**	**4,760**	**97.0**	**0.5**	**0.2**	**1.1**	**1.2**
Aged 35–39	112,198	108,154	722	205	1,471	1,646	96.4	0.6	0.2	1.3	1.5
Aged 40–44	114,212	110,632	622	207	1,322	1,429	96.9	0.5	0.2	1.2	1.3
Aged 45–49	94,435	91,833	473	163	973	993	97.2	0.5	0.2	1.0	1.1
Aged 50–54	80,115	78,301	323	133	666	692	97.7	0.4	0.2	0.8	0.9

(continued)

(continued from previous page)

	total	non-Hispanic					non-Hispanic				
		white	black	Native American	Asian	Hispanic	white	black	Native American	Asian	Hispanic
New Jersey, total	**8,177,791**	**5,557,637**	**1,104,522**	**14,298**	**456,050**	**1,045,284**	**68.0%**	**13.5%**	**0.2%**	**5.6%**	**12.8%**
Total, aged 35 to 54	**2,548,255**	**1,777,432**	**314,209**	**4,469**	**155,268**	**296,877**	**69.8**	**12.3**	**0.2**	**6.1**	**11.7**
Aged 35–39	709,650	466,902	96,044	1,249	46,619	98,836	65.8	13.5	0.2	6.6	13.9
Aged 40–44	707,615	491,267	87,496	1,218	44,593	83,041	69.4	12.4	0.2	6.3	11.7
Aged 45–49	601,477	428,802	71,498	1,141	35,863	64,173	71.3	11.9	0.2	6.0	10.7
Aged 50–54	529,513	390,461	59,171	861	28,193	50,827	73.7	11.2	0.2	5.3	9.6
New Mexico, total	**1,860,397**	**911,758**	**34,026**	**156,717**	**21,335**	**736,561**	**49.0**	**1.8**	**8.4**	**1.1**	**39.6**
Total, aged 35 to 54	**534,718**	**288,748**	**9,965**	**35,284**	**6,445**	**194,276**	**54.0**	**1.9**	**6.6**	**1.2**	**36.3**
Aged 35–39	142,914	70,320	3,075	10,849	1,892	56,778	49.2	2.2	7.6	1.3	39.7
Aged 40–44	146,312	77,036	2,893	10,150	1,857	54,376	52.7	2.0	6.9	1.3	37.2
Aged 45–49	131,311	73,751	2,337	8,146	1,517	45,560	56.2	1.8	6.2	1.2	34.7
Aged 50–54	114,181	67,641	1,660	6,139	1,179	37,562	59.2	1.5	5.4	1.0	32.9
New York, total	**18,146,185**	**11,640,203**	**2,668,358**	**52,425**	**980,588**	**2,804,611**	**64.1**	**14.7**	**0.3**	**5.4**	**15.5**
Total, aged 35 to 54	**5,422,435**	**3,601,592**	**738,085**	**15,363**	**316,411**	**750,984**	**66.4**	**13.6**	**0.3**	**5.8**	**13.8**
Aged 35–39	1,501,243	943,079	221,206	4,404	93,848	238,706	62.8	14.7	0.3	6.3	15.9
Aged 40–44	1,475,903	975,933	201,796	4,331	88,373	205,470	66.1	13.7	0.3	6.0	13.9
Aged 45–49	1,293,077	878,397	169,692	3,677	73,368	167,943	67.9	13.1	0.3	5.7	13.0
Aged 50–54	1,152,212	804,183	145,391	2,951	60,822	138,865	69.8	12.6	0.3	5.3	12.1

(continued)

(continued from previous page)

		non-Hispanic					non-Hispanic				
	total	white	black	Native American	Asian	Hispanic	white	black	Native American	Asian	Hispanic
North Carolina, total	7,777,253	5,747,974	1,725,731	91,637	92,074	119,837	73.9%	22.2%	1.2%	1.2%	1.5%
Total, aged 35 to 54	**2,338,743**	**1,774,427**	**478,091**	**25,367**	**28,558**	**32,300**	**75.9**	**20.4**	**1.1**	**1.2**	**1.4**
Aged 35–39	631,072	469,197	134,858	7,117	8,548	11,352	74.3	21.4	1.1	1.4	1.8
Aged 40–44	635,368	476,431	134,684	6,990	7,985	9,278	75.0	21.2	1.1	1.3	1.5
Aged 45–49	564,812	428,459	116,827	6,127	6,676	6,723	75.9	20.7	1.1	1.2	1.2
Aged 50–54	507,491	400,340	91,722	5,133	5,349	4,947	78.9	18.1	1.0	1.1	1.0
North Dakota, total	**661,689**	**611,587**	**4,711**	**32,145**	**5,694**	**7,552**	**92.4**	**0.7**	**4.9**	**0.9**	**1.1**
Total, aged 35 to 54	**181,849**	**171,673**	**1,080**	**6,200**	**1,406**	**1,490**	**94.4**	**0.6**	**3.4**	**0.8**	**0.8**
Aged 35–39	45,640	42,138	472	2,005	481	544	92.3	1.0	4.4	1.1	1.2
Aged 40–44	50,543	47,643	305	1,803	374	418	94.3	0.6	3.6	0.7	0.8
Aged 45–49	46,847	44,724	203	1,315	294	311	95.5	0.4	2.8	0.6	0.7
Aged 50–54	38,819	37,168	100	1,077	257	217	95.7	0.3	2.8	0.7	0.6
Ohio, total	**11,318,718**	**9,672,043**	**1,305,993**	**20,519**	**136,359**	**183,804**	**85.5**	**11.5**	**0.2**	**1.2**	**1.6**
Total, aged 35 to 54	**3,370,608**	**2,924,940**	**349,919**	**6,584**	**41,015**	**48,150**	**86.8**	**10.4**	**0.2**	**1.2**	**1.4**
Aged 35–39	882,640	755,007	97,727	1,652	12,917	15,337	85.5	11.1	0.2	1.5	1.7
Aged 40–44	932,716	804,511	101,133	1,819	11,345	13,908	86.3	10.8	0.2	1.2	1.5
Aged 45–49	829,399	723,430	84,526	1,700	9,139	10,604	87.2	10.2	0.2	1.1	1.3
Aged 50–54	725,853	641,992	66,533	1,413	7,614	8,301	88.4	9.2	0.2	1.0	1.1

(continued)

(continued from previous page)

	non-Hispanic					non-Hispanic				
	total	white	black	Native American	Asian	Hispanic	white	black	Native American	Asian	Hispanic
Oklahoma, total	**3,372,514**	**2,653,074**	**276,109**	**272,606**	**47,184**	**123,541**	**78.7%**	**8.2%**	**8.1%**	**1.4%**	**3.7%**
Total, aged 35 to 54	**954,869**	**773,987**	**72,728**	**64,286**	**13,706**	**30,162**	**81.1**	**7.6**	**6.7**	**1.4**	**3.2**
Aged 35–39	242,095	189,386	20,916	17,428	4,307	10,058	78.2	8.6	7.2	1.8	4.2
Aged 40–44	260,421	208,835	21,371	17,841	3,696	8,678	80.2	8.2	6.9	1.4	3.3
Aged 45–49	237,979	195,496	17,339	15,461	3,153	6,530	82.1	7.3	6.5	1.3	2.7
Aged 50–54	214,374	180,270	13,102	13,556	2,550	4,896	84.1	6.1	6.3	1.2	2.3
Oregon, total	**3,397,161**	**2,989,829**	**59,602**	**44,738**	**109,680**	**193,312**	**88.0**	**1.8**	**1.3**	**3.2**	**5.7**
Total, aged 35 to 54	**1,050,518**	**941,659**	**17,229**	**12,785**	**31,266**	**47,579**	**89.6**	**1.6**	**1.2**	**3.0**	**4.5**
Aged 35–39	257,986	223,285	5,048	3,546	9,826	16,281	86.5	2.0	1.4	3.8	6.3
Aged 40–44	278,330	248,138	5,002	3,492	8,481	13,217	89.2	1.8	1.3	3.0	4.7
Aged 45–49	271,570	246,616	4,188	3,162	7,222	10,382	90.8	1.5	1.2	2.7	3.8
Aged 50–54	242,632	223,620	2,991	2,585	5,737	7,699	92.2	1.2	1.1	2.4	3.2
Pennsylvania, total	**12,202,050**	**10,460,455**	**1,181,047**	**15,818**	**210,419**	**334,311**	**85.7**	**9.7**	**0.1**	**1.7**	**2.7**
Total, aged 35 to 54	**3,640,614**	**3,171,939**	**318,896**	**4,894**	**61,155**	**83,730**	**87.1**	**8.8**	**0.1**	**1.7**	**2.3**
Aged 35–39	935,727	797,279	90,813	1,309	18,840	27,486	85.2	9.7	0.1	2.0	2.9
Aged 40–44	1,007,440	875,077	90,483	1,391	16,954	23,535	86.9	9.0	0.1	1.7	2.3
Aged 45–49	905,062	795,538	76,007	1,158	13,801	18,558	87.9	8.4	0.1	1.5	2.1
Aged 50–54	792,385	704,045	61,593	1,036	11,560	14,151	88.9	7.8	0.1	1.5	1.8

(continued)

(continued from previous page)

	non-Hispanic						non-Hispanic				
	total	white	black	Native American	Asian	Hispanic	white	black	Native American	Asian	Hispanic
Rhode Island, total	**997,607**	**850,536**	**40,634**	**4,233**	**26,457**	**75,747**	**85.3%**	**4.1%**	**0.4%**	**2.7%**	**7.6%**
Total, aged 35 to 54	**296,168**	**260,337**	**10,624**	**951**	**6,539**	**17,717**	**87.9**	**3.6**	**0.3**	**2.2**	**6.0**
Aged 35–39	80,477	68,717	3,221	257	2,110	6,172	85.4	4.0	0.3	2.6	7.7
Aged 40–44	82,806	72,353	3,232	289	1,835	5,097	87.4	3.9	0.3	2.2	6.2
Aged 45–49	71,237	63,417	2,446	215	1,438	3,721	89.0	3.4	0.3	2.0	5.2
Aged 50–54	61,648	55,850	1,725	190	1,156	2,727	90.6	2.8	0.3	1.9	4.4
South Carolina, total	**3,858,023**	**2,624,084**	**1,151,436**	**8,264**	**30,906**	**43,333**	**68.0**	**29.8**	**0.2**	**0.8**	**1.1**
Total, aged 35 to 54	**1,153,755**	**812,427**	**317,020**	**2,652**	**9,834**	**11,822**	**70.4**	**27.5**	**0.2**	**0.9**	**1.0**
Aged 35–39	305,406	211,560	86,428	728	2,732	3,958	69.3	28.3	0.2	0.9	1.3
Aged 40–44	310,735	215,653	88,289	756	2,712	3,325	69.4	28.4	0.2	0.9	1.1
Aged 45–49	283,550	198,823	79,150	615	2,412	2,550	70.1	27.9	0.2	0.9	0.9
Aged 50–54	254,064	186,391	63,153	553	1,978	1,989	73.4	24.9	0.2	0.8	0.8
South Dakota, total	**777,073**	**697,922**	**5,032**	**59,881**	**5,409**	**8,829**	**89.8**	**0.6**	**7.7**	**0.7**	**1.1**
Total, aged 35 to 54	**214,812**	**198,930**	**1,246**	**11,366**	**1,360**	**1,910**	**92.6**	**0.6**	**5.3**	**0.6**	**0.9**
Aged 35–39	55,323	50,112	486	3,594	458	673	90.6	0.9	6.5	0.8	1.2
Aged 40–44	59,934	55,512	369	3,113	374	566	92.6	0.6	5.2	0.6	0.9
Aged 45–49	54,724	51,132	235	2,630	301	426	93.4	0.4	4.8	0.6	0.8
Aged 50–54	44,831	42,174	156	2,029	227	245	94.1	0.3	4.5	0.5	0.5

(continued)

(continued from previous page)

		non-Hispanic					non-Hispanic				
	total	white	black	Native American	Asian	Hispanic	white	black	Native American	Asian	Hispanic
Tennessee, total	**5,657,161**	**4,607,340**	**925,022**	**12,546**	**54,584**	**57,669**	**81.4%**	**16.4%**	**0.2%**	**1.0%**	**1.0%**
Total, aged 35 to 54	**1,721,308**	**1,427,026**	**256,421**	**4,009**	**17,304**	**16,548**	**82.9**	**14.9**	**0.2**	**1.0**	**1.0**
Aged 35–39	455,997	371,221	73,079	1,043	5,224	5,430	81.4	16.0	0.2	1.1	1.2
Aged 40–44	464,004	379,827	73,417	1,081	4,888	4,791	81.9	15.8	0.2	1.1	1.0
Aged 45–49	421,768	350,135	62,941	1,023	4,052	3,617	83.0	14.9	0.2	1.0	0.9
Aged 50–54	379,539	325,843	46,984	862	3,140	2,710	85.9	12.4	0.2	0.8	0.7
Texas, total	**20,119,335**	**11,272,203**	**2,406,384**	**60,215**	**505,300**	**5,875,233**	**56.0**	**12.0**	**0.3**	**2.5**	**29.2**
Total, aged 35 to 54	**5,788,891**	**3,496,813**	**679,332**	**18,183**	**153,273**	**1,441,290**	**60.4**	**11.7**	**0.3**	**2.6**	**24.9**
Aged 35–39	1,604,353	899,198	200,689	4,820	44,564	455,082	56.0	12.5	0.3	2.8	28.4
Aged 40–44	1,609,846	959,794	197,683	5,054	42,783	404,532	59.6	12.3	0.3	2.7	25.1
Aged 45–49	1,395,154	866,475	160,828	4,480	37,150	326,221	62.1	11.5	0.3	2.7	23.4
Aged 50–54	1,179,538	771,346	120,132	3,829	28,776	255,455	65.4	10.2	0.3	2.4	21.7
Utah, total	**2,207,013**	**1,960,830**	**17,743**	**33,315**	**58,588**	**136,537**	**88.8**	**0.8**	**1.5**	**2.7**	**6.2**
Total, aged 35 to 54	**532,809**	**478,868**	**4,279**	**6,255**	**13,572**	**29,835**	**89.9**	**0.8**	**1.2**	**2.5**	**5.6**
Aged 35–39	146,447	128,499	1,432	2,111	4,499	9,906	87.7	1.0	1.4	3.1	6.8
Aged 40–44	146,722	131,724	1,217	1,750	3,631	8,400	89.8	0.8	1.2	2.5	5.7
Aged 45–49	131,114	119,144	940	1,401	3,048	6,581	90.9	0.7	1.1	2.3	5.0
Aged 50–54	108,526	99,501	690	993	2,394	4,948	91.7	0.6	0.9	2.2	4.6

(continued)

(continued from previous page)

| | | non-Hispanic | | | | | non-Hispanic | | | | |
	total	white	black	Native American	Asian	Hispanic	white	black	Native American	Asian	Hispanic
Vermont, total	**616,803**	**600,653**	**2,777**	**1,793**	**5,717**	**5,863**	**97.4%**	**0.5%**	**0.3%**	**0.9%**	**1.0%**
Total, aged 35 to 54	**197,283**	**192,840**	**760**	**555**	**1,452**	**1,676**	**97.7**	**0.4**	**0.3**	**0.7**	**0.8**
Aged 35–39	49,901	48,516	234	135	438	578	97.2	0.5	0.3	0.9	1.2
Aged 40-44	54,500	53,220	224	174	433	449	97.7	0.4	0.3	0.8	0.8
Aged 45-49	49,920	48,863	195	143	334	385	97.9	0.4	0.3	0.7	0.8
Aged 50-54	42,962	42,241	107	103	247	264	98.3	0.2	0.2	0.6	0.6
Virginia, total	**6,997,006**	**5,061,303**	**1,394,404**	**15,579**	**257,517**	**268,203**	**72.3**	**19.9**	**0.2**	**3.7**	**3.8**
Total, aged 35 to 54	**2,204,636**	**1,632,924**	**408,457**	**5,192**	**81,478**	**76,585**	**74.1**	**18.5**	**0.2**	**3.7**	**3.5**
Aged 35–39	618,298	442,487	122,495	1,503	24,285	27,528	71.6	19.8	0.2	3.9	4.5
Aged 40-44	603,235	439,502	118,270	1,406	22,431	21,626	72.9	19.6	0.2	3.7	3.6
Aged 45-49	522,056	390,503	95,394	1,231	19,060	15,868	74.8	18.3	0.2	3.7	3.0
Aged 50-54	461,047	360,432	72,298	1,052	15,702	11,563	78.2	15.7	0.2	3.4	2.5
Washington, total	**5,858,392**	**4,881,702**	**179,147**	**95,553**	**342,268**	**359,722**	**83.3**	**3.1**	**1.6**	**5.8**	**6.1**
Total, aged 35 to 54	**1,858,249**	**1,589,767**	**55,692**	**26,787**	**98,017**	**87,986**	**85.6**	**3.0**	**1.4**	**5.3**	**4.7**
Aged 35–39	491,912	406,971	17,205	7,804	28,911	31,021	82.7	3.5	1.6	5.9	6.3
Aged 40-44	511,205	434,706	16,640	7,622	27,192	25,045	85.0	3.3	1.5	5.3	4.9
Aged 45-49	461,769	400,504	12,640	6,443	23,338	18,844	86.7	2.7	1.4	5.1	4.1
Aged 50-54	393,363	347,586	9,207	4,918	18,576	13,076	88.4	2.3	1.3	4.7	3.3

(continued)

(continued from previous page)

	total	white	non-Hispanic black	non-Hispanic Native American	non-Hispanic Asian	Hispanic	non-Hispanic white	non-Hispanic black	non-Hispanic Native American	non-Hispanic Asian	non-Hispanic Hispanic
West Virginia, total	**1,840,983**	**1,757,908**	**57,362**	**2,389**	**10,895**	**12,429**	**95.5%**	**3.1%**	**0.1%**	**0.6%**	**0.7%**
Total, aged 35 to 54	**546,015**	**522,753**	**15,926**	**723**	**3,207**	**3,406**	**95.7**	**2.9**	**0.1**	**0.6**	**0.6**
Aged 35–39	125,005	118,889	4,049	168	891	1,008	95.1	3.2	0.1	0.7	0.8
Aged 40–44	143,619	137,106	4,572	187	845	909	95.5	3.2	0.1	0.6	0.6
Aged 45–49	143,156	137,199	4,208	188	781	780	95.8	2.9	0.1	0.5	0.5
Aged 50–54	134,235	129,559	3,097	180	690	709	96.5	2.3	0.1	0.5	0.5
Wisconsin, total	**5,326,324**	**4,731,293**	**318,392**	**44,971**	**97,068**	**134,600**	**88.8**	**6.0**	**0.8**	**1.8**	**2.5**
Total, aged 35 to 54	**1,585,181**	**1,442,980**	**77,794**	**11,294**	**20,518**	**32,595**	**91.0**	**4.9**	**0.7**	**1.3**	**2.1**
Aged 35–39	418,819	373,396	23,773	3,539	7,366	10,745	89.2	5.7	0.8	1.8	2.6
Aged 40–44	440,229	399,498	22,533	3,187	5,449	9,562	90.7	5.1	0.7	1.2	2.2
Aged 45–49	392,496	360,537	18,005	2,579	4,250	7,125	91.9	4.6	0.7	1.1	1.8
Aged 50–54	333,637	309,549	13,483	1,989	3,453	5,163	92.8	4.0	0.6	1.0	1.5
Wyoming, total	**524,700**	**469,445**	**4,418**	**11,790**	**4,702**	**34,345**	**89.5**	**0.8**	**2.2**	**0.9**	**6.5**
Total, aged 35 to 54	**155,195**	**141,790**	**1,179**	**2,543**	**1,265**	**8,418**	**91.4**	**0.8**	**1.6**	**0.8**	**5.4**
Aged 35–39	36,134	32,229	359	710	370	2,466	89.2	1.0	2.0	1.0	6.8
Aged 40–44	42,691	38,792	364	737	353	2,445	90.9	0.9	1.7	0.8	5.7
Aged 45–49	41,508	38,281	292	603	317	2,015	92.2	0.7	1.5	0.8	4.9
Aged 50–54	34,862	32,488	164	493	225	1,492	93.2	0.5	1.4	0.6	4.3

Source: Bureau of the Census, unpublished tables from the Internet web site, <http://www.census.gov> calcuations by New Strategist

Few People in Their Fifties Move

Mobility rates drop sharply as people enter their late forties and early fifties.

By age 50, mobility is uncommon. Only 9 percent of people aged 50 to 54 moved from one house to another between March 1996 and March 1997. Mobility rates fall as people enter middle age because most are committed to a job, own homes they like, and many have children in school. Overall, 16 percent of Americans moved between 1996 and 1997. The mobility rate of people aged 35 to 39 matches the national rate, but falls steadily with age.

Among those who do move, most do not go far. Sixty-six percent of the moves of 35-to-54-year-olds are within the same county. Despite the high mobility rates of young adults, the proportion of Americans aged 45 or older who live in the same community in which they lived at age 16 does not vary much by age. The popular notion that baby boomers, in particular, have moved far from their families is a myth.

♦ While people aged 35 to 54 dominate most markets, they account for just 22 percent of movers.

Mobility rates fall with age

(percent of people aged 35 to 54 who moved between March 1996 and March 1997, by age)

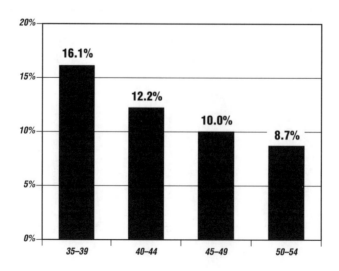

Geographical Mobility, 1996 to 1997

(total number and percent of people aged 1 and older and aged 35 to 54 who moved between March 1996 and March 1997, by type of move; numbers in thousands)

	total	same house (non-movers)	total	same county	total	same state	total	same region	different region	movers from abroad
					different house in the U.S.					
						different county				
							different state			
Total,										
1 or older	**262,976**	**219,585**	**42,088**	**27,740**	**14,348**	**7,960**	**6,389**	**3,220**	**3,168**	**1,303**
Total, 35 to 54	**76,973**	**67,332**	**9,356**	**6,167**	**3,188**	**1,744**	**1,443**	**674**	**769**	**287**
Aged 35 to 39	22,755	18,980	3,659	2,436	1,222	674	548	274	274	117
Aged 40 to 44	21,205	18,539	2,579	1,673	906	496	410	185	225	88
Aged 45 to 49	18,354	16,458	1,841	1,169	672	368	304	130	174	55
Aged 50 to 54	14,659	13,355	1,277	889	388	206	181	85	96	27
Median age	34.7	37.0	26.6	26.3	27.3	27.2	27.4	27.0	27.9	27.3
Total,										
1 or older	**100.0%**	**83.5%**	**16.0%**	**10.5%**	**5.5%**	**3.0%**	**2.4%**	**1.2%**	**1.2%**	**0.5%**
Total, 35 to 54	**100.0**	**87.5**	**12.2**	**8.0**	**4.1**	**2.3**	**1.9**	**0.9**	**1.0**	**0.4**
Aged 35 to 39	100.0	83.4	16.1	10.7	5.4	3.0	2.4	1.2	1.5	0.5
Aged 40 to 44	100.0	87.4	12.2	7.9	4.3	2.3	1.9	0.9	1.1	0.4
Aged 45 to 49	100.0	89.7	10.0	6.4	3.7	2.0	1.7	0.7	0.9	0.3
Aged 50 to 54	100.0	91.1	8.7	6.1	2.6	1.4	1.2	0.6	0.7	0.2

Source: Bureau of the Census, Geographical Mobility: March 1996 to March 1997, *Current Population Reports, P20-510, 1998; calculations by New Strategist*

Mobility Since Age 16, 1996

"When you were 16 years old, were you living in this same city?"

(percent of people aged 18 or older responding by age, 1996)

	same city	different city	different state
Total people	**38%**	**24%**	**38%**
Aged 18 to 24	55	25	20
Aged 25 to 34	43	22	35
Aged 35 to 44	37	25	38
Aged 45 to 54	30	26	44
Aged 55 to 64	34	22	44
Aged 65 to 74	31	27	41
Aged 75 or older	31	25	43

Note: Numbers may not add to 100 because no answer is not shown.
Source: 1996 General Social Survey, National Opinion Research Center, University of Chicago

Boomers Will Move South and West

Fifteen states count as retirement hot spots for boomers.

As the baby-boom generation ages, its decisions about where to live in retirement will bring prosperity to some areas and economic difficulties to others. By 2025, when boomers span the ages of 61 to 79, most will be retired. The Census Bureau's projections of the number of people aged 65 or older by state is a best guess as to where boomers will live in retirement

Between 2000 and 2025, the population aged 65 or older will grow 79 percent nationally. But the elderly population will grow much faster in some states than in others. In 15 states, the 65-or-older population will more than double during those 25 years. The fastest growth is projected for the western states of Utah, Alaska, Idaho, Wyoming, and Colorado. A handful of southern states should also see triple-digit growth including Georgia, Texas, North Carolina, and South Carolina. Fully 24 states will be home to more than 1 million people aged 65 or older in 2025, up from only 9 states today.

◆ In states with below-average growth in the 65-or-older age group, the elderly who remain will be older, less healthy, and less affluent than those who move elsewhere.

◆ States with above-average growth in the 65-or-older population will attract active, affluent retirees. As aging boomers spend their hard-earned wealth, retirement areas in these fortunate states will experience rapid economic growth.

Population Aged 65 or Older by State, 2000 and 2025

(number of people aged 65 or older by state, 2000 and 2025; percent change, 2000–2025; numbers in thousands; ranked by percent change)

	2000	*2025*	*percent change 2000–2025*
Utah	202	495	145.0%
Alaska	38	92	142.1
Idaho	157	374	138.2
Wyoming	62	145	133.9
Colorado	452	1,044	131.0
Washington	685	1,580	130.7
Oregon	471	1,054	123.8
Nevada	219	486	121.9
Arizona	635	1,368	115.4
Georgia	779	1,668	114.1
New Mexico	206	441	114.1
Montana	128	274	114.1
Texas	2,101	4,364	107.7
North Carolina	991	2,004	102.2
South Carolina	478	963	101.5
Florida	2,755	5,453	97.9
Arkansas	377	731	93.9
Virginia	788	1,515	92.3
New Hampshire	142	273	92.3
Tennessee	707	1,355	91.7
California	3,387	6,424	89.7
Vermont	73	138	89.0
Oklahoma	472	888	88.1
Minnesota	596	1,099	84.4
Hawaii	157	289	84.1
Alabama	582	1,069	83.7
Louisiana	523	945	80.7
Kentucky	509	917	80.2
Mississippi	344	615	78.8
United States total	**34,710**	**61,952**	**78.5**
Maine	172	304	76.7
Maryland	589	1,029	74.7
South Dakota	110	188	70.9
Wisconsin	705	1,200	70.2

(continued)

(continued from previous page)

	2000	2025	percent change 2000–2025
Delaware	97	165	70.1%
Nebraska	239	405	69.5
Kansas	359	605	68.5
North Dakota	99	166	67.7
Missouri	755	1,258	66.6
Indiana	763	1,260	65.1
West Virginia	287	460	60.3
Iowa	442	686	55.2
Michigan	1,197	1,821	52.1
New Jersey	1,090	1,654	51.7
Ohio	1,525	2,305	51.1
Illinois	1,484	2,234	50.5
Massachusetts	843	1,252	48.5
Connecticut	461	671	45.6
Rhode Island	148	214	44.6
Pennsylvania	1,899	2,659	40.0
New York	2,358	3,263	38.4
District of Columbia	69	92	33.3

Source: Bureau of the Census, Population Projections for States by Age, Sex, Race and Hispanic Origin: 1995 to 2025, *PPL-47, 1996; calculations by New Strategist*

8

Spending

◆ Despite media stories to the contrary, boomers are not spendthrifts. The spending of householders aged 35 to 54 has yet to match the level of 1990, after adjusting for inflation.

◆ Among all age groups, householders aged 45 to 54 are the biggest spenders. They spent 30 percent more than the average household, or $45,451, in 1997.

◆ Householders aged 35 to 44 spend much more than the average household on a variety of products and services, including school lunches, day care and baby-sitting, computer software, children's clothes, fees for recreational lessons, toys, and bicycles.

◆ Householders aged 45 to 54 spend more than other households on most items, including computer online services, furniture, restaurant meals, clothes, entertainment, personal care products and services, and education.

Note: The Bureau of Labor Statistics' Consumer Expenditure Survey, on which the spending tables are based, presents average spending data for all households in a segment, not just for the purchasers of an item. When examining the spending data that follow, it is important to remember that by including purchasers and nonpurchasers in the calculation of the average, the average spending amount is diluted for items that are not purchased universally. Consequently, for categories purchased by few consumers, the average spending figures are less revealing than the indexes. For universally purchased items such as soaps and detergents, the average spending figures give a more accurate picture of actual spending.

Spending in 1997 Still below 1990 Level

Householders aged 35 to 44 have sharply reduced their spending.

Between 1990 and 1997, householders aged 35 to 44 cut their spending 7.5 percent, after adjusting for inflation. Although the nation experienced both recession and recovery during those years, householders in this age group have yet to spend as much as they did seven years earlier. In contrast to the deep cut in spending by 35-to-44-year-olds, householders aged 45 to 54 cut their spending just 0.5 percent between 1990 and 1997, after adjusting for inflation. The average household spent 0.1 percent less in 1997 than in 1990.

Almost every product and service category saw less spending by 35-to-44-year-olds in 1997 than in 1990. Spending on food away from home fell 17 percent, spending on women's clothes fell 34 percent, and spending on entertainment was down 6 percent. But the average household in the age group spent more on property taxes, personal services (primarily day care expenses), health insurance, and education.

Like their younger counterparts, householders aged 45 to 54 spent less in most product and service categories—although the decline was often less than that for householders aged 35 to 44. Households in the 45-to-54 age group spent more on furniture in 1997 than in 1990. Their spending was also greater for children's clothes, vehicle purchases, and fees and admissions to entertainment events.

♦ Boomers are not big spenders, despite media stories to the contrary. Since the recession of the early 1990s, they have become exceedingly cautious consumers. Businesses must work harder than ever to convince them to part with their paychecks.

Average Spending of Householders Aged 35 to 54, 1990 and 1997

(average annual spending of total consumer units and consumer units aged 35 to 54, 1990 and 1997; percent change, 1990–97; in 1997 dollars)

	total consumer units			aged 35 to 44			aged 45 to 54		
	1990	1997	percent change 1990–97	1990	1997	percent change 1990–97	1990	1997	percent change 1990–97
Number of consumer units (in 000s)	96,968	105,576	8.9%	21,003	24,560	16.9%	14,855	19,343	30.2%
Average before-tax income	$39,160	$39,926	2.0	$50,603	$48,788	-3.6	$53,358	$55,260	3.6
Average annual spending	34,852	34,819	-0.1	43,709	40,413	-7.5	45,451	45,239	-0.5
FOOD	**$5,275**	**$4,801**	**-9.0%**	**$6,607**	**$5,666**	**-14.2%**	**$6,742**	**$6,028**	**-10.6%**
FOOD AT HOME	**3,052**	**2,880**	**-5.6**	**3,849**	**3,382**	**-12.1**	**3,694**	**3,440**	**-6.9**
Cereals and bakery products	**452**	**453**	**0.2**	**583**	**540**	**-7.4**	**540**	**548**	**1.4**
Cereals and cereal products	158	161	1.6	209	197	-5.6	176	189	7.6
Bakery products	295	292	-0.9	375	344	-8.2	365	359	-1.6
Meats, poultry, fish, and eggs	**820**	**743**	**-9.4**	**984**	**865**	**-12.1**	**1,044**	**915**	**-12.3**
Beef	268	224	-16.3	322	264	-17.9	329	284	-13.7
Pork	162	157	-3.1	192	174	-9.2	221	193	-12.7
Other meats	122	96	-21.0	142	120	-15.8	160	111	-30.5
Poultry	133	145	9.3	155	174	12.5	167	172	3.0
Fish and seafood	101	89	-11.6	131	97	-26.2	125	117	-6.6
Eggs	37	33	-10.4	42	35	-16.2	43	38	-11.6
Dairy products	**362**	**314**	**-13.3**	**463**	**387**	**-16.4**	**424**	**359**	**-15.3**
Fresh milk and cream	172	128	-25.5	215	164	-23.7	199	138	-30.6
Other dairy products	190	186	-2.3	248	224	-9.7	226	221	-2.2

(continued)

(continued from previous page)

	total consumer units			aged 35 to 44			aged 45 to 54		
	1990	1997	percent change 1990–97	1990	1997	percent change 1990–97	1990	1997	percent change 1990–97
Fruits and vegetables	**$501**	**$476**	**–5.0%**	**$602**	**$525**	**–12.8%**	**$575**	**$558**	**–2.9%**
Fresh fruits	156	150	–3.8	173	161	–7.0	177	174	–1.6
Fresh vegetables	145	143	–1.3	178	151	–15.2	172	174	1.2
Processed fruits	114	102	–10.7	140	117	–16.4	128	117	–8.4
Processed vegetables	86	80	–6.9	109	95	–13.1	98	93	–5.3
Other food at home	**916**	**895**	**–2.3**	**1,217**	**1,066**	**–12.4**	**1,110**	**1,060**	**–4.5**
Sugar and other sweets	115	114	–1.2	152	130	–14.6	146	139	–4.9
Fats and oils	84	81	–3.0	108	88	–18.6	102	94	–7.8
Miscellaneous foods	413	403	–2.3	567	501	–11.7	484	462	–4.5
Nonalcoholic beverages	262	245	–6.3	336	294	–12.6	328	292	–10.9
Food prepared by household on trips	**43**	**52**	**21.0**	**53**	**52**	**–1.5**	**50**	**73**	**45.0**
FOOD AWAY FROM HOME	**2,224**	**1,921**	**–13.6**	**2,758**	**2,283**	**–17.2**	**3,048**	**2,588**	**–15.1**
ALCOHOLIC BEVERAGES	**360**	**309**	**–14.1**	**454**	**348**	**–23.4**	**398**	**358**	**–10.0**
HOUSING	**10,687**	**11,272**	**5.5**	**13,569**	**13,415**	**–1.1**	**12,802**	**13,892**	**8.5**
SHELTER	**5,939**	**6,344**	**6.8**	**7,622**	**7,864**	**3.2**	**7,143**	**7,829**	**9.6**
Owned dwellings	**3,626**	**3,935**	**8.5**	**5,310**	**5,244**	**–1.2**	**4,856**	**5,586**	**15.0**
Mortgage interest and charges	2,231	2,225	–0.3	3,783	3,448	–8.9	3,224	3,396	5.4
Property taxes	733	971	32.4	882	1,054	19.5	873	1,303	49.2
Maintenance, repairs, insurance, other	663	738	11.3	645	743	15.2	759	887	16.9
Rented dwellings	**1,883**	**1,983**	**5.3**	**1,880**	**2,234**	**18.8**	**1,499**	**1,515**	**1.0**

(continued)

(continued from previous page)

	total consumer units			aged 35 to 44			aged 45 to 54		
	1990	*1997*	*percent change 1990–97*	*1990*	*1997*	*percent change 1990–97*	*1990*	*1997*	*percent change 1990–97*
Other lodging	**$429**	**$426**	**–0.6%**	**$432**	**$386**	**–10.7%**	**$788**	**$729**	**–7.5%**
UTILITIES, FUELS, PUBLIC SERVICES	**2,321**	**2,412**	**3.9**	**2,644**	**2,694**	**1.9**	**2,894**	**2,890**	**–0.2**
Natural gas	302	301	–0.4	336	327	–2.8	376	321	–14.6
Electricity	931	909	–2.3	1,056	1,015	–3.9	1,163	1,114	–4.2
Fuel oil and other fuels	123	108	–12.1	134	108	–19.3	136	147	7.8
Telephone services	727	809	11.3	837	921	10.0	921	952	3.4
Water and other public services	237	286	20.7	281	323	14.9	300	357	19.1
HOUSEHOLD SERVICES	**548**	**548**	**0.1**	**749**	**724**	**–3.3**	**387**	**554**	**43.2**
Personal services	269	263	–2.2	435	450	3.5	66	146	120.2
Other household expenses	279	285	2.2	314	274	–12.8	321	409	27.6
HOUSEKEEPING SUPPLIES	**499**	**455**	**–8.7**	**607**	**524**	**–13.6**	**593**	**552**	**–6.9**
Laundry and cleaning supplies	139	116	–16.4	174	139	–20.3	168	137	–18.6
Other household products	210	210	0.0	268	249	–7.0	243	258	6.1
Postage and stationery	150	129	–13.9	163	136	–16.7	182	157	–13.6
HOUSEHOLD FURNISHINGS AND EQUIPMENT	**1,382**	**1,512**	**9.4**	**1,948**	**1,609**	**–17.4**	**1,784**	**2,066**	**15.8**
Household textiles	122	79	–35.0	152	80	–47.5	178	116	–34.9
Furniture	381	387	1.7	501	430	–14.2	459	515	12.1
Floor coverings	113	78	–31.0	188	57	–69.7	184	70	–62.0

(continued)

(continued from previous page)

	total consumer units			aged 35 to 44			aged 45 to 54		
	1990	1997	percent change 1990–97	1990	1997	percent change 1990–97	1990	1997	percent change 1990–97
Major appliances	$181	$169	–6.4%	$212	$181	–14.8%	$215	$193	–10.2%
Small appliances, misc. housewares	92	92	–0.1	108	97	–10.2	122	131	7.8
Miscellaneous household equipment	494	707	43.2	786	764	–2.8	624	1,041	66.9
APPAREL AND SERVICES	**1,987**	**1,729**	**–13.0**	**2,839**	**2,062**	**–27.4**	**2,660**	**2,107**	**–20.8**
Men and boys	**483**	**407**	**–15.7**	**690**	**496**	**–28.1**	**701**	**550**	**–21.6**
Men, 16 and over	398	323	–18.8	516	333	–35.4	618	457	–26.0
Boys, 2 to 15	86	84	–2.3	173	163	–5.9	84	93	11.4
Women and girls	**826**	**680**	**–17.7**	**1,205**	**793**	**–34.2**	**1,111**	**834**	**–25.0**
Women, 16 and over	720	574	–20.2	954	578	–39.4	1,017	719	–29.3
Girls, 2 to 15	107	106	–0.8	251	215	–14.2	95	115	21.6
Children under 2	**86**	**77**	**–10.4**	**85**	**90**	**6.2**	**71**	**51**	**–28.4**
Footwear	**276**	**315**	**14.0**	**426**	**390**	**–8.5**	**354**	**347**	**–1.9**
Other apparel products, services	**317**	**250**	**–21.1**	**433**	**293**	**–32.4**	**424**	**325**	**–23.3**
TRANSPORTATION	**6,287**	**6,457**	**2.7**	**7,465**	**7,254**	**–2.8**	**8,652**	**8,734**	**0.9**
Vehicle purchases	**2,614**	**2,736**	**4.7**	**3,098**	**3,038**	**–1.9**	**3,643**	**3,704**	**1.7**
Cars and trucks, new	1,423	1,229	–13.6	1,659	1,378	–16.9	2,054	1,808	–12.0
Cars and trucks, used	1,164	1,464	25.8	1,410	1,594	13.1	1,556	1,849	18.8
Other vehicles	27	43	59.2	31	67	118.2	33	47	41.8
Gasoline and motor oil	**1,286**	**1,098**	**–14.6**	**1,529**	**1,294**	**–15.4**	**1,708**	**1,430**	**–16.3**
Other vehicle expenses	**2,016**	**2,230**	**10.6**	**2,438**	**2,556**	**4.9**	**2,747**	**3,079**	**12.1**

(continued)

(continued from previous page)

	total consumer units			aged 35 to 44			aged 45 to 54		
	1990	1997	percent change 1990–97	1990	1997	percent change 1990–97	1990	1997	percent change 1990–97
Vehicle finance charges	$368	$293	–20.5%	$485	$349	–28.1%	$527	$388	–26.3%
Maintenance and repairs	**723**	**682**	**–5.7**	**850**	**788**	**–7.3**	**949**	**942**	**–0.8**
Vehicle insurance	**691**	**755**	**9.2**	**799**	**837**	**4.7**	**963**	**994**	**3.2**
Vehicle rental, leases, licenses, other	**233**	**501**	**114.7**	**303**	**582**	**91.9**	**308**	**755**	**144.9**
Public transportation	**371**	**393**	**6.0**	**400**	**365**	**–8.8**	**553**	**522**	**–5.5**
HEALTH CARE	**1,817**	**1,841**	**1.3**	**1,738**	**1,605**	**–7.6**	**1,961**	**1,945**	**–0.8**
Health insurance	713	881	23.5	596	748	25.6	716	845	18.0
Medical services	690	531	–23.1	793	547	–31.0	815	658	–19.3
Drugs	309	320	3.4	225	210	–6.6	290	303	4.6
Medical supplies	104	108	3.5	123	100	–18.6	139	139	0.2
ENTERTAINMENT	**1,746**	**1,813**	**3.8**	**2,256**	**2,129**	**–5.6**	**2,414**	**2,416**	**0.1**
Fees and admissions	456	471	3.4	647	574	–11.3	538	679	26.2
Television, radio, sound equipment	558	577	3.5	716	671	–6.3	727	683	–6.0
Pets, toys, playground equipment	339	327	–3.5	441	403	–8.6	503	395	–21.5
Other entertainment supplies, equipment, services	394	439	11.4	451	481	6.7	647	659	1.8
PERSONAL CARE PRODUCTS AND SERVICES	**447**	**528**	**18.1**	**549**	**586**	**6.8**	**587**	**637**	**8.5**
READING	**188**	**164**	**–12.7**	**231**	**160**	**–30.7**	**226**	**205**	**–9.3**

(continued)

(continued from previous page)

	total consumer units			aged 35 to 44			aged 45 to 54		
	1990	1997	percent change 1990–97	1990	1997	percent change 1990–97	1990	1997	percent change 1990–97
EDUCATION	**$499**	**$571**	**14.5%**	**$571**	**$604**	**5.8%**	**$899**	**$1,068**	**18.8%**
TOBACCO PRODUCTS AND SMOKING SUPPLIES	**336**	**264**	**–21.5**	**388**	**329**	**–15.2**	**443**	**312**	**–29.6**
MISCELLANEOUS	**1,034**	**847**	**–18.1**	**1,422**	**989**	**–30.5**	**1,347**	**1,106**	**–17.9**
Cash contributions	1,002	1,001	–0.1	1,076	945	–12.2	1,595	1,431	–10.3
Personal insurance and pensions	3,183	3,223	1.3	4,544	4,322	–4.9	4,724	4,998	5.8
Life and other personal insurance	424	379	–10.5	545	383	–29.8	682	604	–11.4
Pensions and Social Security	2,761	2,844	3.0	3,998	3,939	–1.5	4,043	4,394	8.7
PERSONAL TAXES	**3,625**	**3,241**	**–10.6**	**5,490**	**4,278**	**–22.1**	**4,998**	**4,863**	**–2.7**
Federal income taxes	2,848	2,468	–13.3	4,346	3,244	–25.4	3,931	3,757	–4.4
State and local income taxes	685	645	–5.9	1,014	897	–11.6	950	941	–1.0
Other taxes	92	129	40.1	130	137	5.2	117	164	40.6
GIFTS	**1,119**	**1,059**	**–5.3**	**1,102**	**910**	**–17.4**	**2,178**	**1,789**	**–17.9**
FOOD	**117**	**68**	**–41.7**	**112**	**74**	**–33.8**	**290**	**130**	**–55.1**
HOUSING	**285**	**273**	**–4.2**	**287**	**246**	**–14.4**	**521**	**426**	**–18.2**
HOUSEKEEPING SUPPLIES	**43**	**37**	**–13.9**	**50**	**46**	**–8.6**	**45**	**39**	**–14.2**
Household textiles	17	8	–53.5	16	6	–62.4	25	12	–51.1
Appliances and misc. housewares	33	27	–18.6	29	18	–38.9	48	42	–12.3
Major appliances	9	6	–30.2	9	3	–65.1	16	10	–37.4
Small appliances, misc. housewares	25	21	–14.5	21	15	–28.1	31	31	1.0

(continued)

(continued from previous page)

	total consumer units			aged 35 to 44			aged 45 to 54		
	1990	1997	percent change 1990–97	1990	1997	percent change 1990–97	1990	1997	percent change 1990–97
Misc. household equipment	$61	$66	7.5%	$79	$60	–23.7%	$85	$105	23.9%
Other housing	131	135	2.7	114	115	0.7	318	229	–28.0
APPAREL AND SERVICES	**290**	**252**	**–13.0**	**303**	**229**	**–24.5**	**447**	**379**	**–15.2**
Males, 2 and over	75	61	–18.6	70	44	–37.1	126	95	–24.9
Females, 2 and over	117	81	–30.6	144	83	–42.2	178	110	–38.2
Children under 2	38	33	–13.3	34	33	–4.0	56	39	–31.0
Other apparel products, services	**59**	**77**	**30.6**	**55**	**69**	**24.9**	**86**	**136**	**58.2**
Jewelry and watches	31	49	59.6	31	40	30.3	34	96	179.2
All other apparel products, services	28	29	2.7	25	29	18.1	53	40	–24.2
TRANSPORTATION	**65**	**57**	**–12.4**	**49**	**29**	**–41.0**	**168**	**84**	**–50.1**
HEALTH CARE	**55**	**30**	**–45.7**	**55**	**19**	**–65.6**	**104**	**48**	**–54.0**
ENTERTAINMENT	**81**	**99**	**22.1**	**72**	**84**	**15.9**	**122**	**147**	**20.9**
Toys, games, hobbies, tricycles	31	41	33.6	27	35	29.6	39	44	12.0
Other entertainment	50	58	15.2	45	49	7.8	82	103	25.2
EDUCATION	**118**	**155**	**31.5**	**92**	**101**	**9.7**	**411**	**446**	**8.4**
ALL OTHER GIFTS	**108**	**125**	**15.7**	**129**	**127**	**–1.5**	**115**	**129**	**11.8**

Note: The Bureau of Labor Statistics uses consumer units rather than households as the sampling unit in the Consumer Expenditure Survey. For the definition of consumer unit, see the Glossary. Spending on gifts is included in the preceding product and service categories.
Source: Bureau of Labor Statistics, 1990 and 1997 Consumer Expenditure Surveys; calculations by New Strategist

Householders Aged 35 to 44 Spend More Than the Average Household

Most households in the age group include children, which accounts for their above-average spending.

Households headed by people aged 35 to 44 spent 16 percent more than the average household, $40,413 versus $34,819 in 1997. Spending by these householders is particularly high for items commonly purchased by parents with children under age 18. Householders aged 35 to 44 spend 56 percent more than the average household on video games, 37 percent more on computer software, 31 percent more on toys and games, 25 percent more on ready-to-eat cereal, and 21 percent more on computer online services.

This age group spends less than the average household on some surprising items. Spending on postage, for example, is 19 percent below that of the average household (reflecting their preference for e-mailing over letter writing). The age group spends only an average amount on men's and women's clothes. It spends 7 percent less than average on new cars, and 19 percent less on contributions to charities.

◆ The spending of householders aged 35 to 44 reveals not only their lifestage needs but also the preferences of boomers for casual clothes, electronic communication, and sport utility vehicles.

Average and Indexed Spending of Householders Aged 35 to 44, 1997

(average annual spending of total consumer units and average annual and indexed spending of consumer units headed by 35-to-44-year-olds, 1997)

	average spending of total consumer units	consumer units headed by 35-to-44-year-olds	
		average spending	indexed spending*
Number of consumer units (in 000s)	105,576	24,560	–
Average before-tax income	$39,926.00	$48,788.00	122
Average annual spending	34,819.38	40,413.46	116
FOOD	**$4,801.35**	**$5,665.85**	**118**
FOOD AT HOME	2,880.00	3,382.48	117
Cereals and bakery products	**453.00**	**540.15**	**119**
Cereals and cereal products	161.39	196.61	122
Flour	8.79	9.43	107
Prepared flour mixes	15.04	19.05	127
Ready-to-eat and cooked cereals	91.15	114.00	125
Rice	18.37	19.05	104
Pasta, cornmeal, and other cereal products	28.03	35.07	125
Bakery products	291.60	343.54	118
Bread	83.43	89.66	107
White bread	40.89	45.92	112
Bread, other than white	42.55	43.74	103
Crackers and cookies	68.27	82.04	120
Cookies	45.01	55.15	123
Crackers	23.26	26.89	116
Frozen and refrigerated bakery products	23.35	29.40	126
Other bakery products	116.56	142.44	122
Biscuits and rolls	40.96	48.86	119
Cakes and cupcakes	34.51	47.73	138
Bread and cracker products	4.45	4.24	95
Sweetrolls, coffee cakes, doughnuts	23.13	26.44	114
Pies, tarts, turnovers	13.50	15.17	112
Meats, poultry, fish, and eggs	**743.12**	**864.74**	**116**
Beef	223.55	264.29	118
Ground beef	82.77	101.60	123

(continued)

	average spending of total consumer units	consumer units headed by 35-to-44-year-olds	
		average spending	indexed spending*
Roast	$40.48	$46.98	116
Chuck roast	13.02	14.17	109
Round roast	12.85	16.21	126
Other roast	14.61	16.60	114
Steak	87.48	101.23	116
Round steak	16.70	20.57	123
Sirloin steak	23.01	24.15	105
Other steak	47.76	56.50	118
Other beef	12.81	14.48	113
Pork	157.13	173.54	110
Bacon	25.42	27.36	108
Pork chops	39.23	48.05	122
Ham	37.28	43.33	116
Ham, not canned	35.12	41.24	117
Canned ham	2.16	2.09	97
Sausage	24.12	26.42	110
Other pork	31.07	28.38	91
Other meats	96.03	119.84	125
Frankfurters	22.83	29.95	131
Lunch meats (cold cuts)	65.55	80.68	123
Bologna, liverwurst, salami	23.82	27.11	114
Other lunch meats	41.73	53.57	128
Lamb, organ meats, and others	7.92	9.21	116
Lamb and organ meats	7.34	9.06	123
Mutton, goat, and game	0.58	0.15	26
Poultry	145.01	174.47	120
Fresh and frozen chickens	113.38	137.55	121
Fresh and frozen whole chickens	29.77	32.82	110
Fresh and frozen chicken parts	83.61	104.73	125
Other poultry	31.63	36.92	117
Fish and seafood	88.54	97.44	110
Canned fish and seafood	14.18	15.20	107
Fresh fish and shellfish	50.95	53.16	104
Frozen fish and shellfish	23.41	29.09	124
Eggs	32.59	35.17	108

(continued)

(continued from previous page)

	average spending of total consumer units	consumer units headed by 35-to-44-year-olds	
		average spending	indexed spending*
Dairy products	**$313.68**	**$387.33**	**123**
Fresh milk and cream	128.12	163.53	128
Fresh milk, all types	118.78	152.57	128
Cream	9.34	10.96	117
Other dairy products	185.56	223.79	121
Butter	14.63	15.76	108
Cheese	94.33	118.35	125
Ice cream and related products	52.91	63.18	119
Miscellaneous dairy products	23.69	26.50	112
Fruits and vegetables	**475.62**	**524.54**	**110**
Fresh fruits	150.47	161.39	107
Apples	28.47	33.84	119
Bananas	31.44	30.60	97
Oranges	17.62	17.88	101
Citrus fruits, excluding oranges	13.42	13.32	99
Other fresh fruits	59.52	65.75	110
Fresh vegetables	142.75	151.18	106
Potatoes	26.15	27.57	105
Lettuce	19.27	19.68	102
Tomatoes	23.87	24.30	102
Other fresh vegetables	73.46	79.63	108
Processed fruits	102.28	117.19	115
Frozen fruits and fruit juices	15.02	17.89	119
Frozen orange juice	8.44	9.63	114
Frozen fruits	2.02	2.01	100
Frozen fruit juices, excluding orange juice	4.57	6.25	137
Canned fruits	13.97	14.24	102
Dried fruits	6.03	6.35	105
Fresh fruit juice	19.82	24.20	122
Canned and bottled fruit juice	47.43	54.50	115
Processed vegetables	80.13	94.78	118
Frozen vegetables	26.57	33.80	127
Canned and dried vegetables and juices	53.56	60.98	114
Canned beans	11.79	13.81	117
Canned corn	7.26	8.67	119
Canned miscellaneous vegetables	16.80	17.81	106
Dried peas	0.23	0.54	235

(continued)

	average spending of total consumer units	consumer units headed by 35-to-44-year-olds	
		average spending	indexed spending*
Dried beans	2.58	3.51	136
Dried miscellaneous vegetables	7.18	7.59	106
Dried processed vegetables	0.22	0.50	227
Frozen vegetable juices	0.28	0.29	104
Fresh and canned vegetable juices	7.22	8.26	114
Other food at home	**894.58**	**1,065.72**	**119**
Sugar and other sweets	114.30	130.34	114
Candy and chewing gum	69.26	80.12	116
Sugar	18.93	20.54	109
Artificial sweeteners	3.48	2.94	84
Jams, preserves, other sweets	22.63	26.74	118
Fats and oils	81.05	87.97	109
Margarine	11.74	13.30	113
Fats and oils	24.50	25.59	104
Salad dressings	24.68	26.84	109
Nondairy cream and imitation milk	8.50	8.35	98
Peanut butter	11.63	13.89	119
Miscellaneous foods	403.06	500.74	124
Frozen prepared foods	77.61	100.07	129
Frozen meals	20.73	24.49	118
Other frozen prepared foods	56.88	75.58	133
Canned and packaged soups	32.87	37.51	114
Potato chips, nuts, and other snacks	84.53	112.75	133
Potato chips and other snacks	66.83	94.45	141
Nuts	17.70	18.30	103
Condiments and seasonings	86.12	102.21	119
Salt, spices, and other seasonings	19.07	22.92	120
Olives, pickles, relishes	10.54	13.00	123
Sauces and gravies	39.86	50.09	126
Baking needs and miscellaneous products	16.65	16.20	97
Other canned/packaged prepared foods	121.94	148.20	122
Prepared salads	15.05	16.97	113
Prepared desserts	9.95	11.57	116
Baby food	27.86	33.21	119
Miscellaneous prepared foods	68.44	86.41	126
Vitamin supplements	0.64	0.04	6

(continued)

(continued from previous page)

	average spending of total consumer units	consumer units headed by 35-to-44-year-olds	
		average spending	indexed spending*
Nonalcoholic beverages	$244.51	$294.29	120
Cola	90.51	113.88	126
Other carbonated drinks	42.94	53.55	125
Coffee	48.80	49.25	101
Roasted coffee	32.65	33.07	101
Instant and freeze-dried coffee	16.15	16.18	100
Noncarbonated fruit flavored drinks, including nonfrozen lemonade	19.22	26.73	139
Tea	14.76	14.34	97
Nonalcoholic beer	0.34	0.77	226
Other nonalcoholic beverages and ice	27.93	35.77	128
Food prepared by household on out-of-town trips	51.65	52.39	101
FOOD AWAY FROM HOME	**1,921.35**	**2,283.38**	**119**
Meals at restaurants, carry-outs, other	**1,477.51**	**1,848.95**	**125**
Lunch	501.92	658.91	131
Dinner	740.70	881.45	119
Snacks and nonalcoholic beverages	119.38	166.43	139
Breakfast and brunch	115.51	142.17	123
Board (including at school)	**51.88**	**43.86**	**85**
Catered affairs	**83.52**	**2.66**	**3**
Food on out-of-town trips	**223.90**	**222.60**	**99**
School lunches	**54.03**	**130.28**	**241**
Meals as pay	**30.51**	**35.01**	**115**
ALCOHOLIC BEVERAGES	**$309.22**	**$347.95**	**113**
At home	**180.13**	**205.81**	**114**
Beer and ale	90.92	110.11	121
Whiskey	13.40	18.42	137
Wine	55.32	56.83	103
Other alcoholic beverages	20.50	20.46	100
Away from home	**129.09**	**142.13**	**110**
Beer and ale	39.50	44.04	111
Wine	24.30	27.32	112
Other alcoholic beverages	32.81	40.38	123
Alcoholic beverages purchased on trips	32.48	30.39	94

(continued)

(continued from previous page)

	average spending of total consumer units	consumer units headed by 35-to-44-year-olds	
		average spending	indexed spending*
HOUSING	**$11,272.04**	**$13,414.61**	**119**
SHELTER	**6,343.87**	**7,863.64**	**124**
Owned dwellings**	**3,934.87**	**5,243.95**	**133**
Mortgage interest and charges	2,225.26	3,447.83	155
Mortgage interest	2,109.06	3,291.39	156
Interest paid, home equity loan	57.21	84.15	147
Interest paid, home equity line of credit	58.84	72.07	122
Prepayment penalty charges	0.16	0.21	131
Property taxes	971.15	1,053.52	108
Maintenance, repairs, insurance, other expenses	738.46	742.60	101
Homeowner's and related insurance	230.91	229.49	99
Fire and extended coverage	8.02	9.47	118
Homeowner's insurance	222.88	220.02	99
Ground rent	37.16	27.12	73
Maintenance and repair services	365.61	357.04	98
Painting and papering	45.31	50.06	110
Plumbing and water heating	36.61	25.58	70
Heat, air conditioning, electrical work	63.28	58.95	93
Roofing and gutters	72.99	70.76	97
Other repair and maintenance services	124.47	129.90	104
Repair/replacement of hard surface flooring	21.17	20.14	95
Repair of built-in appliances	1.79	1.64	92
Maintenance and repair materials	83.91	114.86	137
Paints, wallpaper, and supplies	18.33	23.99	131
Tools/equipment for painting, wallpapering	1.97	2.58	131
Plumbing supplies and equipment	6.87	6.14	89
Electrical supplies, heating/cooling equipment	4.55	7.38	162
Hard surface flooring, repair and replacement	7.13	9.16	128
Roofing and gutters	7.77	14.81	191
Plaster, paneling, siding, windows, doors, screens, awnings	14.97	16.55	111
Patio, walk, fence, driveway, masonry, brick, and stucco work	0.92	0.61	66
Landscape maintenance	5.19	7.59	146
Miscellaneous supplies and equipment	16.21	26.05	161
Insulation, other maintenance/repair	9.22	12.08	131

(continued)

(continued from previous page)

	average spending of total consumer units	consumer units headed by 35-to-44-year-olds	
		average spending	indexed spending*
Finish basement, remodel rooms, build patios, walks, etc.	$6.99	$13.97	200
Property management and security	19.58	13.54	69
Property management	16.49	11.80	72
Management and upkeep services for security	3.09	1.74	56
Parking	1.30	0.56	43
Rented dwellings	**1,983.18**	**2,233.86**	**113**
Rent	1,876.81	2,103.55	112
Rent as pay	72.36	86.16	119
Maintenance, insurance, and other expenses	34.02	44.15	130
Tenant's insurance	9.76	8.17	84
Maintenance and repair services	16.62	29.09	175
Repair or maintenance services	15.42	28.98	188
Repair and replacement of hard surface flooring	1.17	0.10	9
Repair of built-in appliances	0.03	–	–
Maintenance and repair materials	7.63	6.89	90
Paint, wallpaper, and supplies	1.57	1.46	93
Painting and wallpapering	0.17	0.16	94
Plastering, paneling, roofing, gutters, etc.	1.22	0.63	52
Patio, walk, fence, driveway, masonry, brick, and stucco work	0.02	0.00	0
Plumbing supplies and equipment	0.36	0.53	147
Electrical supplies, heating and cooling equipment	0.08	0.26	325
Miscellaneous supplies and equipment	2.94	3.02	103
Insulation, other maintenance and repair	1.04	1.27	122
Materials for additions, finishing basements, remodeling rooms	1.65	1.69	102
Construction materials for jobs not started	0.25	0.06	24
Hard surface flooring	0.74	0.23	31
Landscape maintenance	0.53	0.59	111
Other lodging	**425.82**	**385.83**	**91**
Owned vacation homes	133.69	105.91	79
Mortgage interest and charges	58.02	63.41	109
Mortgage interest	56.46	63.17	112
Interest paid, home equity loan	0.66	0.25	38
Interest paid, home equity line of credit	0.89	–	–

(continued)

(continued from previous page)

	average spending of total consumer units	consumer units headed by 35-to-44-year-olds	
		average spending	indexed spending*
Property taxes	$54.83	$34.89	64
Maintenance, insurance, and other expenses	20.84	7.60	36
Homeowner's and related insurance	5.03	2.23	44
Homeowner's insurance	4.67	1.60	34
Fire and extended coverage	0.36	0.64	178
Ground rent	1.63	0.05	3
Maintenance and repair services	9.66	2.19	23
Maintenance and repair materials	0.81	1.37	169
Property management and security	3.41	1.64	48
Property management	2.96	1.58	53
Management and upkeep services for security	0.45	0.06	13
Parking	0.29	0.13	45
Housing while attending school	66.35	42.03	63
Lodging on out-of-town trips	225.77	237.89	105
UTILITIES, FUELS & PUBLIC SERVICES	**2,412.30**	**2,694.15**	**112**
Natural gas	**300.96**	**326.66**	**109**
Natural gas (renter)	60.81	84.62	139
Natural gas (owner)	238.55	240.87	101
Natural gas (vacation)	1.60	1.17	73
Electricity	**908.67**	**1,014.56**	**112**
Electricity (renter)	212.54	265.16	125
Electricity (owner)	687.53	741.84	108
Electricity (vacation)	8.60	7.56	88
Fuel oil and other fuels	**107.72**	**108.35**	**101**
Fuel oil	55.18	48.88	89
Fuel oil (renter)	4.92	7.81	159
Fuel oil (owner)	49.77	40.26	81
Fuel oil (vacation)	0.49	0.82	167
Coal	0.99	2.57	260
Coal (renter)	0.02	0.08	400
Coal (owner)	0.97	2.49	257
Bottled/tank gas	43.84	48.77	111
Gas (renter)	4.66	6.98	150
Gas (owner)	36.37	39.04	107
Gas (vacation)	2.81	2.74	98

(continued)

(continued from previous page)

	average spending of total consumer units	consumer units headed by 35-to-44-year-olds	
		average spending	indexed spending*
Wood and other fuels	$7.72	$8.13	105
Wood and other fuels (renter)	1.53	1.52	99
Wood and other fuels (owner)	5.80	6.55	113
Wood and other fuels (vacation)	0.39	0.06	15
Telephone services	**809.05**	**921.33**	**114**
Telephone services in home city, excluding mobile car phones	756.44	856.35	113
Telephone services for mobile car phones	52.61	64.98	124
Water and other public services	**285.90**	**323.25**	**113**
Water and sewerage maintenance	207.28	237.82	115
Water and sewerage maintenance (renter)	28.28	41.25	146
Water and sewerage maintenance (owner)	176.95	194.77	110
Water and sewerage maintenance (vacation)	2.06	1.80	87
Trash and garbage collection	76.00	81.47	107
Trash and garbage collection (renter)	8.78	12.50	142
Trash and garbage collection (owner)	65.66	67.85	103
Trash and garbage collection (vacation)	1.56	1.13	72
Septic tank cleaning	2.62	3.95	151
Septic tank cleaning (renter)	0.19	0.14	74
Septic tank cleaning (owner)	2.41	3.82	159
HOUSEHOLD OPERATIONS	**548.50**	**723.73**	**132**
Personal services	**263.10**	**449.78**	**171**
Baby-sitting and child care in your own home	34.39	79.36	231
Baby-sitting and child care in someone else's home	37.37	55.40	148
Care for elderly, invalids, handicapped, etc.	26.95	9.45	35
Adult day care centers	3.79	2.99	79
Day care centers, nurseries, and preschools	160.60	302.58	188
Other household expenses	**285.40**	**273.95**	**96**
Housekeeping services	75.34	76.38	101
Gardening, lawn care services	72.44	50.56	70
Water softening services	4.51	4.67	104
Nonclothing laundry and dry cleaning, sent out	10.20	11.39	112
Nonclothing laundry and dry cleaning, coin-operated	4.91	5.24	107
Termite/pest control services	11.55	16.00	139
Other home services	15.94	13.52	85
Termite/pest control products	0.12	0.10	83

(continued)

	average spending of total consumer units	consumer units headed by 35-to-44-year-olds	
		average spending	indexed spending*
Moving, storage, and freight express	$34.75	$42.19	121
Appliance repair, including service center	13.50	12.51	93
Reupholstering and furniture repair	10.87	8.03	74
Repairs/rentals of lawn/garden equipment, hand/power tools, etc.	5.13	4.53	88
Appliance rental	1.05	1.16	110
Rental of office equipment for nonbusiness use	0.43	0.09	21
Repair of miscellaneous household equipment and furnishings	1.53	0.11	7
Repair of computer systems for nonbusiness use	2.47	2.45	99
Computer information services	20.65	25.01	121
HOUSEKEEPING SUPPLIES	**454.93**	**523.62**	**115**
Laundry and cleaning supplies	**115.85**	**138.58**	**120**
Soaps and detergents	65.05	81.34	125
Other laundry cleaning products	50.80	57.24	113
Other household products	**210.07**	**249.06**	**119**
Cleansing and toilet tissue, paper towels, and napkins	64.42	76.90	119
Miscellaneous household products	89.90	117.18	130
Lawn and garden supplies	55.74	54.98	99
Postage and stationery	**129.01**	**135.98**	**105**
Stationery, stationery supplies, giftwrap	62.61	82.64	132
Postage	62.53	50.79	81
Delivery services	3.88	2.55	66
HOUSEHOLD FURNISHINGS & EQUIPMENT	**1,512.44**	**1,609.47**	**106**
Household textiles	**79.12**	**79.76**	**101**
Bathroom linens	11.13	12.10	109
Bedroom linens	34.28	35.09	102
Kitchen and dining room linens	2.40	2.39	100
Curtains and draperies	16.73	17.01	102
Slipcovers and decorative pillows	2.10	2.05	98
Sewing materials for household items	11.20	9.69	87
Other linens	1.28	1.43	112
Furniture	**387.34**	**430.19**	**111**
Mattresses and springs	46.56	48.26	104
Other bedroom furniture	63.99	84.12	131

(continued)

(continued from previous page)

	average spending of total consumer units	consumer units headed by 35-to-44-year-olds	
		average spending	indexed spending*
Sofas	$93.81	$108.04	115
Living room chairs	47.42	42.02	89
Living room tables	20.60	29.02	141
Kitchen and dining room furniture	48.69	43.19	89
Infants' furniture	9.87	6.50	66
Outdoor furniture	13.61	16.82	124
Wall units, cabinets, and other furniture	42.81	52.23	122
Floor coverings	**77.74**	**57.26**	**74**
Wall-to-wall carpeting	38.82	43.57	112
Wall-to-wall carpeting (renter)	1.94	2.98	154
Wall-to-wall carpeting, installed	1.37	1.95	142
Wall-to-wall carpeting, not installed carpet squares	0.56	1.03	184
Wall-to-wall carpeting, replacement (owner)	36.88	40.59	110
Wall-to-wall carpeting, not installed carpet squares	2.68	0.62	23
Wall-to-wall carpeting, installed	34.20	39.97	117
Room-size rugs and other floor covering, nonpermanent	38.93	13.69	35
Major appliances	**169.18**	**181.31**	**107**
Dishwashers (built-in), garbage disposals, range hoods (renter)	0.82	0.79	96
Dishwashers (built-in), garbage disposals, range hoods (owner)	11.65	9.90	85
Refrigerators and freezers (renter)	9.52	9.85	103
Refrigerators and freezers (owner)	48.08	53.62	112
Washing machines (renter)	5.46	8.88	163
Washing machines (owner)	17.56	19.39	110
Clothes dryers (renter)	4.40	6.86	156
Clothes dryers (owner)	11.82	13.73	116
Cooking stoves, ovens (renter)	2.83	5.08	180
Cooking stoves, ovens (owner)	19.23	17.91	93
Microwave ovens (renter)	2.96	2.50	84
Microwave ovens (owner)	6.63	7.13	108
Portable dishwashers (renter)	0.41	0.42	102
Portable dishwashers (owner)	0.26	0.61	235
Window air conditioners (renter)	1.69	3.50	207
Window air conditioners (owner)	3.24	3.69	114

(continued)

(continued from previous page)

	average spending of total consumer units	consumer units headed by 35-to-44-year-olds	
		average spending	indexed spending*
Electric floor cleaning equipment	$15.68	$13.31	85
Sewing machines	3.55	2.11	59
Miscellaneous household appliances	**3.39**	**2.01**	**59**
Small appliances and miscellaneous housewares	91.91	96.98	106
Housewares	66.12	75.41	114
Plastic dinnerware	1.75	2.17	124
China and other dinnerware	8.86	13.73	155
Flatware	4.68	4.24	91
Glassware	8.25	5.66	69
Silver serving pieces	2.31	1.58	68
Other serving pieces	1.74	1.98	114
Nonelectric cookware	15.05	10.28	68
Tableware, nonelectric kitchenware	23.48	35.77	152
Small appliances	25.79	21.57	84
Small electric kitchen appliances	16.67	15.57	93
Portable heating and cooling equipment	9.12	6.00	66
Miscellaneous household equipment	**707.15**	**763.97**	**108**
Window coverings	13.71	10.30	75
Infants' equipment	7.05	6.70	95
Laundry and cleaning equipment	13.70	15.79	115
Outdoor equipment	18.42	12.58	68
Clocks	4.51	5.22	116
Lamps and lighting fixtures	12.53	15.43	123
Other household decorative items	134.12	127.85	95
Telephones and accessories	96.54	105.33	109
Lawn and garden equipment	39.37	42.12	107
Power tools	16.31	27.76	170
Office furniture for home use	10.61	10.88	103
Hand tools	9.29	11.69	126
Indoor plants and fresh flowers	52.33	52.73	101
Closet and storage items	8.94	10.62	119
Rental of furniture	3.41	4.44	130
Luggage	9.72	10.12	104
Computers and computer hardware, nonbusiness use	162.66	191.32	118
Computer software and accessories, nonbusiness use	24.72	33.88	137
Telephone answering devices	3.31	3.88	117

(continued)

(continued from previous page)

	average spending of total consumer units	consumer units headed by 35-to-44-year-olds	
		average spending	indexed spending*
Calculators	$1.92	$3.30	172
Business equipment for home use	2.33	3.51	151
Other hardware	23.27	20.05	86
Smoke alarms (owner)	0.86	0.97	113
Smoke alarms (renter)	0.19	0.11	58
Other household appliances (owner)	8.78	11.37	129
Other household appliances (renter)	1.47	1.42	97
Miscellaneous household equipment and parts	27.10	24.59	91
APPAREL AND SERVICES	**$1,729.06**	**$2,061.83**	**119**
Men's apparel	**322.98**	**332.61**	**103**
Suits	35.18	36.50	104
Sportcoats and tailored jackets	15.19	13.57	89
Coats and jackets	29.80	32.74	110
Underwear	12.52	10.33	83
Hosiery	9.91	11.87	120
Nightwear	2.93	1.58	54
Accessories	30.27	25.99	86
Sweaters and vests	15.84	15.86	100
Active sportswear	12.24	17.43	142
Shirts	75.81	77.50	102
Pants	64.52	69.70	108
Shorts and shorts sets	13.76	14.60	106
Uniforms	2.25	1.03	46
Costumes	2.79	3.91	140
Boys' (aged 2 to 15) apparel	**83.88**	**163.40**	**195**
Coats and jackets	8.33	15.48	186
Sweaters	2.81	4.45	158
Shirts	18.34	37.53	205
Underwear	3.08	6.00	195
Nightwear	1.94	4.19	216
Hosiery	3.66	5.72	156
Accessories	3.94	8.92	226
Suits, sportcoats, and vests	2.89	4.93	171
Pants	21.85	43.95	201
Shorts and shorts sets	8.66	16.11	186
Uniforms	4.41	7.82	177

(continued)

	average spending of total consumer units	consumer units headed by 35-to-44-year-olds	
		average spending	indexed spending*
Active sportswear	$2.65	$6.03	228
Costumes	1.33	2.26	170
Women's apparel	**574.26**	**578.03**	**101**
Coats and jackets	44.33	41.01	93
Dresses	84.25	96.29	114
Sportcoats and tailored jackets	2.77	1.35	49
Sweaters and vests	40.39	47.33	117
Shirts, blouses, and tops	93.73	82.76	88
Skirts	18.35	17.80	97
Pants	70.48	64.09	91
Shorts and shorts sets	22.34	16.60	74
Active sportswear	29.74	42.58	143
Nightwear	24.73	27.05	109
Undergarments	29.71	31.32	105
Hosiery	22.88	25.45	111
Suits	38.30	30.60	80
Accessories	45.42	40.49	89
Uniforms	3.20	9.39	293
Costumes	3.64	3.93	108
Girls' (aged 2 to 15) apparel	**106.01**	**214.71**	**203**
Coats and jackets	6.50	11.26	173
Dresses and suits	13.42	23.83	178
Shirts, blouses, and sweaters	25.74	58.08	226
Skirts and pants	19.49	40.93	210
Shorts and shorts sets	9.67	17.54	181
Active sportswear	6.86	15.08	220
Underwear and nightwear	6.75	13.27	197
Hosiery	5.29	9.48	179
Accessories	5.64	11.79	209
Uniforms	3.17	6.90	218
Costumes	3.48	6.55	188
Children under age 2	**77.05**	**90.00**	**117**
Coats, jackets, and snowsuits	3.28	3.53	108
Outerwear including dresses	15.01	16.06	107
Underwear	43.93	54.31	124
Nightwear and loungewear	4.38	4.46	102
Accessories	10.45	11.64	111

(continued)

(continued from previous page)

	average spending of total consumer units	consumer units headed by 35-to-44-year-olds	
		average spending	indexed spending*
Footwear	**$314.52**	**$390.13**	**124**
Men's	100.43	121.33	121
Boys'	27.90	49.32	177
Women's	157.11	156.94	100
Girls'	29.08	62.53	215
Other apparel products and services	**250.35**	**292.95**	**117**
Material for making clothes	4.07	3.73	92
Sewing patterns and notions	4.82	6.49	135
Watches	29.70	54.58	184
Jewelry	142.02	150.84	106
Shoe repair and other shoe services	2.38	2.13	89
Coin-operated apparel laundry and dry cleaning	20.79	24.07	116
Apparel alteration, repair, and tailoring services	6.10	4.83	79
Clothing rental	3.85	5.31	138
Watch and jewelry repair	5.08	5.63	111
Professional laundry, dry cleaning	31.24	35.18	113
Clothing storage	0.30	0.16	53
TRANSPORTATION	**$6,456.86**	**$7,253.68**	**112**
VEHICLE PURCHASES	**2,735.76**	**3,038.45**	**111**
Cars and trucks, new	**1,228.89**	**1,377.87**	**112**
New cars	700.22	653.04	93
New trucks	528.67	724.82	137
Cars and trucks, used	**1,463.52**	**1,594.01**	**109**
Used cars	895.31	881.13	98
Used trucks	568.22	712.88	125
Other vehicles	**43.35**	**66.57**	**154**
New motorcycles	26.39	41.56	157
Used motorcycles	15.32	19.66	128
GASOLINE AND MOTOR OIL	**1,097.52**	**1,294.35**	**118**
Gasoline	985.31	1,176.02	119
Diesel fuel	10.10	8.50	84
Gasoline on out-of-town trips	89.11	92.56	104
Motor oil	12.10	16.34	135
Motor oil on out-of-town trips	0.90	0.93	103

(continued)

(continued from previous page)

	average spending of total consumer units	consumer units headed by 35-to-44-year-olds	
		average spending	indexed spending*
OTHER VEHICLE EXPENSES	**$2,230.41**	**$2,556.18**	**115**
Vehicle finance charges	**292.81**	**349.36**	**119**
Automobile finance charges	161.70	179.63	111
Truck finance charges	116.10	151.93	131
Motorcycle and plane finance charges	1.52	2.89	190
Other vehicle finance charges	13.49	14.91	111
Maintenance and repairs	**681.62**	**788.13**	**116**
Coolant, additives, brake, transmission fluids	5.70	7.04	124
Tires	87.94	108.28	123
Parts, equipment, and accessories	51.31	63.72	124
Vehicle audio equipment	2.00	6.89	345
Vehicle products	6.95	11.88	171
Miscellaneous auto repair, servicing	51.74	71.15	138
Body work and painting	32.29	29.33	91
Clutch, transmission repair	47.92	58.63	122
Drive shaft and rear-end repair	5.73	4.88	85
Brake work	55.82	57.79	104
Repair to steering or front-end	17.41	23.61	136
Repair to engine cooling system	19.98	23.29	117
Motor tune-up	45.05	55.26	123
Lube, oil change, and oil filters	54.29	53.80	99
Front-end alignment, wheel balance, rotation	12.13	13.25	109
Shock absorber replacement	4.98	4.71	95
Gas tank repair, replacement	1.20	2.79	233
Tire repair and other repair work	29.63	32.66	110
Vehicle air conditioning repair	19.07	17.40	91
Exhaust system repair	18.52	21.52	116
Electrical system repair	29.34	28.79	98
Motor repair, replacement	75.45	85.91	114
Auto repair service policy	7.16	5.55	78
Vehicle insurance	**754.99**	**836.91**	**111**
Vehicle rental, leases, licenses, other charges	**500.99**	**581.78**	**116**
Leased and rented vehicles	331.25	385.87	116
Rented vehicles	41.03	42.76	104
Auto rental	7.73	7.76	100
Auto rental, out-of-town trips	26.78	28.46	106

(continued)

(continued from previous page)

	average spending of total consumer units	consumer units headed by 35-to-44-year-olds	
		average spending	indexed spending*
Truck rental	$1.85	$2.08	112
Truck rental, out-of-town trips	4.29	4.21	98
Leased vehicles	290.22	343.11	118
Car lease payments	162.28	171.51	106
Cash downpayment (car lease)	16.16	6.56	41
Termination fee (car lease)	1.81	1.74	96
Truck lease payments	98.37	148.38	151
Cash downpayment (truck lease)	10.63	14.60	137
Termination fee (truck lease)	0.97	0.32	33
State and local registration	94.62	103.56	109
Driver's license	7.42	8.50	115
Vehicle inspection	8.74	9.72	111
Parking fees	28.20	32.36	115
Parking fees in home city, excluding residence	24.37	28.61	117
Parking fees, out-of-town trips	3.83	3.76	98
Tolls	13.19	23.41	177
Tolls on out-of-town trips	4.32	4.31	100
Towing charges	5.04	6.29	125
Automobile service clubs	8.19	7.75	95
PUBLIC TRANSPORTATION	**393.16**	**364.71**	**93**
Airline fares	248.82	240.65	97
Intercity bus fares	10.51	9.16	87
Intracity mass transit fares	55.77	56.95	102
Local transportation on out-of-town trips	12.61	12.37	98
Taxi fares and limousine service on trips	7.40	7.27	98
Taxi fares and limousine service	9.51	10.21	107
Intercity train fares	21.19	13.64	64
Ship fares	26.40	12.12	46
School bus	0.95	2.33	245
HEALTH CARE	**$1,840.71**	**$1,605.01**	**87**
HEALTH INSURANCE	**881.28**	**748.39**	**85**
Commercial health insurance	**203.37**	**207.78**	**102**
Traditional fee-for-service health plan (not BCBS)	100.09	97.16	97
Preferred provider health plan (not BCBS)	103.29	110.62	107
Blue Cross, Blue Shield	**192.51**	**178.58**	**93**
Traditional fee-for-service health plan	62.93	44.20	70

(continued)

(continued from previous page)

	average spending of total consumer units	consumer units headed by 35-to-44-year-olds	
		average spending	indexed spending*
Preferred provider health plan	$46.45	$64.49	139
Health maintenance organization	47.39	66.00	139
Commercial Medicare supplement	31.92	0.47	1
Other BCBS health insurance	3.82	3.43	90
Health maintenance plans (HMOs)	**229.07**	**300.72**	**131**
Medicare payments	**160.92**	**22.46**	**14**
Commercial Medicare supplements/			
other health insurance	**95.40**	**38.84**	**41**
Commercial Medicare supplement (not BCBS)	60.66	9.08	15
Other health insurance (not BCBS)	34.74	29.76	86
MEDICAL SERVICES	**531.04**	**546.91**	**103**
Physician's services	133.59	150.05	112
Dental services	203.56	225.91	111
Eye care services	27.14	24.01	88
Service by professionals other than physician	37.03	50.13	135
Lab tests, X-rays	22.93	20.16	88
Hospital room	35.07	34.51	98
Hospital services other than room	52.37	32.98	63
Care in convalescent or nursing home	13.09	2.18	17
Repair of medical equipment	0.62	–	–
Other medical services	5.64	6.97	124
DRUGS	**320.44**	**210.09**	**66**
Nonprescription drugs	75.43	66.55	88
Nonprescription vitamins	28.43	25.88	91
Prescription drugs	216.58	117.65	54
MEDICAL SUPPLIES	**107.95**	**99.63**	**92**
Eyeglasses and contact lenses	59.73	58.33	98
Hearing aids	11.42	5.44	48
Topicals and dressings	29.47	32.24	109
Medical equipment for general use	2.43	1.38	57
Supportive/convalescent medical equipment	2.62	1.20	46
Rental of medical equipment	0.60	–0.24	–40
Rental of supportive, convalescent medical equipment	1.67	1.27	76
ENTERTAINMENT	**$1,813.28**	**$2,129.11**	**117**
FEES AND ADMISSIONS	**470.74**	**573.83**	**122**

(continued)

(continued from previous page)

	average spending of total consumer units	consumer units headed by 35-to-44-year-olds	
		average spending	indexed spending*
Recreation expenses, out-of-town trips	$24.70	$24.91	101
Social, recreation, civic club membership	75.12	69.41	92
Fees for participant sports	72.62	77.89	107
Participant sports, out-of-town trips	30.30	37.54	124
Movie, theater, opera, ballet	86.71	98.19	113
Movie, other admissions, out-of-town trips	41.93	47.78	114
Admission to sports events	33.51	46.85	140
Admission to sports events, out-of-town trips	13.98	15.92	114
Fees for recreational lessons	67.17	130.42	194
Other entertainment services, out-of-town trips	24.70	24.91	101
TELEVISION, RADIO, SOUND EQUIPMENT	**577.33**	**671.45**	**116**
Television	**403.51**	**443.51**	**110**
Community antenna or cable TV	262.34	279.52	107
Black and white TV sets	0.67	1.08	161
Color TV, console	25.17	30.50	121
Color TV, portable/table model	39.96	42.24	106
VCRs and video disc players	26.58	26.76	101
Video cassettes, tapes, and discs	22.15	25.71	116
Video game hardware and software	19.74	30.76	156
Repair of TV, radio, and sound equipment	6.65	6.81	102
Rental of television sets	0.24	0.14	58
Radios and sound equipment	**173.81**	**227.94**	**131**
Radios	11.76	5.40	46
Tape recorders and players	6.57	9.95	151
Sound components and component systems	29.86	38.83	130
Miscellaneous sound equipment	0.63	0.66	105
Sound equipment accessories	5.23	4.68	89
Satellite dishes	3.41	4.83	142
Compact disc, tape, record, video mail order clubs	10.59	11.19	106
Records, CDs, audio tapes, needles	39.41	50.54	128
Rental of VCR, radio, sound equipment	0.45	0.59	131
Musical instruments and accessories	23.96	39.46	165
Rental and repair of musical instruments	1.64	3.94	240
Rental of video cassettes, tapes, discs, films	40.30	57.87	144
PETS, TOYS, PLAYGROUND EQUIPMENT	**326.53**	**402.62**	**123**
Pets	**198.03**	**235.01**	**119**

(continued)

(continued from previous page)

	average spending of total consumer units	consumer units headed by 35-to-44-year-olds	
		average spending	indexed spending*
Pet food	$87.23	$97.85	112
Pet purchase, supplies, and medicines	40.15	58.86	147
Pet services	17.17	18.29	107
Veterinary services	53.49	60.01	112
Toys, games, hobbies, and tricycles	**127.68**	**167.61**	**131**
Playground equipment	**0.82**	–	–
OTHER ENTERTAINMENT SUPPLIES, EQUIPMENT, SERVICES	**438.68**	**481.22**	**110**
Unmotored recreational vehicles	**37.97**	**9.13**	**24**
Boats without motor and boat trailers	8.48	2.81	33
Trailers and other attachable campers	29.49	6.31	21
Motorized recreational vehicles	**145.96**	**128.91**	**88**
Motorized campers	26.17	9.84	38
Other vehicles	10.62	17.01	160
Motor boats	109.17	102.07	93
Rental of recreational vehicles	**3.35**	**1.79**	**53**
Outboard motors	**3.27**	**4.39**	**134**
Docking and landing fees	**9.52**	**5.04**	**53**
Sports, recreation, exercise equipment	**128.96**	**186.99**	**145**
Athletic gear, game tables, exercise equipment	60.02	89.60	149
Bicycles	15.27	24.44	160
Camping equipment	9.34	13.86	148
Hunting and fishing equipment	16.11	20.00	124
Winter sports equipment	5.50	10.25	186
Water sports equipment	4.52	7.87	174
Other sports equipment	16.29	19.27	118
Rental and repair of miscellaneous sports equipment	1.91	1.69	88
Photographic equipment and supplies	**89.92**	**119.12**	**132**
Film	21.36	28.47	133
Other photographic supplies	1.07	0.40	37
Film processing	29.36	37.19	127
Repair and rental of photographic equipment	0.49	1.02	208
Photographic equipment	14.19	21.52	152
Photographer fees	23.45	30.51	130
Fireworks	**3.98**	**4.39**	**110**

(continued)

(continued from previous page)

	average spending of total consumer units	consumer units headed by 35-to-44-year-olds	
		average spending	indexed spending*
Souvenirs	$0.74	$1.49	201
Visual goods	3.15	3.14	100
Pinball, electronic video games	11.85	16.83	142

PERSONAL CARE PRODUCTS AND SERVICES

PERSONAL CARE PRODUCTS AND SERVICES	**$527.62**	**$586.32**	**111**
Personal care products	**241.86**	**288.04**	**119**
Hair care products	51.00	65.04	128
Hair accessories	6.89	9.08	132
Wigs and hairpieces	1.22	0.85	70
Oral hygiene products	26.96	33.38	124
Shaving products	11.45	12.94	113
Cosmetics, perfume, and bath products	109.99	123.63	112
Deodorants, feminine hygiene, miscellaneous products	29.80	37.87	127
Electric personal care appliances	4.56	5.26	115
Personal care services	**285.76**	**298.28**	**104**
Personal care services (female)	188.30	184.46	98
Personal care services (male)	97.25	113.67	117
Repair of personal care appliances	0.20	0.14	70

READING

READING	**$163.58**	**$159.88**	**98**
Newspaper subscriptions	51.70	41.03	79
Newspaper, nonsubscriptions	17.18	18.20	106
Magazine subscriptions	22.62	20.76	92
Magazines, nonsubscriptions	11.55	13.41	116
Books purchased through book clubs	10.18	8.67	85
Books not purchased through book clubs	49.50	57.22	116
Encyclopedia and other reference book sets	0.85	0.60	71

EDUCATION

EDUCATION	**$570.70**	**$604.14**	**106**
College tuition	326.09	239.60	73
Elementary/high school tuition	90.14	175.15	194
Other school tuition	19.26	21.75	113
Other school expenses including rentals	27.44	46.94	171
Books, supplies for college	47.87	27.27	57
Books, supplies for elementary, high school	12.22	27.15	222
Books, supplies for day care, nursery school	3.13	6.59	211
Miscellaneous school expenses and supplies	44.55	59.68	134

(continued)

(continued from previous page)

	average spending of total consumer units	consumer units headed by 35-to-44-year-olds	
		average spending	indexed spending*
TOBACCO PRODUCTS AND SMOKING SUPPLIES	**$263.69**	**$329.06**	**125**
Cigarettes	232.31	298.85	129
Other tobacco products	28.78	28.06	97
Smoking accessories	2.60	2.15	83
FINANCIAL PRODUCTS AND SERVICES	**$847.31**	**$988.96**	**117**
Miscellaneous fees, gambling losses	53.32	31.02	58
Legal fees	135.79	188.48	139
Funeral expenses	63.05	40.98	65
Safe deposit box rental	6.69	5.24	78
Checking accounts, other bank service charges	24.51	32.40	132
Cemetery lots, vaults, and maintenance fees	19.65	12.01	61
Accounting fees	48.99	52.61	107
Miscellaneous personal services	39.17	62.30	159
Finance charges, except mortgage and vehicles	249.40	323.98	130
Occupational expenses	102.65	131.14	128
Expenses for other properties	99.61	104.60	105
Interest paid, home equity line of credit (other property)	0.49	–	–
Credit card memberships	3.98	4.20	106
CASH CONTRIBUTIONS	**$1,000.90**	**$944.75**	**94**
Cash contributions to nonhousehold members, including students, alimony, child support	253.98	326.86	129
Gifts of cash, stocks, bonds to nonhousehold members	225.03	112.03	50
Contributions to charities	101.95	82.80	81
Contributions to religious organizations	390.25	396.82	102
Contributions to educational organizations	16.88	14.67	87
Political contributions	6.20	5.39	87
Other contributions	6.61	6.18	93
PERSONAL INSURANCE AND PENSIONS	**$3,223.06**	**$4,322.32**	**134**
Life and other personal insurance	**378.63**	**383.21**	**101**
Life, endowment, annuity, other personal insurance	369.48	375.53	102
Other nonhealth insurance	9.15	7.68	84

(continued)

(continued from previous page)

	average spending of total consumer units	consumer units headed by 35-to-44-year-olds	
		average spending	indexed spending*
Pensions and Social Security	**$2,844.43**	**$3,939.11**	**138**
Deductions for government retirement	81.02	111.64	138
Deductions for railroad retirement	2.26	1.45	64
Deductions for private pensions	339.22	496.46	146
Nonpayroll deposit to retirement plans	376.65	457.99	122
Deductions for Social Security	2,045.27	2,871.57	140
PERSONAL TAXES	**$3,241.49**	**$4,277.55**	**132**
Federal income tax	2,467.90	3,244.02	131
State and local income tax	644.81	896.57	139
Other taxes	128.78	136.96	106
GIFTS*	**$1,059.44**	**$910.36**	**86**
FOOD	**67.73**	**74.37**	**110**
Cakes and cupcakes	2.73	6.63	243
Cheese	3.16	7.58	240
Fresh fruits	6.23	8.31	133
Candy and chewing gum	11.56	11.28	98
Board (including at school)	23.79	16.13	68
HOUSING	**273.22**	**245.98**	**90**
Housekeeping supplies	**36.73**	**46.50**	**127**
Miscellaneous household products	6.62	9.75	147
Lawn and garden supplies	2.04	4.10	201
Stationery, stationery supplies, giftwrap	20.71	26.30	127
Postage	4.08	2.90	71
Household textiles	**8.35**	**5.66**	**68**
Bedroom linens	4.18	3.01	72
Appliances and miscellaneous housewares	**27.34**	**18.37**	**67**
Major appliances	6.41	3.35	52
Small appliances and miscellaneous housewares	20.93	15.02	72
China and other dinnerware	2.46	3.32	135
Glassware	3.97	1.27	32
Nonelectric cookware	3.57	0.89	25
Tableware, nonelectric kitchenware	3.76	5.70	152
Small electric kitchen appliances	3.51	1.75	50

(continued)

(continued from previous page)

	average spending of total consumer units	consumer units headed by 35-to-44-year-olds	
		average spending	indexed spending*
Miscellaneous household equipment	**$66.08**	**$60.32**	**91**
Infants' equipment	2.43	0.57	23
Other household decorative items	24.94	19.78	79
Telephones and accessories	3.14	2.70	86
Indoor plants, fresh flowers	16.63	14.40	87
Computers and hardware, nonbusiness use	7.19	11.85	165
Other housing	**134.72**	**115.13**	**85**
Repair or maintenance services	5.04	0.87	17
Housing while attending school	36.57	22.63	62
Natural gas (renter)	3.26	2.48	76
Electricity (renter)	13.58	13.17	97
Telephone services in home city, excluding mobile car phone	16.34	10.81	66
Water, sewerage maintenance (renter)	2.61	2.27	87
Baby-sitting and child care, someone else's home	3.73	3.48	93
Day care centers, nurseries, and preschools	19.65	29.47	150
Housekeeping services	4.07	7.01	172
Gardening, lawn care service	4.24	2.80	66
Moving, storage, freight express	2.59	2.03	78
Infants' furniture	2.07	0.73	35
APPAREL AND SERVICES	**252.24**	**229.18**	**91**
Men and boys, aged 2 or older	**61.29**	**43.80**	**71**
Men's coats and jackets	2.99	3.17	106
Men's accessories	4.73	5.09	108
Men's sweaters and vests	3.45	1.59	46
Men's active sportswear	3.31	2.64	80
Men's shirts	12.60	9.20	73
Men's pants	7.88	3.37	43
Boys' shirts	4.76	3.17	67
Boys' pants	3.25	3.89	120
Women and girls, aged 2 or older	**81.19**	**82.98**	**102**
Women's coats and jackets	3.17	3.41	108
Women's dresses	7.83	13.52	173
Women's vests and sweaters	6.06	7.18	118
Women's shirts, tops, blouses	12.70	10.03	79
Women's pants	6.09	3.99	66

(continued)

(continued from previous page)

	average spending of total consumer units	consumer units headed by 35-to-44-year-olds	
		average spending	indexed spending*
Women's shorts and shorts sets	$2.22	$2.64	119
Women's active sportswear	4.13	6.04	146
Women's nightwear	6.03	3.06	51
Women's hosiery	2.19	2.01	92
Women's suits	2.25	1.58	70
Women's accessories	5.86	4.59	78
Girls' dresses and suits	4.80	4.37	91
Girls' shirts, blouses, sweaters	5.38	9.66	180
Girls' skirts and pants	2.72	2.37	87
Children under age 2	**32.52**	**33.27**	**102**
Infant dresses, outerwear	7.54	6.47	86
Infant underwear	15.64	18.55	119
Infant nightwear, loungewear	2.94	2.54	86
Infant accessories	4.41	3.73	85
Other apparel products and services	**77.24**	**69.13**	**90**
Watches	7.41	15.25	206
Jewelry	41.18	24.82	60
Men's footwear	7.81	7.53	96
Boys' footwear	3.24	0.57	18
Women's footwear	11.83	10.07	85
Girls' footwear	3.81	5.43	143
TRANSPORTATION	**56.74**	**28.90**	**51**
New cars	7.05	–	–
New trucks	4.52	–	–
Used cars	9.67	1.85	19
Gasoline on out-of-town trips	13.52	11.91	88
Miscellaneous auto repair, servicing	2.94	1.17	40
Airline fares	6.89	6.20	90
Local transportation on out-of-town trips	2.25	1.26	56
Ship fares	3.09	2.70	87
HEALTH CARE	**30.35**	**18.76**	**62**
Physician services	2.23	2.29	103
Dental services	4.76	3.10	65
Hospital service other than room	2.79	1.41	51
Care in convalescent or nursing home	8.05	0.83	10
Prescription drugs	2.17	0.88	41

(continued)

(continued from previous page)

	average spending of total consumer units	consumer units headed by 35-to-44-year-olds	
		average spending	indexed spending*
ENTERTAINMENT	**$98.92**	**$84.35**	**85**
Toys, games, hobbies, tricycles	40.95	35.38	86
Movie, other admissions, out-of-town trips	7.77	6.81	88
Admission to sports events, out-of-town trips	2.59	2.27	88
Fees for recreational lessons	3.33	3.24	97
Community antenna or cable TV	3.96	3.14	79
Color TV, portable/table model	2.88	1.74	60
VCRs and video disc players	2.84	1.63	57
Video game hardware and software	2.17	1.50	69
Tape recorders and players	2.93	4.77	163
Sound components and component systems	2.09	3.47	166
Musical instruments and accessories	2.13	0.91	43
Veterinary services	2.18	1.34	61
Athletic gear, game tables, exercise equipment	5.97	3.29	55
EDUCATION	**155.44**	**101.49**	**65**
College tuition	119.23	68.54	57
Elementary, high school tuition	10.29	13.20	128
Other school expenses, including rentals	4.33	3.53	82
College books, supplies	9.80	5.58	57
Miscellaneous school supplies	8.35	6.57	79
ALL OTHER GIFTS	**124.80**	**127.34**	**102**
Out-of-town trip expenses	46.85	32.74	70

*The index compares the spending of consumer units headed by 35-to-44-year-olds with the spending of the average consumer unit by dividing the spending of 35-to-44-year-olds by average spending in each category and multiplying by 100. An index of 100 means the spending of 35-to-44-year-olds in the category equals average spending. An index of 132 means the spending of 35-to-44-year-olds is 32 percent above average, while an index of 75 means the spending of 35-to-44-year-olds is 25 percent below average.

** This figure does not include the amount paid for mortgage principle, which is considered an asset.

*** Expenditures on gifts are also included in the preceding product and service categories. Food spending, for example, includes the amount spent on food gifts. Only gift categories with spending of $2.00 or more by the average consumer unit are shown.

Note: The Bureau of Labor Statistics uses consumer units rather than households as the sampling unit in the Consumer Expenditure Survey. For the definition of consumer unit, see the Glossary. (–) means the sample is too small to make a reliable estimate.

Source: Bureau of Labor Statistics, unpublished data from the 1997 Consumer Expenditure Survey; calculations by New Strategist

Householders Aged 45 to 54 Spend the Most

Households headed by 45-to-54-year-olds spend 30 percent more than the average household.

Householders aged 45 to 54 spent $45,239 in 1997, versus $34,819 spent by the average household. Households headed by 45-to-54-year-olds are the nation's biggest spenders. The spending of this age group has become increasingly important over the past few years because of the reduction in spending by householders aged 35 to 44. In 1990, householders aged 45 to 54 spent just $1,742 more than those aged 35 to 44. By 1997, they spent fully $4,826 more.

Householders aged 45 to 54 spend big on most discretionary items. They spend 21 percent more than the average household on restaurant meals, 57 percent more on computer online services, and 33 percent more on entertainment. The age group spends much more than those aged 35 to 44 on men's and women's clothing and 60 percent more than the average household on new cars. Because many 45-to-54-year-olds have children in college, they spend twice as much as the average household on college tuition.

◆ While many advertisers believe young adults are the nation's big spenders, they're wrong. Marketers who target the 45-to-54 age group are likely to boost their bottom lines.

Average and Indexed Spending of Householders Aged 45 to 54, 1997

(average annual spending of total consumer units and average annual and indexed spending of consumer units headed by 45-to-54-year-olds, 1997)

	average spending of total consumer units	consumer units headed by 45-to-54-year-olds	
		average spending	indexed spending*
Number of consumer units (in 000s)	105,576	19,343	-
Average before-tax income	$39,926.00	$55,260.00	138
Average annual spending	34,819.38	45,238.96	130
FOOD	**$4,801.35**	**$6,028.36**	**126**
FOOD AT HOME	**2,880.00**	**3,440.35**	**119**
Cereals and bakery products	**453.00**	**548.14**	**121**
Cereals and cereal products	161.39	188.99	117
Flour	8.79	9.47	108
Prepared flour mixes	15.04	18.37	122
Ready-to-eat and cooked cereals	91.15	105.77	116
Rice	18.37	23.60	128
Pasta, cornmeal, and other cereal products	28.03	31.78	113
Bakery products	291.60	359.15	123
Bread	83.43	100.88	121
White bread	40.89	48.45	118
Bread, other than white	42.55	52.43	123
Crackers and cookies	68.27	81.94	120
Cookies	45.01	54.04	120
Crackers	23.26	27.89	120
Frozen and refrigerated bakery products	23.35	27.39	117
Other bakery products	116.56	148.95	128
Biscuits and rolls	40.96	55.68	136
Cakes and cupcakes	34.51	44.61	129
Bread and cracker products	4.45	6.31	142
Sweetrolls, coffee cakes, doughnuts	23.13	25.53	110
Pies, tarts, turnovers	13.50	16.84	125
Meats, poultry, fish, and eggs	**743.12**	**915.48**	**123**
Beef	223.55	284.29	127
Ground beef	82.77	93.67	113

(continued)

(continued from previous page)

	average spending of total consumer units	consumer units headed by 45-to-54-year-olds	
		average spending	indexed spending*
Roast	$40.48	$50.31	124
Chuck roast	13.02	15.79	121
Round roast	12.85	16.90	132
Other roast	14.61	17.62	121
Steak	87.48	125.50	143
Round steak	16.70	23.61	141
Sirloin steak	23.01	31.08	135
Other steak	47.76	70.80	148
Other beef	12.81	14.81	116
Pork	157.13	192.98	123
Bacon	25.42	29.49	116
Pork chops	39.23	45.91	117
Ham	37.28	49.18	132
Ham, not canned	35.12	46.23	132
Canned ham	2.16	2.95	137
Sausage	24.12	26.27	109
Other pork	31.07	42.13	136
Other meats	96.03	111.00	116
Frankfurters	22.83	26.96	118
Lunch meats (cold cuts)	65.55	72.80	111
Bologna, liverwurst, salami	23.82	25.53	107
Other lunch meats	41.73	47.27	113
Lamb, organ meats, and others	7.92	11.24	142
Lamb and organ meats	7.34	9.34	127
Mutton, goat, and game	0.58	1.90	328
Poultry	145.01	172.34	119
Fresh and frozen chickens	113.38	130.89	115
Fresh and frozen whole chickens	29.77	32.76	110
Fresh and frozen chicken parts	83.61	98.14	117
Other poultry	31.63	41.44	131
Fish and seafood	88.54	116.59	132
Canned fish and seafood	14.18	16.17	114
Fresh fish and shellfish	50.95	69.34	136
Frozen fish and shellfish	23.41	31.08	133
Eggs	32.59	38.29	117

(continued)

(continued from previous page)

	average spending of total consumer units	consumer units headed by 45-to-54-year-olds	
		average spending	indexed spending*
Dairy products	**$313.68**	**$358.82**	**114**
Fresh milk and cream	128.12	138.04	108
Fresh milk, all types	118.78	126.85	107
Cream	9.34	11.19	120
Other dairy products	185.56	220.78	119
Butter	14.63	18.17	124
Cheese	94.33	112.21	119
Ice cream and related products	52.91	60.40	114
Miscellaneous dairy products	23.69	30.01	127
Fruits and vegetables	**475.62**	**557.78**	**117**
Fresh fruits	150.47	173.73	115
Apples	28.47	34.08	120
Bananas	31.44	35.53	113
Oranges	17.62	21.40	121
Citrus fruits, excluding oranges	13.42	16.43	122
Other fresh fruits	59.52	66.30	111
Fresh vegetables	142.75	173.82	122
Potatoes	26.15	32.11	123
Lettuce	19.27	24.02	125
Tomatoes	23.87	29.53	124
Other fresh vegetables	73.46	88.16	120
Processed fruits	102.28	116.82	114
Frozen fruits and fruit juices	15.02	16.33	109
Frozen orange juice	8.44	9.49	112
Frozen fruits	2.02	2.57	127
Frozen fruit juices, excluding orange juice	4.57	4.27	93
Canned fruits	13.97	17.14	123
Dried fruits	6.03	6.11	101
Fresh fruit juice	19.82	22.61	114
Canned and bottled fruit juice	47.43	54.63	115
Processed vegetables	80.13	93.41	117
Frozen vegetables	26.57	32.33	122
Canned and dried vegetables and juices	53.56	61.08	114
Canned beans	11.79	13.33	113
Canned corn	7.26	7.26	100
Canned miscellaneous vegetables	16.80	20.49	122
Dried peas	0.23	0.18	78

(continued)

(continued from previous page)

	average spending of total consumer units	consumer units headed by 45-to-54-year-olds	
		average spending	indexed spending*
Dried beans	$2.58	$2.63	102
Dried miscellaneous vegetables	7.18	9.23	129
Dried processed vegetables	0.22	0.11	50
Frozen vegetable juices	0.28	0.22	79
Fresh and canned vegetable juices	7.22	7.64	106
Other food at home	**894.58**	**1,060.13**	**119**
Sugar and other sweets	114.30	139.23	122
Candy and chewing gum	69.26	87.68	127
Sugar	18.93	21.03	111
Artificial sweeteners	3.48	4.36	125
Jams, preserves, other sweets	22.63	26.17	116
Fats and oils	81.05	93.90	116
Margarine	11.74	13.13	112
Fats and oils	24.50	27.63	113
Salad dressings	24.68	30.97	125
Nondairy cream and imitation milk	8.50	9.83	116
Peanut butter	11.63	12.34	106
Miscellaneous foods	403.06	462.17	115
Frozen prepared foods	77.61	95.25	123
Frozen meals	20.73	24.07	116
Other frozen prepared foods	56.88	71.19	125
Canned and packaged soups	32.87	33.39	102
Potato chips, nuts, and other snacks	84.53	101.88	121
Potato chips and other snacks	66.83	79.48	119
Nuts	17.70	22.40	127
Condiments and seasonings	86.12	107.55	125
Salt, spices, and other seasonings	19.07	23.40	123
Olives, pickles, relishes	10.54	11.91	113
Sauces and gravies	39.86	51.69	130
Baking needs and miscellaneous products	16.65	20.55	123
Other canned/packaged prepared foods	121.94	124.09	102
Prepared salads	15.05	21.22	141
Prepared desserts	9.95	12.58	126
Baby food	27.86	11.85	43
Miscellaneous prepared foods	68.44	77.39	113
Vitamin supplements	0.64	1.04	163

(continued)

(continued from previous page)

	average spending of total consumer units	consumer units headed by 45-to-54-year-olds	
		average spending	indexed spending*
Nonalcoholic beverages	$244.51	$292.19	120
Cola	90.51	109.97	122
Other carbonated drinks	42.94	55.55	129
Coffee	48.80	57.12	117
Roasted coffee	32.65	38.33	117
Instant and freeze-dried coffee	16.15	18.79	116
Noncarbonated fruit flavored drinks, including nonfrozen lemonade	19.22	19.78	103
Tea	14.76	17.93	121
Nonalcoholic beer	0.34	0.07	21
Other nonalcoholic beverages and ice	27.93	31.77	114
Food prepared by household on out-of-town trips	51.65	72.64	141
FOOD AWAY FROM HOME	**1,921.35**	**2,588.01**	**135**
Meals at restaurants, carry-outs, other	**1,477.51**	**1,784.31**	**121**
Lunch	501.92	593.04	118
Dinner	740.70	918.48	124
Snacks and nonalcoholic beverages	119.38	140.26	117
Breakfast and brunch	115.51	132.53	115
Board (including at school)	**51.88**	**116.18**	**224**
Catered affairs	**83.52**	**277.09**	**332**
Food on out-of-town trips	**223.90**	**314.95**	**141**
School lunches	**54.03**	**70.28**	**130**
Meals as pay	**30.51**	**25.21**	**83**
ALCOHOLIC BEVERAGES	**$309.22**	**$358.16**	**116**
At home	**180.13**	**216.44**	**120**
Beer and ale	90.92	99.42	109
Whiskey	13.40	13.19	98
Wine	55.32	82.46	149
Other alcoholic beverages	20.50	21.37	104
Away from home	**129.09**	**141.72**	**110**
Beer and ale	39.50	37.78	96
Wine	24.30	26.96	111
Other alcoholic beverages	32.81	35.29	108
Alcoholic beverages purchased on trips	32.48	41.70	128

(continued)

(continued from previous page)

	average spending of total consumer units	consumer units headed by 45-to-54-year-olds	
		average spending	indexed spending*
HOUSING	**$11,272.04**	**$13,892.48**	**123**
SHELTER	**6,343.87**	**7,829.37**	**123**
Owned dwellings**	**3,934.87**	**5,586.10**	**142**
Mortgage interest and charges	2,225.26	3,396.22	153
Mortgage interest	2,109.06	3,152.04	149
Interest paid, home equity loan	57.21	101.77	178
Interest paid, home equity line of credit	58.84	142.12	242
Prepayment penalty charges	0.16	0.28	175
Property taxes	971.15	1,302.73	134
Maintenance, repairs, insurance, other expenses	738.46	887.15	120
Homeowner's and related insurance	230.91	305.76	132
Fire and extended coverage	8.02	8.70	108
Homeowner's insurance	222.88	297.06	133
Ground rent	37.16	24.92	67
Maintenance and repair services	365.61	423.07	116
Painting and papering	45.31	62.94	139
Plumbing and water heating	36.61	37.85	103
Heat, air conditioning, electrical work	63.28	78.03	123
Roofing and gutters	72.99	79.97	110
Other repair and maintenance services	124.47	129.57	104
Repair/replacement of hard surface flooring	21.17	33.26	157
Repair of built-in appliances	1.79	1.47	82
Maintenance and repair materials	83.91	104.74	125
Paints, wallpaper, and supplies	18.33	32.04	175
Tools/equipment for painting, wallpapering	1.97	3.44	175
Plumbing supplies and equipment	6.87	9.77	142
Electrical supplies, heating/cooling equipment	4.55	2.06	45
Hard surface flooring, repair and replacement	7.13	7.61	107
Roofing and gutters	7.77	6.25	80
Plaster, paneling, siding, windows, doors, screens, awnings	14.97	21.55	144
Patio, walk, fence, driveway, masonry, brick, and stucco work	0.92	1.03	112
Landscape maintenance	5.19	6.07	117
Miscellaneous supplies and equipment	16.21	14.93	92
Insulation, other maintenance/repair	9.22	12.90	140

(continued)

(continued from previous page)

	average spending of total consumer units	consumer units headed by 45-to-54-year-olds	
		average spending	indexed spending*
Finish basement, remodel rooms, build patios, walks, etc.	$6.99	$2.04	29
Property management and security	19.58	27.29	139
Property management	16.49	23.14	140
Management and upkeep services for security	3.09	4.15	134
Parking	1.30	1.37	105
Rented dwellings	**1,983.18**	**1,514.76**	**76**
Rent	1,876.81	1,422.79	76
Rent as pay	72.36	70.04	97
Maintenance, insurance, and other expenses	34.02	21.93	64
Tenant's insurance	9.76	11.66	119
Maintenance and repair services	16.62	5.28	32
Repair or maintenance services	15.42	5.08	33
Repair and replacement of hard surface flooring	1.17	0.19	16
Repair of built-in appliances	0.03	0.02	67
Maintenance and repair materials	7.63	4.99	65
Paint, wallpaper, and supplies	1.57	1.39	89
Painting and wallpapering	0.17	0.15	88
Plastering, paneling, roofing, gutters, etc.	1.22	1.67	137
Patio, walk, fence, driveway, masonry, brick, and stucco work	0.02	0.10	500
Plumbing supplies and equipment	0.36	0.20	56
Electrical supplies, heating and cooling equipment	0.08	0.03	38
Miscellaneous supplies and equipment	2.94	0.66	22
Insulation, other maintenance and repair	1.04	0.44	42
Materials for additions, finishing basements, remodeling rooms	1.65	0.22	13
Construction materials for jobs not started	0.25	0.00	0
Hard surface flooring	0.74	–	–
Landscape maintenance	0.53	0.79	149
Other lodging	**425.82**	**728.52**	**171**
Owned vacation homes	133.69	232.71	174
Mortgage interest and charges	58.02	99.30	171
Mortgage interest	56.46	97.75	173
Interest paid, home equity loan	0.66	1.06	161
Interest paid, home equity line of credit	0.89	0.49	55

(continued)

(continued from previous page)

	average spending of total consumer units	consumer units headed by 45-to-54-year-olds	
		average spending	indexed spending*
Property taxes	$54.83	$95.73	175
Maintenance, insurance, and other expenses	20.84	37.67	181
Homeowner's and related insurance	5.03	4.75	94
Homeowner's insurance	4.67	4.51	97
Fire and extended coverage	0.36	0.24	67
Ground rent	1.63	–	–
Maintenance and repair services	9.66	25.22	261
Maintenance and repair materials	0.81	0.91	112
Property management and security	3.41	6.56	192
Property management	2.96	5.81	196
Management and upkeep services for security	0.45	0.76	169
Parking	0.29	0.22	76
Housing while attending school	66.35	165.24	249
Lodging on out-of-town trips	225.77	330.57	146
UTILITIES, FUELS & PUBLIC SERVICES	**2,412.30**	**2,890.43**	**120**
Natural gas	**300.96**	**320.97**	**107**
Natural gas (renter)	60.81	42.60	70
Natural gas (owner)	238.55	276.33	116
Natural gas (vacation)	1.60	2.05	128
Electricity	**908.67**	**1,114.46**	**123**
Electricity (renter)	212.54	168.36	79
Electricity (owner)	687.53	936.99	136
Electricity (vacation)	8.60	9.11	106
Fuel oil and other fuels	**107.72**	**146.87**	**136**
Fuel oil	55.18	83.89	152
Fuel oil (renter)	4.92	3.55	72
Fuel oil (owner)	49.77	79.42	160
Fuel oil (vacation)	0.49	0.92	188
Coal	0.99	0.94	95
Coal (renter)	0.02	–	–
Coal (owner)	0.97	0.94	97
Bottled/tank gas	43.84	51.14	117
Gas (renter)	4.66	2.88	62
Gas (owner)	36.37	45.01	124
Gas (vacation)	2.81	3.24	115

(continued)

	average spending of total consumer units	consumer units headed by 45-to-54-year-olds	
		average spending	indexed spending*
Wood and other fuels	$7.72	$10.90	141
Wood and other fuels (renter)	1.53	0.68	44
Wood and other fuels (owner)	5.80	8.36	144
Wood and other fuels (vacation)	0.39	1.86	477
Telephone services	**809.05**	**951.60**	**118**
Telephone services in home city, excluding mobile car phones	756.44	877.67	116
Telephone services for mobile car phones	52.61	73.93	141
Water and other public services	**285.90**	**356.53**	**125**
Water and sewerage maintenance	207.28	260.01	125
Water and sewerage maintenance (renter)	28.28	23.98	85
Water and sewerage maintenance (owner)	176.95	233.10	132
Water and sewerage maintenance (vacation)	2.06	2.92	142
Trash and garbage collection	76.00	93.56	123
Trash and garbage collection (renter)	8.78	7.50	85
Trash and garbage collection (owner)	65.66	83.91	128
Trash and garbage collection (vacation)	1.56	2.15	138
Septic tank cleaning	2.62	2.96	113
Septic tank cleaning (renter)	0.19	0.76	400
Septic tank cleaning (owner)	2.41	2.21	92
HOUSEHOLD OPERATIONS	**548.50**	**554.40**	**101**
Personal services	**263.10**	**145.82**	**55**
Baby-sitting and child care in your own home	34.39	15.01	44
Baby-sitting and child care in someone else's home	37.37	17.45	47
Care for elderly, invalids, handicapped, etc.	26.95	9.63	36
Adult day care centers	3.79	7.37	194
Day care centers, nurseries, and preschools	160.60	96.36	60
Other household expenses	**285.40**	**408.58**	**143**
Housekeeping services	75.34	123.30	164
Gardening, lawn care services	72.44	111.63	154
Water softening services	4.51	4.85	108
Nonclothing laundry and dry cleaning, sent out	10.20	17.68	173
Nonclothing laundry and dry cleaning, coin-operated	4.91	3.28	67
Termite/pest control services	11.55	10.33	89
Other home services	15.94	19.26	121
Termite/pest control products	0.12	0.13	108

(continued)

(continued from previous page)

	average spending of total consumer units	consumer units headed by 45-to-54-year-olds	
		average spending	indexed spending*
Moving, storage, and freight express	$34.75	$35.22	101
Appliance repair, including service center	13.50	17.87	132
Reupholstering and furniture repair	10.87	16.31	150
Repairs/rentals of lawn/garden equipment, hand/power tools, etc.	5.13	7.86	153
Appliance rental	1.05	0.92	88
Rental of office equipment for nonbusiness use	0.43	1.04	242
Repair of miscellaneous household equipment and furnishings	1.53	3.98	260
Repair of computer systems for nonbusiness use	2.47	2.58	104
Computer information services	20.65	32.35	157
HOUSEKEEPING SUPPLIES	**454.93**	**551.88**	**121**
Laundry and cleaning supplies	**115.85**	**136.88**	**118**
Soaps and detergents	65.05	73.70	113
Other laundry cleaning products	50.80	63.18	124
Other household products	**210.07**	**257.65**	**123**
Cleansing and toilet tissue, paper towels, and napkins	64.42	74.20	115
Miscellaneous household products	89.90	111.69	124
Lawn and garden supplies	55.74	71.77	129
Postage and stationery	**129.01**	**157.36**	**122**
Stationery, stationery supplies, giftwrap	62.61	72.13	115
Postage	62.53	80.45	129
Delivery services	3.88	4.77	123
HOUSEHOLD FURNISHINGS & EQUIPMENT	**1,512.44**	**2,066.39**	**137**
Household textiles	**79.12**	**115.87**	**146**
Bathroom linens	11.13	14.11	127
Bedroom linens	34.28	48.97	143
Kitchen and dining room linens	2.40	4.04	168
Curtains and draperies	16.73	24.34	145
Slipcovers and decorative pillows	2.10	2.51	120
Sewing materials for household items	11.20	19.40	173
Other linens	1.28	2.49	195
Furniture	**387.34**	**514.53**	**133**
Mattresses and springs	46.56	61.05	131
Other bedroom furniture	63.99	102.91	161

(continued)

(continued from previous page)

	average spending of total consumer units	consumer units headed by 45-to-54-year-olds	
		average spending	indexed spending*
Sofas	$93.81	$114.42	122
Living room chairs	47.42	62.43	132
Living room tables	20.60	21.79	106
Kitchen and dining room furniture	48.69	64.61	133
Infants' furniture	9.87	7.22	73
Outdoor furniture	13.61	24.41	179
Wall units, cabinets, and other furniture	42.81	55.67	130
Floor coverings	**77.74**	**70.20**	**90**
Wall-to-wall carpeting	38.82	45.34	117
Wall-to-wall carpeting (renter)	1.94	2.31	119
Wall-to-wall carpeting, installed	1.37	1.79	131
Wall-to-wall carpeting, not installed carpet squares	0.56	0.52	93
Wall-to-wall carpeting, replacement (owner)	36.88	43.03	117
Wall-to-wall carpeting, not installed carpet squares	2.68	8.20	306
Wall-to-wall carpeting, installed	34.20	34.83	102
Room-size rugs and other floor covering, nonpermanent	38.93	24.86	64
Major appliances	**169.18**	**193.45**	**114**
Dishwashers (built-in), garbage disposals, range hoods (renter)	0.82	0.65	79
Dishwashers (built-in), garbage disposals, range hoods (owner)	11.65	12.64	108
Refrigerators and freezers (renter)	9.52	7.26	76
Refrigerators and freezers (owner)	48.08	53.80	112
Washing machines (renter)	5.46	4.97	91
Washing machines (owner)	17.56	19.55	111
Clothes dryers (renter)	4.40	3.33	76
Clothes dryers (owner)	11.82	13.98	118
Cooking stoves, ovens (renter)	2.83	1.04	37
Cooking stoves, ovens (owner)	19.23	25.18	131
Microwave ovens (renter)	2.96	2.00	68
Microwave ovens (owner)	6.63	8.47	128
Portable dishwashers (renter)	0.41	0.07	17
Portable dishwashers (owner)	0.26	0.13	50
Window air conditioners (renter)	1.69	0.76	45
Window air conditioners (owner)	3.24	3.70	114

(continued)

(continued from previous page)

	average spending of total consumer units	consumer units headed by 45-to-54-year-olds	
		average spending	indexed spending*
Electric floor cleaning equipment	$15.68	$19.31	123
Sewing machines	3.55	4.27	120
Miscellaneous household appliances	**3.39**	**12.35**	**364**
Small appliances and miscellaneous housewares	91.91	131.45	143
Housewares	66.12	103.54	157
Plastic dinnerware	1.75	2.11	121
China and other dinnerware	8.86	17.51	198
Flatware	4.68	6.15	131
Glassware	8.25	13.70	166
Silver serving pieces	2.31	4.09	177
Other serving pieces	1.74	2.32	133
Nonelectric cookware	15.05	24.49	163
Tableware, nonelectric kitchenware	23.48	33.16	141
Small appliances	25.79	27.90	108
Small electric kitchen appliances	16.67	20.74	124
Portable heating and cooling equipment	9.12	7.16	79
Miscellaneous household equipment	**707.15**	**1,040.90**	**147**
Window coverings	13.71	18.84	137
Infants' equipment	7.05	3.30	47
Laundry and cleaning equipment	13.70	12.39	90
Outdoor equipment	18.42	60.77	330
Clocks	4.51	4.86	108
Lamps and lighting fixtures	12.53	16.24	130
Other household decorative items	134.12	193.95	145
Telephones and accessories	96.54	133.82	139
Lawn and garden equipment	39.37	61.66	157
Power tools	16.31	23.96	147
Office furniture for home use	10.61	28.17	266
Hand tools	9.29	9.81	106
Indoor plants and fresh flowers	52.33	76.05	145
Closet and storage items	8.94	12.98	145
Rental of furniture	3.41	2.54	74
Luggage	9.72	14.38	148
Computers and computer hardware, nonbusiness use	162.66	266.71	164
Computer software and accessories, nonbusiness use	24.72	38.36	155
Telephone answering devices	3.31	4.01	121

(continued)

	average spending of total consumer units	consumer units headed by 45-to-54-year-olds	
		average spending	indexed spending*
Calculators	$1.92	$2.60	135
Business equipment for home use	2.33	1.79	77
Other hardware	23.27	8.32	36
Smoke alarms (owner)	0.86	0.58	67
Smoke alarms (renter)	0.19	0.10	53
Other household appliances (owner)	8.78	11.90	136
Other household appliances (renter)	1.47	1.08	73
Miscellaneous household equipment and parts	27.10	31.72	117
APPAREL AND SERVICES	**$1,729.06**	**$2,106.72**	**122**
Men's apparel	**322.98**	**456.79**	**141**
Suits	35.18	55.35	157
Sportcoats and tailored jackets	15.19	24.01	158
Coats and jackets	29.80	42.62	143
Underwear	12.52	17.03	136
Hosiery	9.91	16.28	164
Nightwear	2.93	5.07	173
Accessories	30.27	45.85	151
Sweaters and vests	15.84	21.21	134
Active sportswear	12.24	11.39	93
Shirts	75.81	102.80	136
Pants	64.52	92.63	144
Shorts and shorts sets	13.76	19.41	141
Uniforms	2.25	0.81	36
Costumes	2.79	2.34	84
Boys' (aged 2 to 15) apparel	**83.88**	**93.14**	**111**
Coats and jackets	8.33	10.34	124
Sweaters	2.81	3.21	114
Shirts	18.34	20.89	114
Underwear	3.08	4.07	132
Nightwear	1.94	2.22	114
Hosiery	3.66	4.82	132
Accessories	3.94	3.05	77
Suits, sportcoats, and vests	2.89	3.50	121
Pants	21.85	23.05	105
Shorts and shorts sets	8.66	8.87	102
Uniforms	4.41	5.52	125

(continued)

(continued from previous page)

	average spending of total consumer units	consumer units headed by 45-to-54-year-olds	
		average spending	indexed spending*
Active sportswear	$2.65	$2.72	103
Costumes	1.33	0.86	65
Women's apparel	**574.26**	**718.98**	**125**
Coats and jackets	44.33	60.53	137
Dresses	84.25	108.88	129
Sportcoats and tailored jackets	2.77	3.02	109
Sweaters and vests	40.39	47.10	117
Shirts, blouses, and tops	93.73	122.51	131
Skirts	18.35	19.50	106
Pants	70.48	83.32	118
Shorts and shorts sets	22.34	34.29	153
Active sportswear	29.74	30.41	102
Nightwear	$24.73	$37.30	151
Undergarments	29.71	37.08	125
Hosiery	22.88	27.05	118
Suits	38.30	48.05	125
Accessories	45.42	52.97	117
Uniforms	3.20	2.90	91
Costumes	3.64	4.10	113
Girls' (aged 2 to 15) apparel	**106.01**	**115.06**	**109**
Coats and jackets	6.50	7.03	108
Dresses and suits	13.42	16.79	125
Shirts, blouses, and sweaters	25.74	33.04	128
Skirts and pants	19.49	21.18	109
Shorts and shorts sets	9.67	9.62	99
Active sportswear	6.86	0.94	14
Underwear and nightwear	6.75	6.95	103
Hosiery	5.29	5.52	104
Accessories	5.64	6.61	117
Uniforms	3.17	3.31	104
Costumes	3.48	4.08	117
Children under age 2	**77.05**	**50.57**	**66**
Coats, jackets, and snowsuits	3.28	3.11	95
Outerwear including dresses	15.01	12.31	82
Underwear	43.93	24.64	56
Nightwear and loungewear	4.38	4.82	110
Accessories	10.45	5.70	55

(continued)

(continued from previous page)

	average spending of total consumer units	consumer units headed by 45-to-54-year-olds	
		average spending	indexed spending*
Footwear	**$314.52**	**$346.93**	**110**
Men's	100.43	117.18	117
Boys'	27.90	30.25	108
Women's	157.11	178.65	114
Girls'	29.08	20.86	72
Other apparel products and services	**250.35**	**325.25**	**130**
Material for making clothes	4.07	5.31	130
Sewing patterns and notions	4.82	5.99	124
Watches	29.70	13.54	46
Jewelry	142.02	208.88	147
Shoe repair and other shoe services	2.38	3.47	146
Coin-operated apparel laundry and dry cleaning	20.79	21.25	102
Apparel alteration, repair, and tailoring services	6.10	7.81	128
Clothing rental	3.85	5.46	142
Watch and jewelry repair	5.08	5.47	108
Professional laundry, dry cleaning	31.24	47.72	153
Clothing storage	0.30	0.36	120
TRANSPORTATION	**$6,456.86**	**$8,734.16**	**135**
VEHICLE PURCHASES	**2,735.76**	**3,703.95**	**135**
Cars and trucks, new	**1,228.89**	**1,808.24**	**147**
New cars	700.22	1,118.89	160
New trucks	528.67	689.35	130
Cars and trucks, used	**1,463.52**	**1,848.54**	**126**
Used cars	895.31	1,123.41	125
Used trucks	568.22	725.13	128
Other vehicles	**43.35**	**47.17**	**109**
New motorcycles	26.39	–	–
Used motorcycles	15.32	45.06	294
GASOLINE AND MOTOR OIL	**1,097.52**	**1,429.75**	**130**
Gasoline	985.31	1,278.12	130
Diesel fuel	10.10	16.95	168
Gasoline on out-of-town trips	89.11	117.67	132
Motor oil	12.10	15.81	131
Motor oil on out-of-town trips	0.90	1.19	132

(continued)

(continued from previous page)

	average spending of total consumer units	consumer units headed by 45-to-54-year-olds	
		average spending	indexed spending*
OTHER VEHICLE EXPENSES	**$2,230.41**	**$3,078.79**	**138**
Vehicle finance charges	**292.81**	**387.98**	**133**
Automobile finance charges	161.70	211.45	131
Truck finance charges	116.10	155.43	134
Motorcycle and plane finance charges	1.52	1.15	76
Other vehicle finance charges	13.49	19.95	148
Maintenance and repairs	**681.62**	**941.73**	**138**
Coolant, additives, brake, transmission fluids	5.70	7.82	137
Tires	87.94	118.38	135
Parts, equipment, and accessories	51.31	66.92	130
Vehicle audio equipment	2.00	1.39	70
Vehicle products	6.95	8.73	126
Miscellaneous auto repair, servicing	51.74	75.90	147
Body work and painting	32.29	51.18	159
Clutch, transmission repair	47.92	66.71	139
Drive shaft and rear-end repair	5.73	8.31	145
Brake work	55.82	75.72	136
Repair to steering or front-end	17.41	22.14	127
Repair to engine cooling system	19.98	26.49	133
Motor tune-up	45.05	58.87	131
Lube, oil change, and oil filters	54.29	69.48	128
Front-end alignment, wheel balance, rotation	12.13	17.29	143
Shock absorber replacement	4.98	6.70	135
Gas tank repair, replacement	1.20	0.94	78
Tire repair and other repair work	29.63	37.20	126
Vehicle air conditioning repair	19.07	31.16	163
Exhaust system repair	18.52	22.87	123
Electrical system repair	29.34	38.53	131
Motor repair, replacement	75.45	120.61	160
Auto repair service policy	7.16	8.38	117
Vehicle insurance	**754.99**	**993.69**	**132**
Vehicle rental, leases, licenses, other charges	**500.99**	**755.39**	**151**
Leased and rented vehicles	331.25	546.59	165
Rented vehicles	41.03	62.92	153
Auto rental	7.73	13.30	172
Auto rental, out-of-town trips	26.78	40.57	151

(continued)

(continued from previous page)

	average spending of total consumer units	consumer units headed by 45-to-54-year-olds	
		average spending	indexed spending*
Truck rental	$1.85	$3.68	199
Truck rental, out-of-town trips	4.29	4.98	116
Leased vehicles	290.22	483.67	167
Car lease payments	162.28	270.33	167
Cash downpayment (car lease)	16.16	26.71	165
Termination fee (car lease)	1.81	1.89	104
Truck lease payments	98.37	163.66	166
Cash downpayment (truck lease)	10.63	19.37	182
Termination fee (truck lease)	0.97	1.71	176
State and local registration	94.62	121.32	128
Driver's license	7.42	8.95	121
Vehicle inspection	8.74	10.70	122
Parking fees	28.20	33.31	118
Parking fees in home city, excluding residence	24.37	28.26	116
Parking fees, out-of-town trips	3.83	5.05	132
Tolls	13.19	11.13	84
Tolls on out-of-town trips	4.32	6.20	144
Towing charges	5.04	6.48	129
Automobile service clubs	8.19	10.72	131
PUBLIC TRANSPORTATION	**393.16**	**521.67**	**133**
Airline fares	248.82	337.67	136
Intercity bus fares	10.51	13.34	127
Intracity mass transit fares	55.77	70.11	126
Local transportation on out-of-town trips	12.61	14.06	111
Taxi fares and limousine service on trips	7.40	8.26	112
Taxi fares and limousine service	9.51	10.58	111
Intercity train fares	21.19	31.59	149
Ship fares	26.40	35.63	135
School bus	0.95	0.42	44
HEALTH CARE	**$1,840.71**	**$1,944.68**	**106**
HEALTH INSURANCE	**881.28**	**845.27**	**96**
Commercial health insurance	**203.37**	**265.19**	**130**
Traditional fee-for-service health plan (not BCBS)	100.09	123.11	123
Preferred provider health plan (not BCBS)	103.29	142.08	138
Blue Cross, Blue Shield	**192.51**	**200.10**	**104**
Traditional fee-for-service health plan	62.93	81.13	129

(continued)

(continued from previous page)

	average spending of total consumer units	consumer units headed by 45-to-54-year-olds	
		average spending	indexed spending*
Preferred provider health plan	$46.45	$59.68	128
Health maintenance organization	47.39	54.17	114
Commercial Medicare supplement	31.92	2.97	9
Other BCBS health insurance	3.82	2.15	56
Health maintenance plans (HMOs)	**229.07**	**304.40**	**133**
Medicare payments	**160.92**	**35.46**	**22**
Commercial Medicare supplements/			
other health insurance	**95.40**	**40.13**	**42**
Commercial Medicare supplement (not BCBS)	60.66	5.88	10
Other health insurance (not BCBS)	34.74	34.24	99
MEDICAL SERVICES	**531.04**	**657.52**	**124**
Physician's services	133.59	160.27	120
Dental services	203.56	280.79	138
Eye care services	27.14	30.17	111
Service by professionals other than physicians	37.03	48.84	132
Lab tests, X-rays	22.93	28.00	122
Hospital room	35.07	42.36	121
Hospital services other than room	52.37	62.71	120
Care in convalescent or nursing home	13.09	4.15	32
Repair of medical equipment	0.62	–	–
Other medical services	5.64	0.23	4
DRUGS	**320.44**	**303.24**	**95**
Nonprescription drugs	75.43	77.32	103
Nonprescription vitamins	28.43	22.90	81
Prescription drugs	216.58	203.01	94
MEDICAL SUPPLIES	**107.95**	**138.65**	**128**
Eyeglasses and contact lenses	59.73	90.51	152
Hearing aids	11.42	2.90	25
Topicals and dressings	29.47	37.11	126
Medical equipment for general use	2.43	4.99	205
Supportive/convalescent medical equipment	2.62	1.12	43
Rental of medical equipment	0.60	0.62	103
Rental of supportive, convalescent medical equipment	1.67	1.4	84
ENTERTAINMENT	**$1,813.28**	**$2,415.59**	**133**
FEES AND ADMISSIONS	**470.74**	**679.02**	**144**

(continued)

(continued from previous page)

	average spending of total consumer units	consumer units headed by 45-to-54-year-olds	
		average spending	indexed spending*
Recreation expenses, out of town trips	$24.70	$38.20	155
Social, recreation, civic club membership	75.12	104.50	139
Fees for participant sports	72.62	102.37	141
Participant sports, out-of-town trips	30.30	45.90	151
Movie, theater, opera, ballet	86.71	116.99	135
Movie, other admissions, out-of-town trips	41.93	52.61	125
Admission to sports events	33.51	48.15	144
Admission to sports events, out-of-town trips	13.98	17.53	125
Fees for recreational lessons	67.17	114.59	171
Other entertainment services, out-of-town trips	24.70	38.20	155
TELEVISION, RADIO, SOUND EQUIPMENT	**577.33**	**682.70**	**118**
Television	**403.51**	**471.97**	**117**
Community antenna or cable TV	262.34	307.55	117
Black and white TV sets	0.67	1.07	160
Color TV, console	25.17	29.39	117
Color TV, portable/table model	39.96	48.31	121
VCRs and video disc players	26.58	32.01	120
Video cassettes, tapes, and discs	22.15	24.80	112
Video game hardware and software	19.74	21.12	107
Repair of TV, radio, and sound equipment	6.65	7.58	114
Rental of television sets	0.24	0.14	58
Radios and sound equipment	**173.81**	**210.73**	**121**
Radios	11.76	12.54	107
Tape recorders and players	6.57	6.89	105
Sound components and component systems	29.86	36.1	121
Miscellaneous sound equipment	0.63	0.28	44
Sound equipment accessories	5.23	5.36	102
Satellite dishes	3.41	4.63	136
Compact disc, tape, record, video mail order clubs	10.59	14.07	133
Records, CDs, audio tapes, needles	39.41	50.96	129
Rental of VCR, radio, sound equipment	0.45	0.11	24
Musical instruments and accessories	23.96	29.34	122
Rental and repair of musical instruments	1.64	2.09	127
Rental of video cassettes, tapes, discs, films	40.30	48.37	120
PETS, TOYS, PLAYGROUND EQUIPMENT	**326.53**	**394.68**	**121**
Pets	**198.03**	**277.72**	**140**

(continued)

(continued from previous page)

	average spending of total consumer units	consumer units headed by 45-to-54-year-olds	
		average spending	indexed spending*
Pet food	$87.23	$108.16	124
Pet purchase, supplies, and medicines	40.15	51.02	127
Pet services	17.17	32.07	187
Veterinary services	53.49	86.48	162
Toys, games, hobbies, and tricycles	**127.68**	**115.52**	**90**
Playground equipment	**0.82**	**1.43**	**174**
OTHER ENTERTAINMENT SUPPLIES, EQUIPMENT, SERVICES	**438.68**	**659.19**	**150**
Unmotored recreational vehicles	**37.97**	**45.93**	**121**
Boats without motor and boat trailers	8.48	22.30	263
Trailers and other attachable campers	29.49	23.63	80
Motorized recreational vehicles	**145.96**	**259.65**	**178**
Motorized campers	26.17	33.31	127
Other vehicles	10.62	7.91	74
Motor boats	109.17	218.43	200
Rental of recreational vehicles	**3.35**	**2.34**	**70**
Outboard motors	**3.27**	**4.86**	**149**
Docking and landing fees	**9.52**	**24.86**	**261**
Sports, recreation, exercise equipment	**128.96**	**193.05**	**150**
Athletic gear, game tables, exercise equipment	60.02	101.94	170
Bicycles	15.27	16.11	106
Camping equipment	9.34	15.08	161
Hunting and fishing equipment	16.11	20.56	128
Winter sports equipment	5.50	6.8	124
Water sports equipment	4.52	8.19	181
Other sports equipment	16.29	21.67	133
Rental and repair of miscellaneous sports equipment	1.91	2.69	141
Photographic equipment and supplies	**89.92**	**109.26**	**122**
Film	21.36	27.09	127
Other photographic supplies	1.07	0.24	22
Film processing	29.36	38.47	131
Repair and rental of photographic equipment	0.49	0.23	47
Photographic equipment	14.19	16.65	117
Photographer fees	23.45	26.58	113
Fireworks	**3.98**	**0.78**	**20**

(continued)

(continued from previous page)

	average spending of total consumer units	consumer units headed by 45-to-54-year-olds	
		average spending	indexed spending*
Souvenirs	$0.74	$0.47	64
Visual goods	3.15	9.31	296
Pinball, electronic video games	11.85	8.68	73
PERSONAL CARE PRODUCTS			
AND SERVICES	527.62	637.24	121
Personal care products	241.86	293.03	121
Hair care products	51.00	54.57	107
Hair accessories	6.89	9.69	141
Wigs and hairpieces	1.22	1.22	100
Oral hygiene products	26.96	29.82	111
Shaving products	11.45	16.47	144
Cosmetics, perfume, and bath products	109.99	138.76	126
Deodorants, feminine hygiene, miscellaneous products	29.80	37.32	125
Electric personal care appliances	4.56	5.18	114
Personal care services	285.76	344.21	120
Personal care services (female)	188.30	221.30	118
Personal care services (male)	97.25	122.49	126
Repair of personal care appliances	0.20	0.42	210
READING	**$163.58**	**$205.30**	**126**
Newspaper subscriptions	51.70	61.18	118
Newspaper, nonsubscriptions	17.18	20.08	117
Magazine subscriptions	22.62	25.95	115
Magazines, nonsubscriptions	11.55	15.30	132
Books purchased through book clubs	10.18	12.62	124
Books not purchased through book clubs	49.50	69.60	141
Encyclopedia and other reference book sets	0.85	0.58	68
EDUCATION	**$570.70**	**$1,067.94**	**187**
College tuition	326.09	657.12	202
Elementary/high school tuition	90.14	177.85	197
Other school tuition	19.26	39.33	204
Other school expenses including rentals	27.44	38.29	140
Books, supplies for college	47.87	72.19	151
Books, supplies for elementary, high school	12.22	15.48	127
Books, supplies for day care, nursery school	3.13	2.42	77
Miscellaneous school expenses and supplies	44.55	65.26	146

(continued)

(continued from previous page)

	average spending of total consumer units	consumer units headed by 45-to-54-year-olds	
		average spending	indexed spending*
TOBACCO PRODUCTS AND SMOKING SUPPLIES	**$263.69**	**$312.00**	**118**
Cigarettes	232.31	270.93	117
Other tobacco products	28.78	36.40	126
Smoking accessories	2.60	4.68	180
FINANCIAL PRODUCTS AND SERVICES	**$847.31**	**$1,106.49**	**131**
Miscellaneous fees, gambling losses	53.32	60.12	113
Legal fees	135.79	176.31	130
Funeral expenses	63.05	21.16	34
Safe deposit box rental	6.69	8.13	122
Checking accounts, other bank service charges	24.51	32.00	131
Cemetery lots, vaults, and maintenance fees	19.65	13.18	67
Accounting fees	48.99	65.26	133
Miscellaneous personal services	39.17	55.59	142
Finance charges, except mortgage and vehicles	249.40	316.08	127
Occupational expenses	102.65	201.02	196
Expenses for other properties	99.61	151.19	152
Interest paid, home equity line of credit (other property)	0.49	2.02	412
Credit card memberships	3.98	4.43	111
CASH CONTRIBUTIONS	**$1,000.90**	**$1,431.36**	**143**
Cash contributions to nonhousehold members, including students, alimony, child support	253.98	553.08	218
Gifts of cash, stocks, bonds to nonhousehold members	225.03	146.39	65
Contributions to charities	101.95	148.43	146
Contributions to religious organizations	390.25	533.86	137
Contributions to educational organizations	16.88	30.35	180
Political contributions	6.20	10.04	162
Other contributions	6.61	9.21	139
PERSONAL INSURANCE AND PENSIONS	**$3,223.06**	**$4,998.47**	**155**
Life and other personal insurance	**378.63**	**604.14**	**160**
Life, endowment, annuity, other personal insurance	369.48	589.61	160
Other nonhealth insurance	9.15	14.53	159

(continued)

(continued from previous page)

	average spending of total consumer units	consumer units headed by 45-to-54-year-olds	
		average spending	indexed spending*
Pensions and Social Security	**$2,844.43**	**$4,394.33**	**154**
Deductions for government retirement	81.02	169.97	210
Deductions for railroad retirement	2.26	7.13	315
Deductions for private pensions	339.22	558.87	165
Nonpayroll deposit to retirement plans	376.65	619.96	165
Deductions for Social Security	2,045.27	3,038.39	149
PERSONAL TAXES	**$3,241.49**	**$4,863.11**	**150**
Federal income tax	2,467.90	3,757.50	152
State and local income tax	644.81	941.49	146
Other taxes	128.78	164.12	127
GIFTS*	**$1,059.44**	**$1,788.80**	**169**
FOOD	**67.73**	**129.57**	**191**
Cakes and cupcakes	2.73	2.55	93
Cheese	3.16	2.05	65
Fresh fruits	6.23	4.99	80
Candy and chewing gum	11.56	17.89	155
Board (including at school)	23.79	71.99	303
HOUSING	**273.22**	**425.66**	**156**
Housekeeping supplies	**36.73**	**38.84**	**106**
Miscellaneous household products	6.62	7.72	117
Lawn and garden supplies	2.04	1.34	66
Stationery, stationery supplies, giftwrap	20.71	23.52	114
Postage	4.08	2.43	60
Household textiles	**8.35**	**11.71**	**140**
Bedroom linens	4.18	5.59	134
Appliances and miscellaneous housewares	**27.34**	**41.77**	**153**
Major appliances	6.41	10.29	161
Small appliances and miscellaneous housewares	20.93	31.48	150
China and other dinnerware	2.46	4.16	169
Glassware	3.97	7.44	187
Nonelectric cookware	3.57	6.27	176
Tableware, nonelectric kitchenware	3.76	2.62	70
Small electric kitchen appliances	3.51	4.67	133

(continued)

(continued from previous page)

	average spending of total consumer units	consumer units headed by 45-to-54-year-olds	
		average spending	indexed spending*
Miscellaneous household equipment	**$66.08**	**$104.83**	**159**
Infants' equipment	2.43	1.67	69
Other household decorative items	24.94	44.66	179
Telephones and accessories	3.14	4.62	147
Indoor plants, fresh flowers	16.63	25.75	155
Computers and hardware, nonbusiness use	7.19	13.63	190
Other housing	**134.72**	**228.51**	**170**
Repair or maintenance services	5.04	4.02	80
Housing while attending school	36.57	126.35	346
Natural gas (renter)	3.26	3.14	96
Electricity (renter)	13.58	10.66	78
Telephone services in home city, excluding mobile car phone	16.34	13.32	82
Water, sewerage maintenance (renter)	2.61	2.34	90
Baby-sitting and child care, someone else's home	3.73	5.42	145
Day care centers, nurseries, and preschools	19.65	13.37	68
Housekeeping services	4.07	5.34	131
Gardening, lawn care service	4.24	4.71	111
Moving, storage, freight express	2.59	1.82	70
Infants' furniture	2.07	4.62	223
APPAREL AND SERVICES	**252.24**	**379.30**	**150**
Men and boys, aged 2 or older	**61.29**	**94.76**	**155**
Men's coats and jackets	2.99	6.01	201
Men's accessories	4.73	5.28	112
Men's sweaters and vests	3.45	5.35	155
Men's active sportswear	3.31	2.18	66
Men's shirts	12.60	19.37	154
Men's pants	7.88	14.53	184
Boys' shirts	4.76	10.14	213
Boys' pants	3.25	3.19	98
Women and girls, aged 2 or older	**81.19**	**109.95**	**135**
Women's coats and jackets	3.17	5.83	184
Women's dresses	7.83	6.97	89
Women's vests and sweaters	6.06	6.76	112
Women's shirts, tops, blouses	12.70	17.64	139
Women's pants	6.09	11.21	184

(continued)

(continued from previous page)

	average spending of total consumer units	consumer units headed by 45-to-54-year-olds	
		average spending	indexed spending*
Women's shorts and shorts sets	$2.22	$1.96	88
Women's active sportswear	4.13	4.27	103
Women's nightwear	6.03	11.12	184
Women's hosiery	2.19	2.65	121
Women's suits	2.25	3.15	140
Women's accessories	5.86	8.60	147
Girls' dresses and suits	4.80	10.17	212
Girls' shirts, blouses, sweaters	5.38	7.31	136
Girls' skirts and pants	2.72	2.99	110
Children under age 2	**32.52**	**38.58**	**119**
Infant dresses, outerwear	7.54	11.16	148
Infant underwear	15.64	15.54	99
Infant nightwear, loungewear	2.94	4.36	148
Infant accessories	4.41	4.96	112
Other apparel products and services	**77.24**	**136.01**	**176**
Watches	7.41	0.57	8
Jewelry	41.18	95.12	231
Men's footwear	7.81	14.08	180
Boys' footwear	3.24	9.06	280
Women's footwear	11.83	12.28	104
Girls' footwear	3.81	4.28	112
TRANSPORTATION	**56.74**	**84.20**	**148**
New cars	7.05	–	–
New trucks	4.52	–	–
Used cars	9.67	17.25	178
Gasoline on out-of-town trips	13.52	18.89	140
Miscellaneous auto repair, servicing	2.94	13.43	457
Airline fares	6.89	12.83	186
Local transportation on out-of-town trips	2.25	1.98	88
Ship fares	3.09	5.97	193
HEALTH CARE	**30.35**	**47.68**	**157**
Physician services	2.23	5.37	241
Dental services	4.76	11.20	235
Hospital service other than room	2.79	12.38	444
Care in convalescent or nursing home	8.05	3.76	47
Prescription drugs	2.17	2.12	98

(continued)

(continued from previous page)

	average spending of total consumer units	consumer units headed by 45-to-54-year-olds	
		average spending	indexed spending*
ENTERTAINMENT	**$98.92**	**$147.09**	**149**
Toys, games, hobbies, tricycles	40.95	44.22	108
Movie, other admissions, out-of-town trips	7.77	14.09	181
Admission to sports events, out-of-town trips	2.59	4.70	181
Fees for recreational lessons	3.33	9.03	271
Community antenna or cable TV	3.96	3.57	90
Color TV, portable/table model	2.88	7.56	263
VCRs and video disc players	2.84	3.06	108
Video game hardware and software	2.17	3.08	142
Tape recorders and players	2.93	1.38	47
Sound components and component systems	2.09	3.06	146
Musical instruments and accessories	2.13	1.39	65
Veterinary services	2.18	3.98	183
Athletic gear, game tables, exercise equipment	5.97	21.14	354
EDUCATION	**155.44**	**446.18**	**287**
College tuition	119.23	377.48	317
Elementary, high school tuition	10.29	10.74	104
Other school expenses, including rentals	4.33	7.16	165
College books, supplies	9.80	30.38	310
Miscellaneous school supplies	8.35	13.15	157
ALL OTHER GIFTS	**124.80**	**129.12**	**103**
Out-of-town trip expenses	46.85	54.98	117

* The index compares the spending of consumer units headed by 45-to-54-year-olds with the spending of the average consumer unit by dividing the spending of 45-to-54-year-olds by average spending in each category and multiplying by 100. An index of 100 means the spending of 45-to-54-year-olds in the category equals average spending. An index of 132 means the spending of 45-to-54-year-olds is 32 percent above average, while an index of 75 means the spending of 45-to-54-year-olds is 25 percent below average.

** This figure does not include the amount paid for mortgage principle, which is considered an asset.

*** Expenditures on gifts are also included in the preceding product and service categories. Food spending, for example, includes the amount spent on food gifts. Only gift categories with spending of $2.00 or more by the average consumer unit are shown.

Note: The Bureau of Labor Statistics uses consumer units rather than households as the sampling unit in the Consumer Expenditure Survey. For the definition of consumer unit, see the Glossary. (–) means the sample is too small to make a reliable estimate.

Source: Bureau of Labor Statistics, unpublished data from the 1997 Consumer Expenditure Survey; calculations by New Strategist

9

Wealth

◆ Boomers aged 45 to 54 had a median net worth of $90,500 in 1995, much higher than the $48,500 median net worth of those aged 35 to 44.

◆ Americans have little in the way of financial assets, and boomers are no exception. Householders aged 45 to 54 had a median of only $24,800 in financial assets in 1995, while those aged 35 to 44 had just $11,600.

◆ The median value of nonfinancial assets peaks in the 45-to-54 age group at $111,700. The oversized homes of boomers account for this peak, since owned homes are the biggest nonfinancial asset of most households.

◆ More than 80 percent of householders aged 35 to 54 are in debt, with the amount of debt peaking in the 45-to-54 age group at median of $41,000 in 1995.

◆ The homeownership rate of householders aged 35 to 54 stood at 70.5 percent in 1998, while 84 percent of married couples in the age group owned their home.

◆ Among workers aged 45 to 64, most men and women are covered by pensions. Many dual-income baby-boom couples will become dual-pension couples in retirement.

Net Worth Rises with Age

Net worth peaks in the 55-to-64 age group.

The median net worth of American households stood at $56,400 in 1995 (the latest data available). Net worth, which is one of the most important measures of wealth, is what remains after a household's debts are subtracted from its assets.

Net worth rises with age and peaks in the 55-to-64 age group. The youngest householders, under age 35, had a median net worth of just $11,400 in 1995. People in this age group are buying homes, starting careers, and having children. Most take on debt to achieve these goals. Net worth rises in middle age as people pay off their debts. Older boomers (aged 45 to 54) have a median net worth that is nearly double that of younger boomers (aged 35 to 44)—$90,500 versus $48,500 in 1995.

Median net worth peaks in the 55-to-64 age group at $110,800. At this age, many people own their homes free and clear. They have accumulated retirement savings as well. After age 65, net worth slowly declines as people spend their wealth.

♦ For most households, homeownership is the single largest component of net worth. Because older boomers are much more likely to own a home than younger boomers, and because they have had more time to build equity in their homes, their net worth is much greater.

Net worth of older boomers exceeds $90,000

(median net worth of householders aged 35 to 54, 1995)

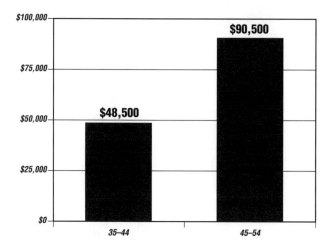

Net Worth of Households by Age of Householder, 1995

(median net worth of households by age of householder, 1995)

	median net worth
Total households	**$56,400**
Under age 35	11,400
Aged 35 to 44	48,500
Aged 45 to 54	90,500
Aged 55 to 64	110,800
Aged 65 to 74	104,100
Aged 75 or older	95,000

Source: Federal Reserve Board, Family Finances in the U.S.: Recent Evidence from the Survey of Consumer Finances, *Federal Reserve Bulletin, January 1997*

Boomers Have Limited Financial Assets

Financial assets of older boomers are much greater than those of younger boomers.

The median value of the financial assets held by the average household stood at just $13,000 in 1995 (the latest data available). The most commonly held financial asset is a transaction account—such as a checking account—owned by 87 percent.

Households headed by people aged 35 to 44 held only $11,600 in financial assets in 1995. Most householders in the age group own transaction accounts as well as retirement accounts—worth a median of $12,000 in 1995. Slightly fewer than one-third own savings bonds, while 29 percent have cash value in a life insurance policy.

The financial assets of householders aged 45 to 54 are more than twice as valuable as those of their younger counterparts—worth $24,800 in 1995. Most people in this age group have transactions accounts and retirement accounts. The retirement accounts were worth a median of $25,000 in 1995. While this amount is substantially above that of the average household, it is far from enough to retire on.

◆ Many baby boomers think personal savings will be their primary source of income in retirement. If so, they must accumulate much more in financial assets than they now have to afford a comfortable retirement.

Older boomers have more

(median financial assets of householders aged 35 to 54, 1995)

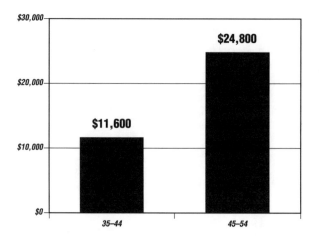

Financial Assets of Householders Aged 35 to 54, 1995

(percent of total households and householders aged 35 to 54 owning financial assets, and median value of asset for owners, by type of asset, 1995)

	total	35 to 44	45 to 54
PERCENT OWNING ASSET			
Any financial asset	**90.8%**	**92.0%**	**92.4%**
Transaction accounts	87.1	87.4	88.9
Certificates of deposit	14.1	8.2	12.5
Savings bonds	22.9	31.0	25.1
Bonds	3.0	1.6	4.6
Stocks	15.3	14.5	17.5
Mutual funds	12.0	10.5	16.0
Retirement accounts	43.0	51.5	54.3
Life insurance	31.4	28.9	37.5
Other managed assets	3.8	3.4	2.9
Other financial assets	11.0	10.5	13.0
MEDIAN VALUE OF ASSET FOR OWNERS			
Any financial asset	**$13,000**	**$11,600**	**$24,800**
Transaction accounts	2,100	2,000	2,700
Certificates of deposit	10,000	6,000	12,000
Savings bonds	1,000	1,000	1,000
Bonds	26,200	11,000	17,000
Stocks	8,000	4,000	10,000
Mutual funds	19,000	10,000	17,500
Retirement accounts	15,600	12,000	25,000
Life insurance	5,000	5,000	6,500
Other managed assets	30,000	10,800	43,000
Other financial assets	3,000	2,000	5,000

Source: Federal Reserve Board, Family Finances in the U.S.: Recent Evidence from the Survey of Consumer Finances, *Federal Reserve Bulletin, January 1997*

Value of Nonfinancial Assets Peaks among Older Boomers

A home is their most valuable asset.

For the average American household, the median value of nonfinancial assets amounted to $83,000 in 1995 (the latest data available). The nonfinancial assets of boomers are worth even more.

Younger boomers, aged 35 to 44, had nonfinancial assets valued at $95,600 in 1995. Most householders in this age group own a car (85 percent) and a home (65 percent). Among householders aged 45 to 54, nonfinancial assets were valued at $111,700 in 1995—the largest among all age groups. Seventy-five percent of householders aged 45 to 54 own a home, and 88 percent own a car.

A home is by far the most valuable asset owned by the average household, and this is true for boomers as well. A median home value of $100,000 for homeowners aged 45-to-54 explains the peak in nonfinancial assets in the age group.

◆ Many boomers have invested in oversized homes as they raise children. If the demand for large homes falls when boomers exit their childrearing years, then the nonfinancial assets of boomers may decline.

Nonfinancial assets greatest for householders aged 45 to 54

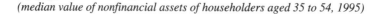

(median value of nonfinancial assets of householders aged 35 to 54, 1995)

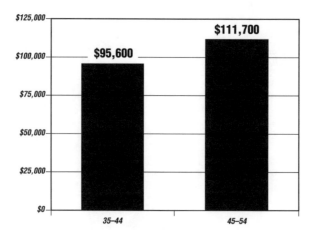

Nonfinancial Assets of Householders Aged 35 to 54, 1995

(percent of total households and householders aged 35 to 54 owning nonfinancial assets, and median value of asset for owners, by type of asset, 1995)

	total	35 to 44	45 to 54
PERCENT OWNING ASSET			
Any nonfinancial asset	**91.1%**	**90.9%**	**93.7%**
Vehicles	84.2	85.1	88.2
Primary residence	64.7	64.6	75.4
Investment real estate	17.5	14.4	23.9
Business	11.0	13.9	14.8
Other nonfinancial asset	9.0	10.2	10.7
MEDIAN VALUE OF ASSET FOR ASSET OWNERS			
Any nonfinancial asset	**$83,000**	**$95,600**	**$111,700**
Vehicles	10,000	10,700	12,400
Primary residence	90,000	95,000	100,000
Investment real estate	50,000	45,000	55,000
Business	41,000	35,000	60,000
Other nonfinancial asset	10,000	9,000	12,000

Source: Federal Reserve Board, Family Finances in the U.S.: Recent Evidence from the Survey of Consumer Finances, *Federal Reserve Bulletin, January 1997*

Boomers Have More Debt Than Most

Debt level peaks in the 45-to-54 age group.

More than 80 percent of householders aged 35 to 54 have debts, exceeding the 75 percent of all households that have debts. The amount of debt held by the 35-to-54 age group also exceeds that of the average household. In 1995 (the latest data available), the average household owed a median of $22,500. Householders aged 35 to 44 owed $37,600, while those aged 45 to 54 owed $41,000.

The majority of boomers had mortgage debt in 1995, compared with a 41 percent minority of all households. Most boomers also have credit card and installment debts—primarily vehicle loans.

For the average householder as well as for boomers, the largest amount they owe is for a mortgage. The median amount owed for mortgage and home equity debt by the average household was $51,000 in 1995. Householders aged 35 to 44 owed an even larger $60,000, while those aged 45 to 54—who have had more time to pay down their mortgage—owed a median of $48,000. Boomers owe a median of $5,600 to $7,000 on installment loans and a median of $1,800 to $2,000 on their credit cards.

◆ As boomers age into their fifties, many will concentrate on paying off their debts. This will curtail their spending even though they will be in their peak earning years.

Debt of Householders Aged 35 to 54, 1995

(percent of total households and householders aged 35 to 54 with debt, and median value of debt for those with debts, by type of debt, 1995)

	total	35 to 44	45 to 54
PERCENT WITH DEBT			
Any debt	**75.2%**	**87.2%**	**86.5%**
Mortgage and home equity	41.1	54.1	61.9
Installment	46.5	60.7	54.0
Other lines of credit	1.9	2.2	2.3
Credit card	47.8	55.8	57.3
Investment real estate	6.3	6.5	10.4
Other debt	9.0	11.1	14.1
MEDIAN VALUE OF DEBT FOR DEBTOR HOUSEHOLDS			
Any debt	**$22,500**	**$37,600**	**$41,000**
Mortgage and home equity	51,000	60,000	48,000
Installment	6,100	5,600	7,000
Other lines of credit	3,500	2,000	5,700
Credit card	1,500	1,800	2,000
Investment real estate	28,000	30,000	28,100
Other debt	2,000	1,700	2,500

Source: Federal Reserve Board, Family Finances in the U.S.: Recent Evidence from the Survey of Consumer Finances, _Federal Reserve Bulletin, January 1997_

Most Boomers Are Homeowners

More than 75 percent of Americans aged 50 to 54 own a home.

After a slow start in the housing market, boomers are joining the ranks of homeowners in force. In 1998, 70.5 percent of householders aged 35 to 54 were homeowners—above the 66 percent homeownership rate for all households.

Boomers have been slow to buy homes because housing prices were escalating rapidly during the 1970s and 1980s as they entered the housing market. In addition, because many postponed marriage, they did not have the two incomes necessary to afford a mortgage payment. Now boomers are playing catch-up, boosting the nation's homeownership rate and driving housing starts to record levels.

Among baby-boom households, married couples are most likely to own a home. In 1998, 84 percent of couples aged 35 to 54 were homeowners, with the share peaking at 89 percent among those aged 50 to 54.

◆ Homeownership in the U.S. is now at a record high. With most 35-to-54-year-olds owning a home, and with homeownership nearly universal among couples in the age group, boomers are well-positioned to build wealth.

Homeownership of Householders Aged 35 to 54, 1998

(number and percent of total householders and householders aged 35 to 54 who own their home, by household type, 1998; numbers in thousands)

		owners	
	number	*number*	*percent*
Total households	**102,528**	**67,873**	**66.2%**
Total aged 35 to 54	43,490	30,671	70.5
Aged 35 to 44	23,943	15,909	66.4
Aged 45 to 54	19,547	14,762	75.5
Aged 35 to 39	11,838	7,463	63.0
Aged 40 to 44	12,105	8,446	69.8
Aged 45 to 49	10,601	7,778	73.4
Aged 50 to 54	8,946	6,984	78.1
Married couples	**54,317**	**43,964**	**80.9**
Total aged 35 to 54	25,914	21,711	83.8
Aged 35 to 44	14,180	11,478	80.9
Aged 45 to 54	11,734	10,233	87.2
Aged 35 to 39	6,941	5,488	79.1
Aged 40 to 44	7,239	5,990	82.7
Aged 45 to 49	6,239	5,336	85.5
Aged 50 to 54	5,495	4,897	89.1

Source: Bureau of the Census, detailed tables from Household and Family Characteristics: March 1998, *Current Population Reports, P20-515, 1998; calculations by New Strategist*

Pensions Cover about One-Half of Middle-Aged Workers

Women are almost as likely to have pension coverage as men.

Among workers with earnings in 1996, 42 percent were covered by a pension. Pension coverage is slightly greater among working men (44 percent) than working women (40 percent).

Among workers in the age group closest to retirement (45 to 64—an age group that includes the older half of the baby-boom generation), at least half are covered by a pension. Fifty-seven percent of working men aged 45 to 64 are covered, as are 50 percent of working women in the age group.

Pension coverage is lower in the 25 to 44 age group (which includes the younger half of the baby-boom generation). Forty-eight percent of working men and 45 percent of working women aged 25 to 44 have pension coverage.

♦ Millions of baby-boom women will have pension coverage in old age because of their propensity to work. Consequently, many of today's dual-income couples will be dual-pension couples in retirement.

Most 45-to-64-year-olds are covered by pensions

(percent of workers aged 45 to 64 with earnings in 1996 covered by pensions, by sex, 1997)

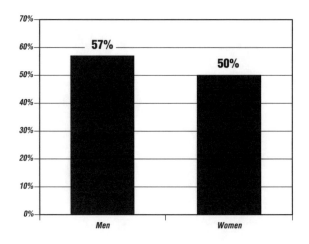

Pension Coverage by Sex and Age, 1997

(number and percent of workers with earnings in 1996 covered by pensions, by sex and age, 1997; numbers in thousands)

	number	percent
Total workers with coverage	**59,923**	**41.9%**
Men with coverage	**33,363**	**43.8**
Aged 15 to 24	1,501	12.0
Aged 25 to 44	18,768	48.4
Aged 45 to 64	12,456	56.5
Aged 65 or older	639	22.5
Women with coverage	**26,560**	**39.8**
Aged 15 to 24	1,176	10.3
Aged 25 to 44	15,091	45.0
Aged 45 to 64	9,815	50.0
Aged 65 or older	478	22.4

Source: Bureau of the Census, Statistical Abstract of the United States: 1998

For More Information

The federal government is a rich source of accurate and reliable data about almost every aspect of American life. Below are the web site addresses of the federal agencies collecting the data analyzed in this book, as well as the web site addresses of other organizations whose data appear here. Also listed are the phone numbers of organizations mentioned in this book, as well as government subject specialists, arranged alphabetically by topic. A list of State Data Centers and Small Business Development Centers appears here as well. Researchers can contact these centers for help in tracking down demographic and economic information.

Web Site Addresses

Bureau of the Census	http://www.census.gov
Bureau of Labor Statistics	http://www.bls.gov
Current Population Survey home page	http://www.bls.census.gov/cps
Consumer Expenditure Survey home page	http://www.bls.gov/csxhome.htm
Employee Benefit Research Institute	http://www.ebri.org
National Center For Education Statistics	http://nces.ed.gov
National Center For Health Statistics	http://www.cdc.gov/nchswww
National Endowment for the Arts	http://arts.endow.gov
National Opinion Research Center	http://www.norc.uchicago.edu

Telephone Numbers of Subject Specialists and Organizations

Absences from work, Staff	202-606-6378
Aging population, Staff	301-457-2422
Ancestry, Staff	301-457-2403
Apportionment, Ed Byerly	301-457-2381
Census, 1990 tabulations, Staff	301-457-2422
Census, 2000 plans, Arthur Cresce/John Stuart	301-457-3947/3949
Census Bureau Customer Services	301-457-4100
Child care, Martin O'Connell/Lynne Casper	301-457-2416
Children, Staff	301-457-2465
Citizenship, Staff	301-457-2403
College graduate job outlook, Mark Mittelhauser	202-606-5707
Commuting, Phil Salopek/Celia Boertlein	301-457-2454
Consumer Expenditure Survey, Staff	202-606-6900
Contingent workers, Sharon Cohany	202-606-6378
County population, Staff	301-457-2422
Crime, Kathleen Creighton	301-457-3925
Current employment analysis, Philip Rones	202-606-6378
Current Population Survey (general information), Staff	301-457-4100
Demographic surveys (general information), Staff	301-457-3773
Disability, Jack McNeil/Bob Bennefield	301-763-8300/8213
Discouraged workers, Staff	202-606-6378

Census Regional Offices

Atlanta, GA	404-730-3833/3964
Boston, MA	617-424-0510/0565
Charlotte, NC	704-344-6144/6548
Chicago, IL	708-562-1740/1791
Dallas, TX	214-640-4470/4434
Denver, CO	303-969-7750/6769
Detroit, MI	313-259-1875/5169
Kansas City, KS	913-551-6711/5839
Los Angeles, CA	818-904-6339/6249
New York, NY	212-264-4730/3863
Philadelphia, PA	215-656-7578/7550
Seattle, WA	206-553-5835/5859

State Data Centers And Business/Industry Data Centers

Below are listed the State Data Center and Business/Industry Data Center (BIDC) lead agency contacts only. Lead data centers are usually state government agencies, universities, or libraries that head up a network of affiliate centers. Every state has a State Data Center. The asterisks (*) identify states that also have Business/Industry Data Centers. In some states, one agency serves as the lead for both the State Data Centers and the Business/Industry Data Centers. The Business/Industry Data Center is listed separately if there is a separate agency serving as the lead.

Alabama, Annette Watters, University of Alabama	205-348-6191
Alaska, Kathryn Lizik, Department of Labor	907-465-2437
*Arizona, Betty Jeffries, Department of Security	602-542-5984
Arkansas, Sarah Breshears, University of Arkansas at Little Rock	501-569-8530
California, Linda Gage, Department of Finance	916-323-4086
Colorado, Rebecca Picaso, Department of Local Affairs	303-866-2156
Connecticut, Bill Kraynak, Office of Policy & Management	860-418-6230
*Delaware, Mike Mahaffie, Development Office	302-739-4271
District of Columbia, Herb Bixhorn, Mayor's Office of Planning	202-727-6533
*Florida, Pam Schenker, Dept. of Labor & Employment Security	850-488-1048
Georgia, Robert Giacomini, Georgia Institute of Technology	404-894-9416
Guam, Rose Deaver, Department of Commerce	011-671-475-0325/6
Hawaii, Jan Nakamoto, Dept. of Business, Econ. Dev., & Tourism	808-586-2493
Idaho, Alan Porter, Department of Commerce	208-334-2470
Illinois, Suzanne Ebetsch, Bureau of the Budget	217-782-1381
*Indiana, Sylvia Andrews, State Library	317-232-3733
Indiana BIDC, Carol Rogers, Business Research Center	317-274-2205
Iowa, Beth Henning, State Library	515-281-4350
Kansas, Marc Galbraith, State Library	913-296-3296
*Kentucky, Ron Crouch, University of Louisville	502-852-7990
Louisiana, Karen Paterson, Office of Planning & Budget	504-342-7410

*Maine .... [Currently being reorganized]
*Maryland, Jane Traynham, Office of Planning 410-767-4450
*Massachusetts, John Gaviglio, Mass. Inst. for Social and Econ. Res 413-545-3460
Michigan, Carolyn Lauer, Dept. of Management & Budget 517-373-7910
*Minnesota, David Birkholz, State Demographer's Office 612-296-2557
Minnesota BIDC, David Rademacher, State Dem. Office 612-297-3255
*Mississippi, Rachael McNeely, University of Mississippi 601-232-7288
Mississippi BIDC, Deloise Tate, Dept. of Econ. & Comm. Dev 601-359-3593
*Missouri, Debra Pitts, State Library 573-526-7648
Missouri BIDC, Steve Garrotto, Small Business Dev. Centers 573-882-0344
*Montana, Patricia Roberts, Department of Commerce 406-444-2896
Nebraska, Jerome Deichert, University of Nebraska-Omaha 402-595-2311
Nevada, Linda Nary, State Library & Archives 702-687-8326
New Hampshire, Thomas Duffy, Office of State Planning 603-271-2155
*New Jersey, David Joye, Department of Labor 609-984-2595
*New Mexico, Kevin Kargacin, University of New Mexico 505-277-6626
*New York, Staff, Department of Economic Development 518-474-1141
*North Carolina, Staff, State Library 919-733-6418
North Dakota, Richard Rathge, State University 701-231-8621
Northern Mariana Islands, Juan Borja, Dept. of Commerce 011-670-664-3034
*Ohio, Barry Bennett, Department of Development 614-466-2115
*Oklahoma, Jeff Wallace, Department of Commerce 405-815-5184
Oregon, George Hough, Portland State Univ. .... 503-725-5159 / 1-800-547-8887x5159
*Pennsylvania, Diane Shoop, Penns. State Univ. at Harrisburg 717-948-6336
Puerto Rico, Lillian Torres Aguirre, Planning Bd. .... 787-728-4430 / 723-6200x2502
Rhode Island, Paul Egan, Department of Administration 401-277-6493
South Carolina, Mike MacFarlane, Budget & Control Board 803-734-3780
South Dakota, Theresa Bendert, Univ. of South Dakota 605-677-5287
Tennessee, Don Walli, State Planning Office 615-741-1676
Texas, Steve Murdock, Texas A&M University .... 409-845-5115 / 5332
*Utah, David Abel, Office of Planning & Budget 801-538-1036
Vermont, Sybil McShane, Department of Libraries 802-828-3261
*Virginia, Don Lillywhite, Virginia Employment Commission 804-786-8026
Virgin Islands, Frank Mills, Univ. of the Virgin Islands 340-693-1027
*Washington, Yi Zhao, Office of Financial Management 360-902-0599
*West Virginia, Delphine Coffey, Office of Comm. & Industrial Dev. 304-558-4010
West Virginia BIDC, Randy Childs, Center for Econ. Research 304-293-7832
*Wisconsin, Robert Naylor, Department of Administration 608-266-1927
Wisconsin BIDC, David Mohn, Univ. of Wisconsin-Madison 608-262-3097
Wyoming, Wenlin Liu, Dept. of Administration & Fiscal Control 307-777-7504

Glossary

adjusted for inflation Incomes and changes in income have been adjusted for the rise in the cost of living, or the consumer price index (CPI-U-XI). In this book, any year-to-year changes in income or spending are shown in inflation-adjusted dollars.

Asian In this book, the term "Asian" includes both Asians and Pacific Islanders.

baby boom Americans born between 1946 and 1964.

baby bust Americans born between 1965 and 1976; also known as Generation X.

central city The largest city in a metropolitan area is called the central city. The balance of the metropolitan area outside the central city is regarded as the "suburbs."

consumer unit (on spending tables only) For convenience, the terms consumer unit and household are used interchangeably in the spending section of this book, although consumer units are somewhat different from the Census Bureau's households. A consumer unit comprises all related members of a household or a financially independent member of a household. A household may consist of more than one consumer unit.

dual-earner couple A married couple in which both the householder and the householder's spouse are in the labor force.

earnings One type of income. *See also* Income.

employed All civilians who did any work as paid employees or farmers/self-employed workers, or who worked 15 hours or more as unpaid farm workers or in a family-owned business, during the reference period. All those who have jobs but are temporarily absent from their jobs due to illness, bad weather, vacation, labor management dispute, or personal reasons are considered employed.

expenditure The transaction cost including excise and sales taxes of goods and services acquired during the survey period. The full cost of each purchase is recorded even though full payment may not have been made at the date of purchase. Average expenditure figures may be artificially low for infrequently purchased items such as cars because figures are calculated using all consumer units within a demographic segment rather than just purchasers. Expenditure estimates include money spent on gifts for others.

family A group of two or more people (one of whom is the householder) related by birth, marriage, or adoption and living in the same household.

family household A household maintained by a householder who lives with one or more people related to him or her by blood, marriage, or adoption.

female/male householder A woman/man who maintains a household without a spouse present. May head family or nonfamily household.

full-time employment Full-time employment is 35 or more hours of work per week during a majority of the weeks worked.

full-time, year-round Indicates 50 or more weeks of full-time employment during the previous calendar year.

geographic regions The four major regions and nine census divisions of the United States are the state groupings as shown below:

Northeast:
—New England: Connecticut, Maine, Massachusetts, New Hampshire, Rhode Island, and Vermont
—Middle Atlantic: New Jersey, New York, and Pennsylvania

Midwest:
—East North Central: Illinois, Indiana, Michigan, Ohio, and Wisconsin
—West North Central: Iowa, Kansas, Minnesota, Missouri, Nebraska, North Dakota, and South Dakota

South:
—South Atlantic: Delaware, District of Columbia, Florida, Georgia, Maryland, North Carolina, South Carolina, Virginia, and West Virginia
—East South Central: Alabama, Kentucky, Mississippi, and Tennessee
—West South Central: Arkansas, Louisiana, Oklahoma, and Texas

West:
—Mountain: Arizona, Colorado, Idaho, Montana, Nevada, New Mexico, Utah, and Wyoming
—Pacific: Alaska, California, Hawaii, Oregon, and Washington

Generation X Americans born between 1965 and 1976; also known as the baby-bust generation.

Hispanic Persons who identify their origin as Mexican, Puerto Rican, Central or South American, or some other Hispanic origin. Persons of Hispanic origin may be of any race. In other words, there are black Hispanics, white Hispanics, Asian Hispanics, and Native American Hispanics.

household All the persons who occupy a housing unit. A household includes the related family members and all the unrelated persons, if any, such as lodgers, foster children, wards, or employees who share the housing unit. A person living alone is counted as a household. A group of unrelated people who share a housing unit as roommates or unmarried partners is also counted as a household. Households do not include group quarters such as college dormitories, prisons, or nursing homes.

household, race/ethnicity of Households are categorized according to the race or ethnicity of the householder only.

householder The householder is the person (or one of the persons) in whose name the housing unit is owned or rented or, if there is no such person, any adult member. With married couples, the householder may be either the husband or the wife. The householder is the reference person for the household.

householder, age of The age of the householder is used to categorize households into age groups. Married couples, for example, are classified according to the age of either the husband or the wife, depending on which one identified him- or herself as the householder.

income Money received in the preceding calendar year by a person aged 15 or older from any of the following sources: (1) earnings from longest job (or self-employment); (2) earnings from jobs other than longest job; (3) unemployment compensation; (4) workers' compensation; (5) Social Security; (6) Supplemental Security income; (7) public assistance; (8) veterans' payments; (9) survivor benefits; (10) disability benefits; (11) retirement pensions; (12) interest; (13) dividends; (14) rents and royalties or estates and trusts; (15) educational assistance; (16) alimony; (17) child support; (18) financial assistance from outside the household, and other periodic income. Income is reported in several ways in this book. Household income is the combined income of all household members. Income of a person is all income accruing to the person from all sources. Earnings is the amount of money a person receives from his or her job.

job tenure The length of time a person has been employed continuously by the same employer.

labor force The labor force tables in this book are for the civilian labor force, which includes both the employed and the unemployed—people who are looking for work.

labor force participation rate The percentage of the civilian noninstitutional population that is in the civilian labor force, which includes both the employed and the unemployed.

married couples with/without children under age 18 Refers to married couples with/without own children under age 18 living in the same household. Couples without children under age 18 may be parents of grown children who live elsewhere, or they could be childless couples.

median The median is the value that divides the population or households into two equal portions: one below and one above the median. Medians can be calculated for income, age, and many other characteristics.

median income The amount that divides the income distribution into two equal groups, one-half having incomes above the median, one-half having incomes below the median. The median for households or families is based on all households or families. The median for persons is based on all persons aged 15 or older with income.

metropolitan area An area qualifies for recognition as a metropolitan area if it includes a city of at least 50,000 population, or it includes a Census Bureau–defined urban-

ized area of at least 50,000 with a total metropolitan population of at least 100,000 (75,000 in New England). In addition to the county containing the main city or urbanized area, a metropolitan area may include other counties having strong commuting ties to the central county.

Millennial generation Americans born between 1997 and 1994.

nonfamily household A household maintained by a householder who lives alone or with people to whom he or she is not related.

nonfamily householder A householder who lives alone or with nonrelatives.

non-Hispanic People who did not identify themselves as Hispanic on the Current Population Survey or the 1990 Census are classified as non-Hispanic. Non-Hispanics may be of any race.

nonmetropolitan area Counties that are not classified as metropolitan areas.

occupation Occupational classification is based on the kind of work a person did at his or her job during the previous calendar year. If a person changed jobs during the year, the data refer to the occupation of the job held the longest during that year.

outside central city The portion of a metropolitan county or counties that falls outside of the central city or cities; generally regarded as the suburbs.

own children Own children in a family are sons and daughters, including stepchildren and adopted children, of the householder. The totals include never-married children living away from home in college dormitories.

owner occupied A housing unit is owner occupied if the owner lives in the unit, even if it is mortgaged or not fully paid for. A cooperative or condominium unit is owner occupied only if the owner lives in it. All other occupied units are classified as renter occupied.

part-time or full-time employment Part-time is less than 35 hours of work per week in a majority of the weeks worked during the year. Full-time is 35 or more hours of work per week during a majority of the weeks worked.

percent change The change (either positive or negative) in a measure that is expressed as a proportion of the starting measure. When median income changes from $20,000 to $25,000, for example, this is a 25 percent increase.

percentage point change The change (either positive or negative) in a value which is already expressed as a percentage. When the labor force participation rate changes from 70 percent to 75 percent, for example, this is a 5 percentage point increase.

poverty level The official income threshold below which families and persons are classified as living in poverty. The threshold rises each year with inflation and varies depending on family size and age of householder. In 1997, the poverty threshold for a family of four was $16,400.

proportion or share The value of a part expressed as a percentage of the whole. If there are 4 million people aged 25 and 3 million of them are white, then the white proportion is 75 percent.

race Race is self-reported and appears in four categories in this book: white, black, Native American, and Asian. A household is assigned the race of the householder.

rounding Percentages are rounded to the nearest one-tenth of a percent; therefore, the percentages in a distribution do not always add to exactly 100.0 percent, al-

though totals are always shown as 100.0. Moreover, individual figures are rounded to the nearest 1,000 without being adjusted to group totals, which are independently rounded; percentages are based on the unrounded numbers.

self-employment A person is categorized as self-employed if he or she was self-employed in the job held longest during the reference period. People who report self-employment from a second job are excluded, but those who report wage-and-salary income from a second job are included. Unpaid workers in family businesses are excluded. Self-employment statistics include only nonagricultural workers and exclude people who work for themselves in incorporated businesses.

sex ratio The number of men per 100 women.

suburbs *See* Outside central city.

unemployed Unemployed people are those who, during the survey period, had no employment but were available and looking for work. Those who were laid off from their jobs and were waiting to be recalled are also classified as unemployed.

Bibliography

Bureau of the Census
> Internet web site, http://www.census.gov
> ——1998 Current Population Survey, unpublished data
> ——*Educational Attainment in the United States: March 1998*, detailed tables from Current Population Reports, P20-513, 1998
> ——*Geographic Mobility: March 1996 to March 1997*, Current Population Reports, P20-510, 1998
> ——*Household and Family Characteristics: March 1998*, detailed tables from Current Population Reports, P20-515, 1998
> ——*Marital Status and Living Arrangements: March 1998*, Current Population Reports, P20-514, 1998
> ——*Money Income in the United States: 1997*, Current Population Reports, P60-200, 1998
> ——*Population Projections of the United States by Age, Sex, Race, and Hispanic Origin: 1995 to 2050*, Current Population Reports, P25-1130, 1996
> ——*Poverty in the United States: 1997*, Current Population Reports, P60-201, 1998
> ——*Projections of the Total Population of States: 1995 to 2025*; PPL-47, 1996
> ——*School Enrollment—Social and Economic Characteristics of Students: October 1996*, Current Population Reports, P20-500, 1998
> ——*Statistical Abstract of the United States: 1998* (118th edition) Washington, DC 1998
> ——*U.S. Population Estimates, by Age, Sex, Race, and Hispanic Origin: 1980 to 1991*, Current Population Reports, P25-1095, 1993
> ——*Voting and Registration in the Election of November 1996*, Current Population Reports, P20-504, 1998

Bureau of Labor Statistics
> Internet web site, http://www.bls.gov
> ——1997 Consumer Expenditure Survey, unpublished data
> ——*Contingent and Alternative Employment Arrangements*, February 1997
> ——*Employment and Earnings*, January 1991
> ——*Employment and Earnings*, January 1999
> ——*Handbook of Labor Statistics*, Bulletin 2340, 1989
> ——*Monthly Labor Review*, November 1997
> ——*Work at Home in 1997*, USDL 98-93

Consumer Health Products Association
> ——*Self Medication in the '90s: Practices and Perceptions*, 1992

Employee Benefit Research Institute, Mathew Greenwald & Associates, Inc., and American Savings Education Council
> ——Internet web site, http://www.ebri.org
> ——1997 Retirement Confidence Survey

Federal Reserve Board
    ——*Family Finances in the U.S.: Recent Evidence from the Survey of Consumer Finances*, Federal Reserve Bulletin, January 1997

HealthFocus
    P. O. Box 7174, Des Moines, IA 50309-7174, 515-274-1307
    ——*1997 HealthFocus Trend Report*

National Center for Health Statistics
    Internet web site, http://www.cdc.gov/nchswww
    ——*Ambulatory Care Visits to Physician Offices, Hospital Outpatient Departments, and Emergency Departments: United States, 1996*, Vital and Health Statistics, Series 13, No. 135, 1998
    ——*Births and Deaths: Preliminary Data for 1997*, National Vital Statistics Report, Vol. 47, No. 4, 1998
    ——*Current Estimates from the National Health Interview Survey, 1995*, Series 10, No. 199, 1998
    ——*Deaths: Final Data for 1996*, National Vital Statistics Report, Vol. 47, No. 9, 1998
    ——*Health, United States, 1996-97*
    ——*Health, United States, 1998*
    ——*Report of Final Natality Statistics, 1996*, Monthly Vital Statistics Report, Vol. 46, No. 11 Supplement, 1998

National Endowment for the Arts
    Internet web site, http://arts.endow.gov
    ——*1997 Survey of Public Participation in the Arts, Summary Report*, 1998

National Opinion Research Center
    Internet web site, http://www.norc.uchicago.edu
    ——1976 General Social Survey, unpublished data
    ——1994 General Social Survey, unpublished data
    ——1996 General Social Survey, unpublished data

U.S. Department of Agriculture
    Internet web site http://www.barc.usda.gov
    ——1994–95 National Survey on Recreation and the Environment, Forest Service
    ——ARS Food Surveys Research Group, *1994 and 1995 Continuing Survey of Food Intakes by Individuals*
    ——ARS Food Surveys Research Group, *1994 and 1995 Diet and Health Knowledge Survey*

U.S. Substance Abuse and Mental Health Services Administration
    Internet wet site http://www.samhsa.gov
    ——*National Household Survey on Drug Abuse, 1997*

Index

earnings by educational attainment, 145–46;

eating away from home, 75–76;

educational attainment, 53–55, 58–59;

employment status, 160–63;

food consumption, 72–74;

frequency of exercise, 84–85;

full-time workers, 174–75;

income, 128–29, 132–37;

job tenure of, 178–79;

labor force participation, 158–63;

life expectancy, 109, 112;

living alone, 187–93, 208–11;

living arrangements, 210–11;

marital status, 214–19;

participation in the labor force, projected, 184–85;

part-time workers, 174–75;

pensions for, 348–49;

population, 222–23, 230–31, 235–41;

poverty rate, 155–56;

school enrollment, 62–63;

self-employed, 176–77;

smoking behavior by age, 89–90

mental disability, 108

metabolic conditions, 104

migration, 234

milk and milk products, consumption by sex, 74

mobility, geographic, 266–68

mortgage debt, 344–45

mothers worked during childhood, by age group, 14

mother's working, impact on children, opinions by age group, 27

motor boating, 87

muscle aches, 99

musculoskeletal conditions,
  acute, 101;
  chronic, 103

mutual funds, 340–41

Native Americans:
  births, 80
  by Hispanic origin, 227–28, 248–65;
  population, 227–28, 248–65

nervous conditions, 104

net worth, personal, 338–339

newspaper readership by age group, 35

occupation, 168–173

outdoor recreational activities, 86–88

outlook on life, 6–9

outpatient department visits, 106

overweight problems, 99

parents at home during childhood, by age, 12–13

parents still living, by age, 22

part-time workers, by sex, 174–75

pensions, percent covered by, 348–49

personal care products and services:
  consumer spending by detailed product category, 303, 330;
  consumer spending trends, 279

physician office visits, 106

picnicking, 87

pneumonia, 101, 110–11

political behavior, by age, 42–46

political influence, belief in, by age, 43

political party identification, by age, 45

political philosophy, by age, 44

population, 221–71:
  by age and sex, 222–23, 229–31, 234–41;
  by race and Hispanic origin, 226–28, 248–65;
  by region, 229–33;
  by state, 234–65;
  projections, 224–25, 232–33, 242–47, 269–70

poverty rate, 155–56

privacy and computers, attitudes toward, by age group, 40–41;

public transportation:
  consumer spending on by detailed product category, 299, 324;
  consumer spending trends, 279

reading:
  consumer spending by detailed product category, 303, 330;
  consumer spending trends, 279

recreational activities, 86–88

marital status, 216, 219;
poverty rate, 155–56
White Americans. *See also* White non-
Hispanic Americans:
births, 80
by Hispanic origin, 226–28, 248–65;
educational attainment, 53, 58–61;
employment status, 162–65;
household types, 187, 190, 193, 196, 200;
households with children, 196, 200;
income, 118, 121, 132, 136, 138, 142;
labor force, 157, 162–65;
life expectancy, 112;
marital status, 216, 219;
population, 226–28, 248–65;
poverty rate, 155–56
White, non-Hispanic Americans
income, 122, 137–38, 143;
population, 226–28, 248–65;
women:
alternative work arrangements, by type,
180–81;
baby-boom population, by single year age-
group, 222–23;
earnings by educational attainment,
149–52;
eating away from home, 75–76;
employment status, 164–65;
food consumption, 72–74;
frequency of exercise by, 84–85;
full-time workers, 174–75;
income, 130–31, 138–43;
job tenure of, 178–79;
labor force participation, 158–61, 164–65,
184–85;
life expectancy, 112;
living alone, 188–93, 208–09, 212–13;
living alone by income, 122–27;
living arrangements, 212–13;
marital status, 214–19;
participation in the labor force, projected,
184–85;
part-time workers, 174–75;
pensions for, 348–49;

population, 222–23, 230–31, 235–41;
poverty rate, 155–56;
school enrollment, 62–63;
self-employed, 176–77;
smoking behavior by age, 89–90
work arrangements, alternative, 180–81
workers:
at home, 182–83;
by occupation, 168–173;
contract, 180–81;
full-time, by sex, 174–75;
on call, 180–81;
part-time, by sex, 174–75;
temporary, 180–81